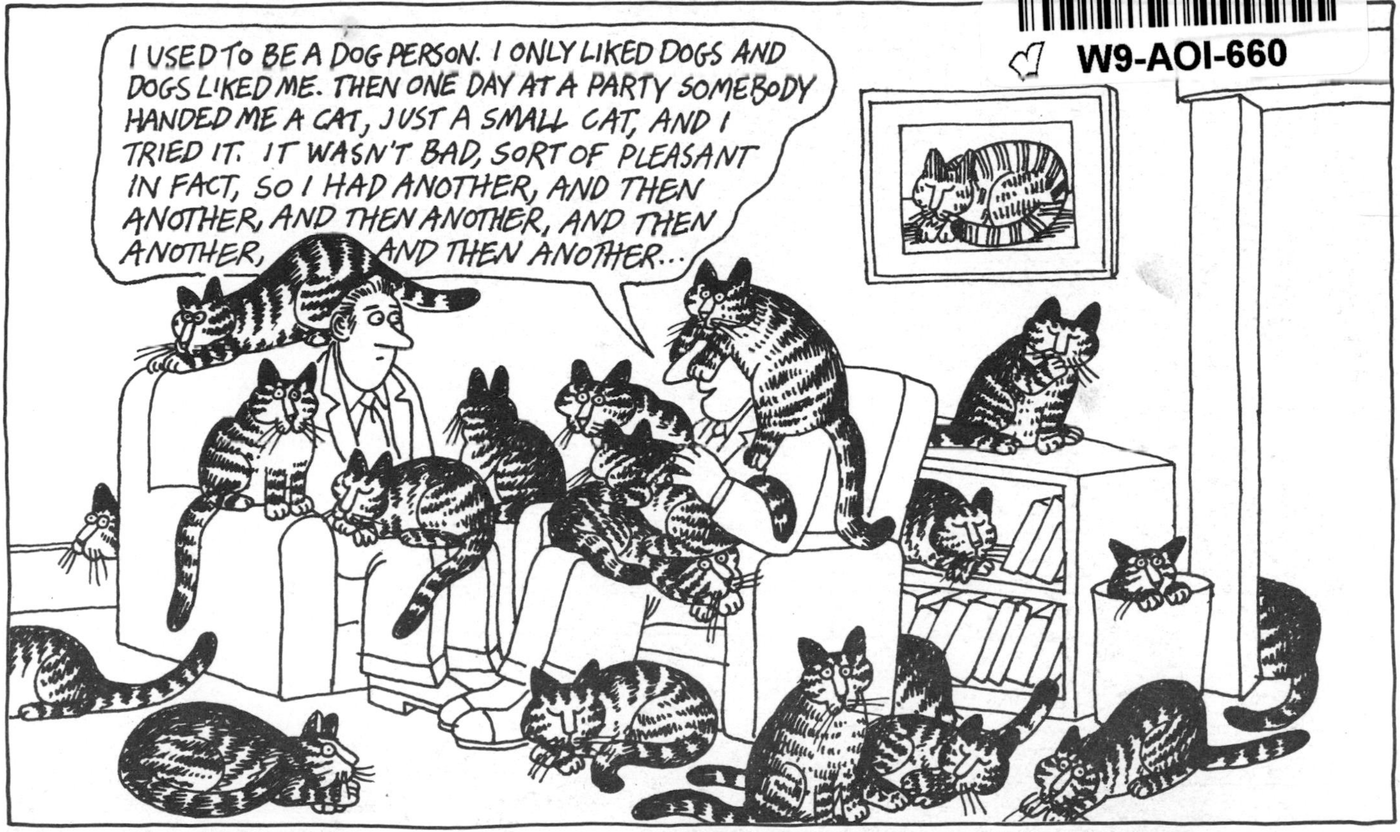
I USED TO BE A DOG PERSON. I ONLY LIKED DOGS AND DOGS LIKED ME. THEN ONE DAY AT A PARTY SOMEBODY HANDED ME A CAT, JUST A SMALL CAT, AND I TRIED IT. IT WASN'T BAD, SORT OF PLEASANT IN FACT, SO I HAD ANOTHER, AND THEN ANOTHER, AND THEN ANOTHER, AND THEN ANOTHER, AND THEN ANOTHER...

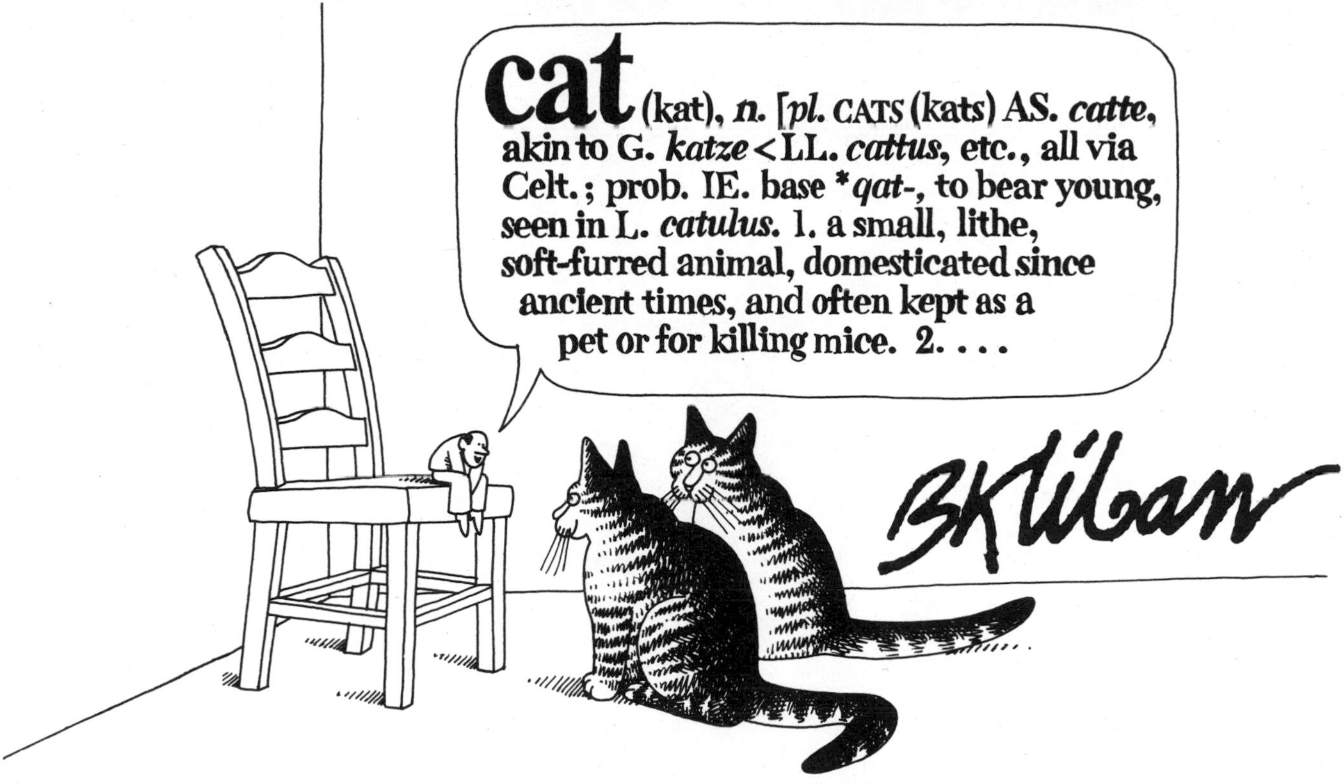
cat (kat), n. [pl. CATS (kats) AS. catte, akin to G. katze <LL. cattus, etc., all via Celt.; prob. IE. base *qat-, to bear young, seen in L. catulus. 1. a small, lithe, soft-furred animal, domesticated since ancient times, and often kept as a pet or for killing mice. 2. . . .
B Kliban

Seventeenth Anniversary Edition

Workman Publishing, New York

Kliban, B.
Cat (kat), n. ... / by B. Kliban.
p. cm.
ISBN 1-56305-284-9 (paper): $7.95
1. Cats—Caricatures and cartoons. 2. American wit and humor.
Pictorial. I. Title.
NC1429.K58A4 1992
741.5'973—dc 20   92-7121
                                        CIP

Workman books are available at special discounts when purchased in bulk
for premiums and sales promotions as well as for fund-raising or educational use.
Special editions or book excerpts can also be created to specification.
For details, contact the Special Sales Director at the address below.

Workman Publishing Company
708 Broadway
New York, NY 10003

Manufactured in the United States of America
First printing March 1975
First printing of the anniversary edition April 1992
3 5 7 9 10 8 6 4 2

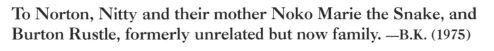

To Norton, Nitty and their mother Noko Marie the Snake, and
Burton Rustle, formerly unrelated but now family. —B.K. (1975)

For Hap, always. —J.K.K. (1992)

Introduction

by Art Spiegelman

I'm a mouse man, myself. It's even been said that *MAUS*, my comic book memoir that portrays nazis as cats, has set ailurophiles back a good 500 years—back to when cats were burned as witches' familiars. So, maybe I'm uniquely disqualified to introduce the book that single-handedly made "cat" a household word.

On the other hand, Zazou, my own jumbo-sized orange-and-white meatloaf (who, at this very moment, is mercilessly batting a drawing pencil around the studio), seems to know enough not to take my work personally. And when I met Hap Kliban in 1987, three years before his premature death, he seemed amused (in his kind of depressed and laid-back way) that cats could be used as an emblem of evil. His own furry little carnivores are goggle-eyed, all-knowing innocents, but like Walt Whitman they contain multitudes.

Hap thought he was just doodling (his first cat scratchings were casually discovered in his files by *Playboy* cartoon editor Michelle Urry), but the unassuming little book now in your paws has become something of a classic. It's sold many hundreds of thousands of copies since it came out in 1975 and has never been out of print. Even the book's odd squat, horizontal format has since become a standard, the premier format of choice for any volume wishing to announce itself as an indispensable collection of cartoon hilarity.

Unwittingly, in the best American "create-a-need-then-fill-it" tradition, Hap spawned an industry. He discovered a previously uncharted population of cat-crazies, a diverse, broad and hip audience not limited to maiden aunts who swoon over perennial cuddly kitten calendars. His own whimsical drawings somehow managed to survive wanton merchandising success—everything from coffee mugs to maternity smocks—with their mysteries amazingly intact.

For the record, you should know that Hap also invented a new kind of gag cartoon, the kind with a third-person caption instead of a line of dialogue below. (For an example, class, turn to "Quick as a wink, the sly cat had eaten Monroe's cheese sandwich" somewhere in the middle of this unpaged volume.) Gary Larson, Glen Baxter and millions of other cartoonists owe Hap for this. He's up there in the Gag Cartoonist Hall of Fame (which is located somewhere near the Pantheon of Immortal Garage Mechanics, but never mind). He's kind of a wrinkled-collar Saul Steinberg, in that his gag cartoons aren't exactly "gags" at all. They're Funny Drawings. Actually, just drawings that happen to be funny. They don't telegraph their jokes. Looking at them is like eavesdropping into someone's sketchbook, except most sketchbooks aren't hilarious, and Kliban's drawings can make you wet yourself if you don't get to the litter box in time.

Kliban was generous enough to include his "How to Draw a Qat" lessons in this book, but nobody drew cats like Kliban. Solemn, simultaneously omniscient and dim-witted, they have all the Rubenesque grace of a 1950 Buick. What they're not, is cute. They're not cloying little Hello Kitties nor are they malevolent Garfields (though Jim Davis' cat was obviously sired by a defective Kliban seed). If anything, they're distant cousins to Krazy Kat, multidimensional in a 2-D world. Despite the dictionary definition on the title page, Kliban's cats are as difficult to pin down and define as any real cat, and that is their ineffable magic.

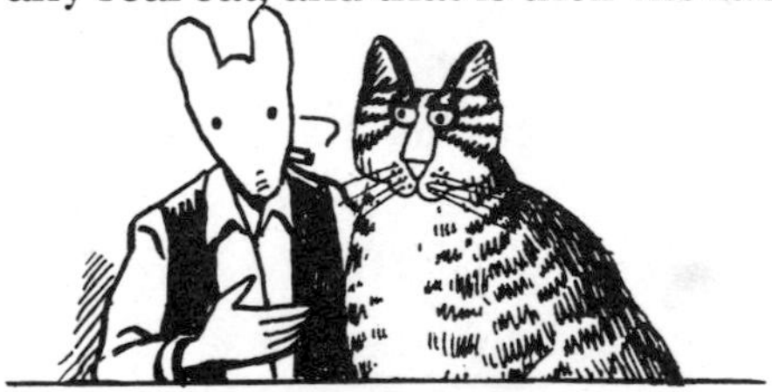

art spiegelman

New York, 1992

How to draw a Qat

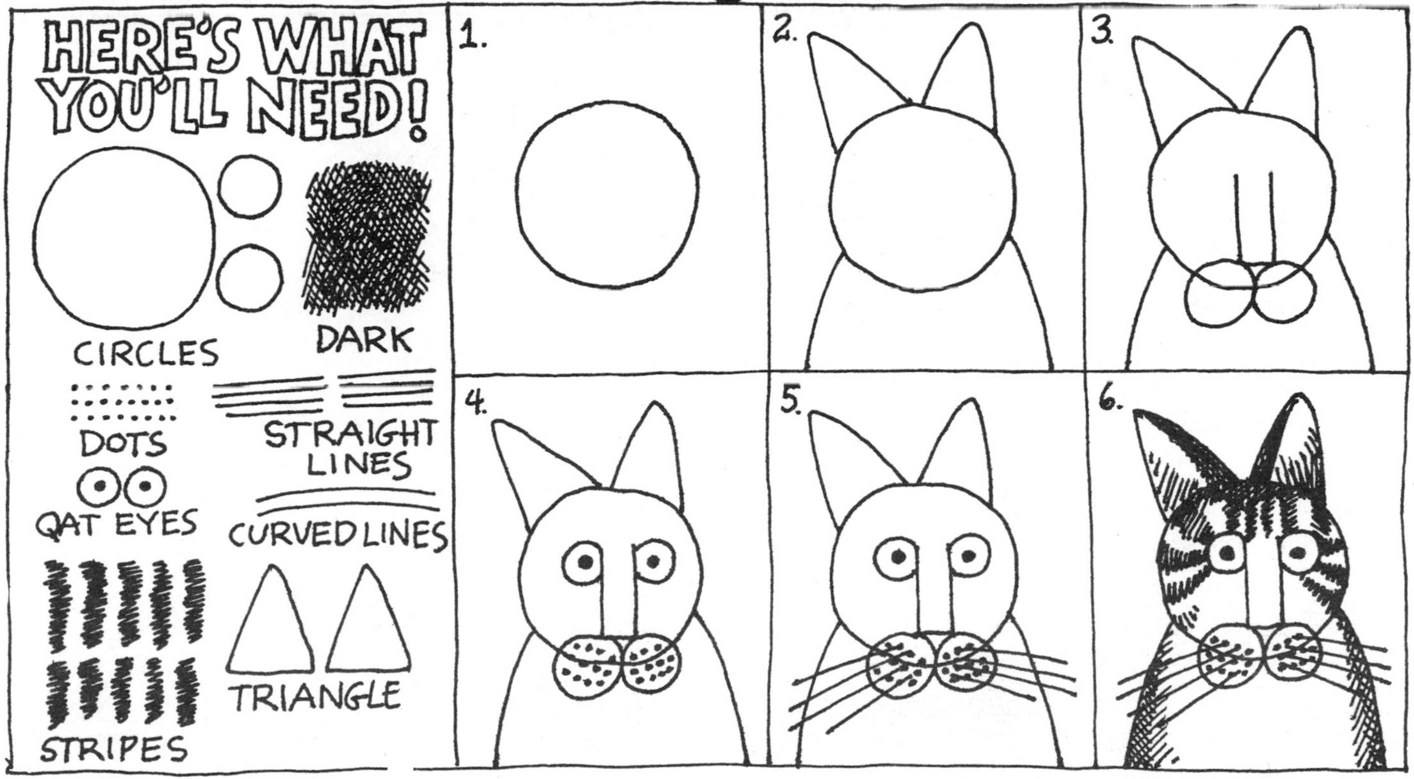
HERE'S WHAT YOU'LL NEED!
CIRCLES
DARK
DOTS
STRAIGHT LINES
QAT EYES
CURVED LINES
STRIPES
TRIANGLE
1.
2.
3.
4.
5.
6.

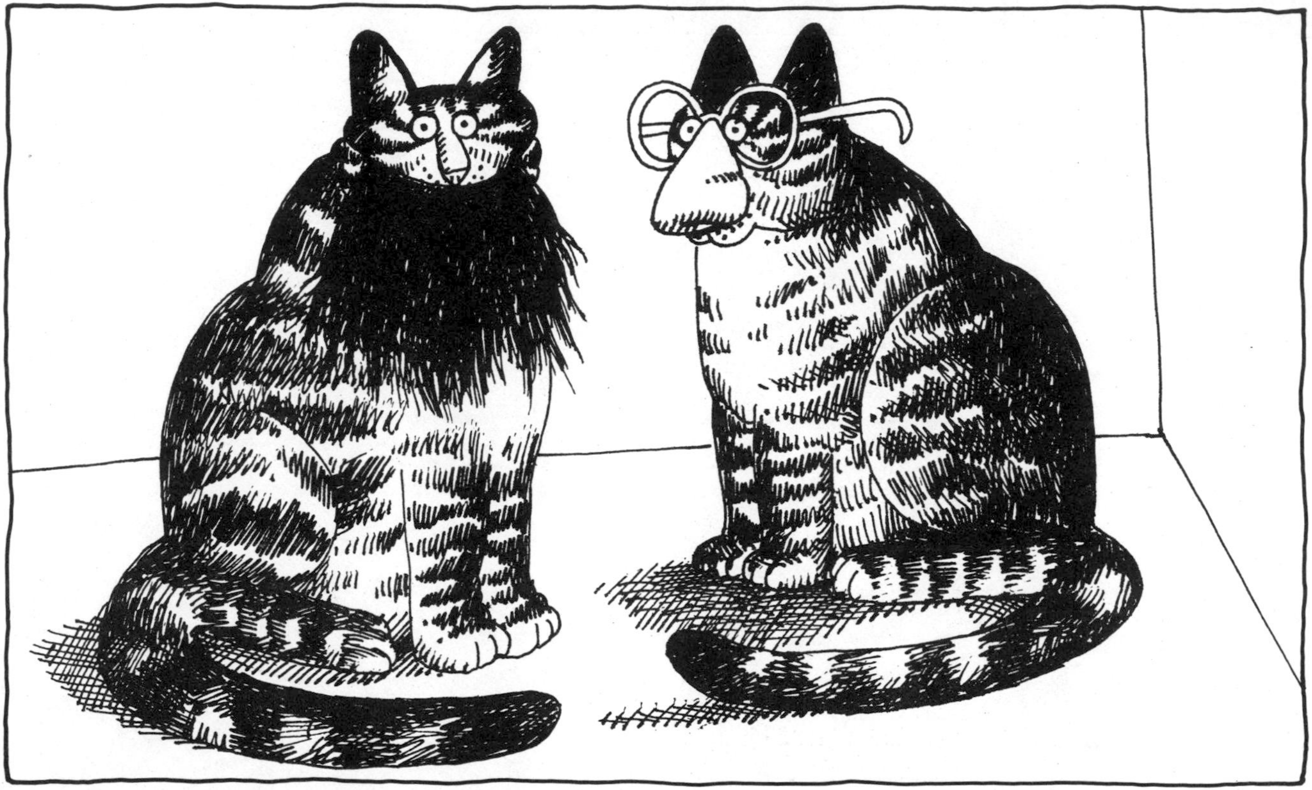

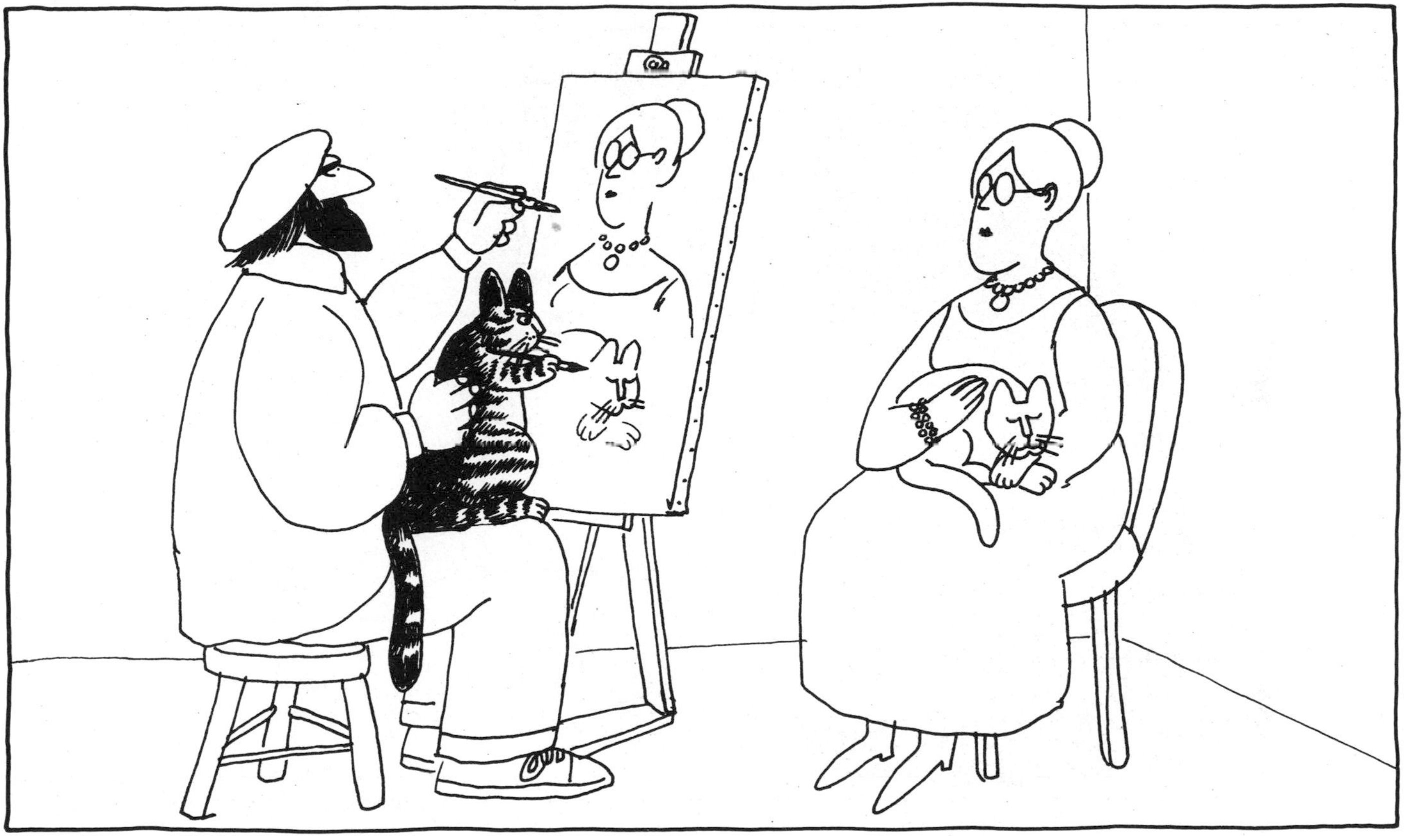

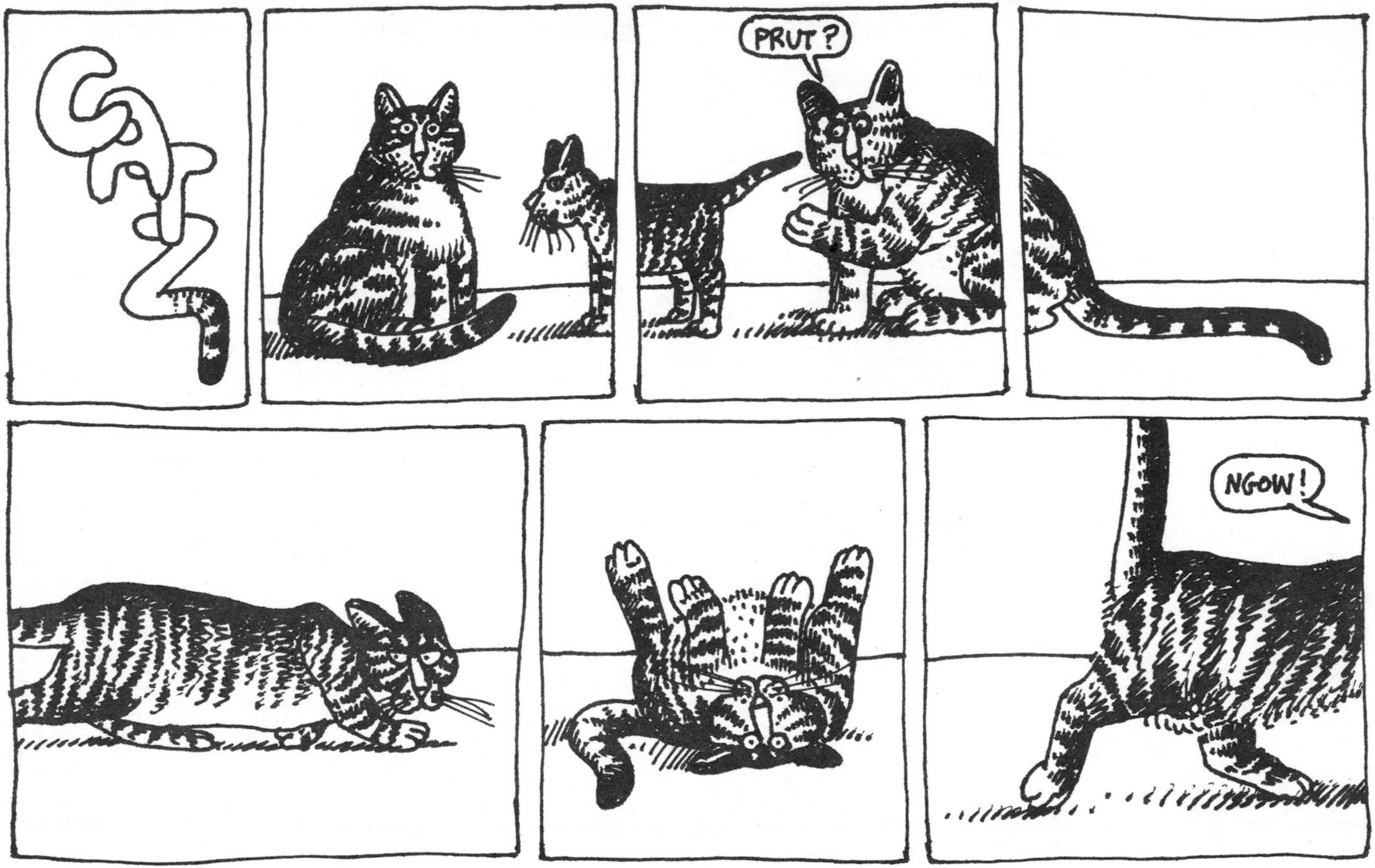
CATZ
PRUT?
NGOW!

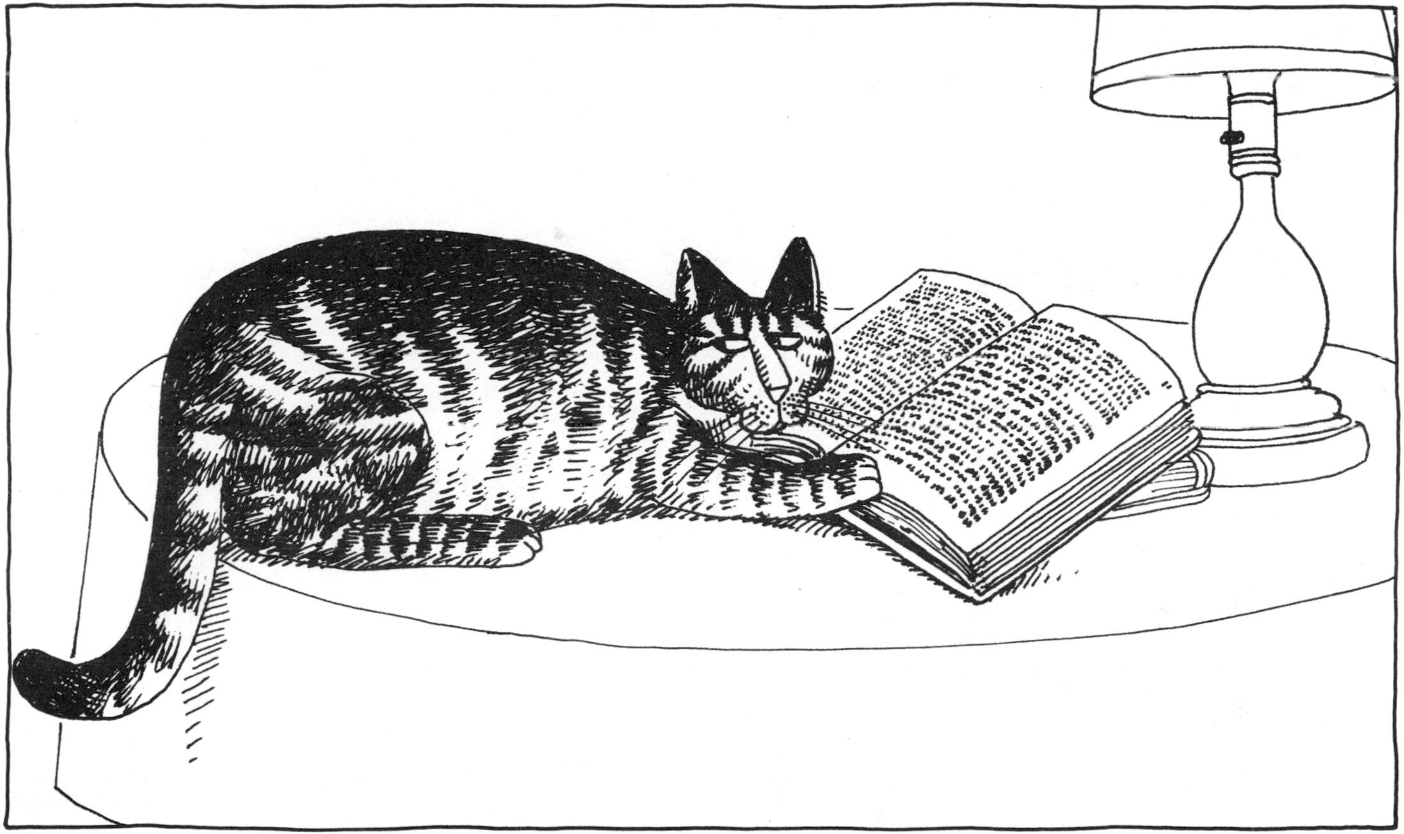

Wanda & Her Cats

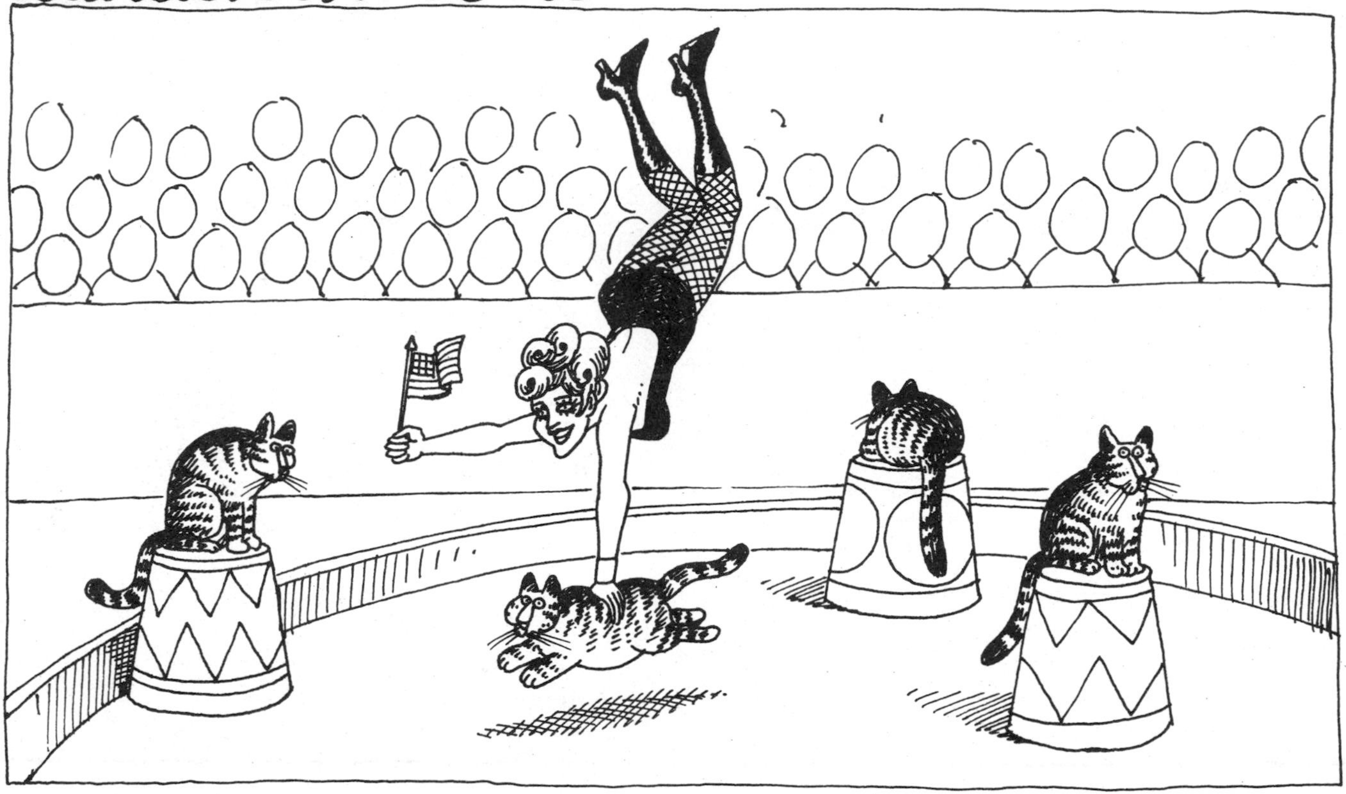

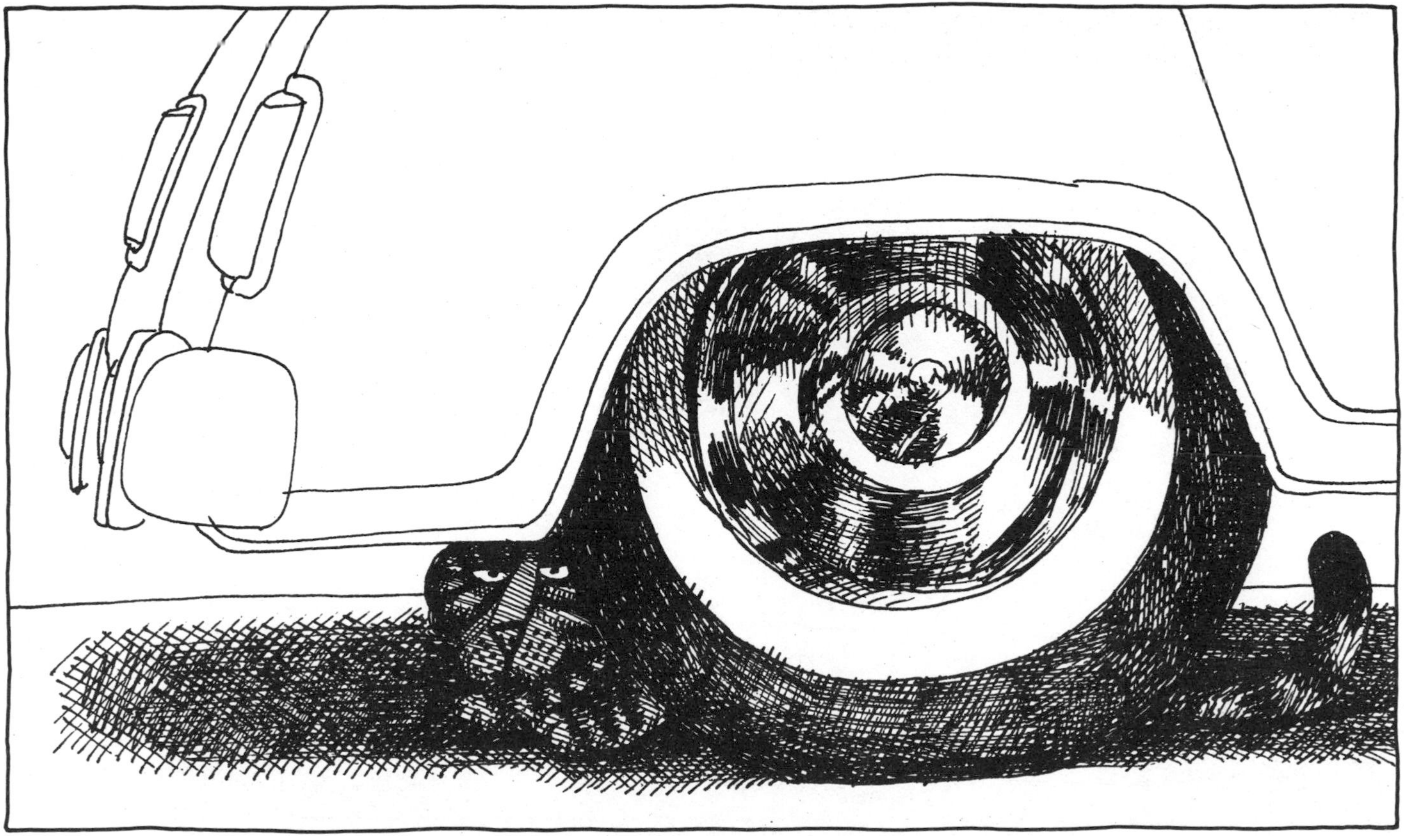

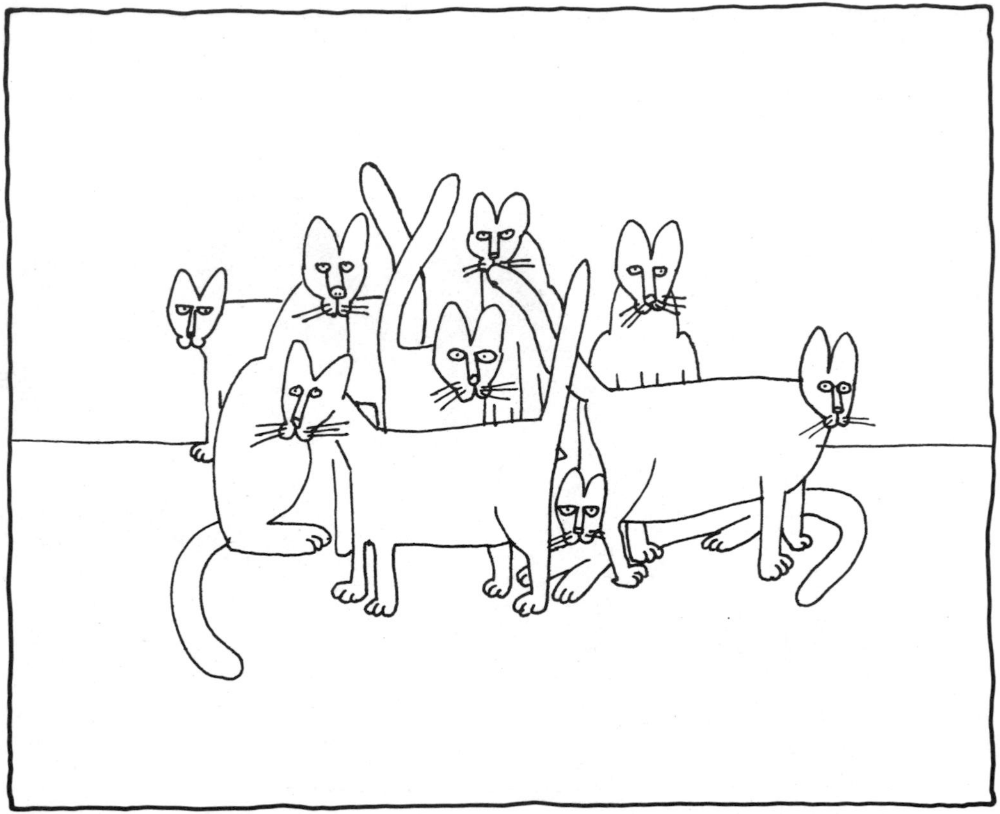

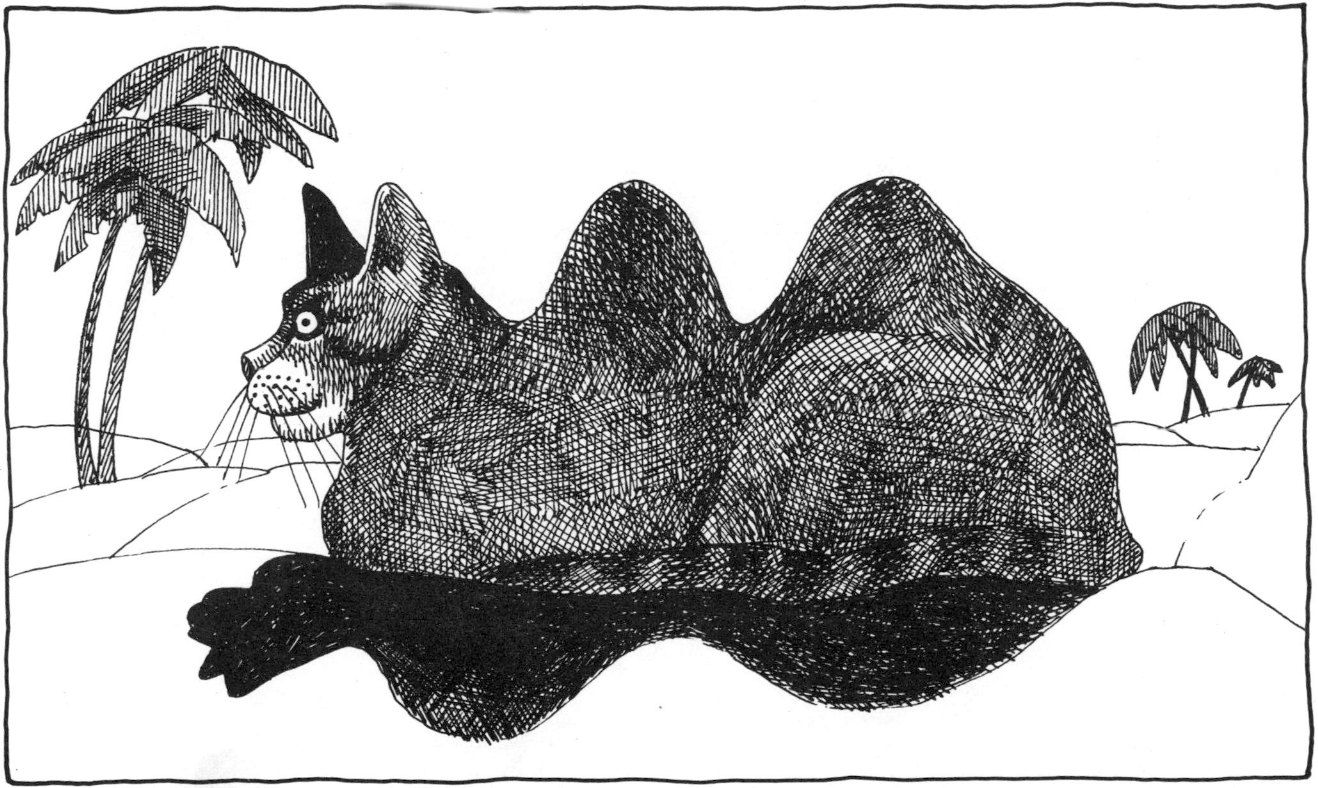

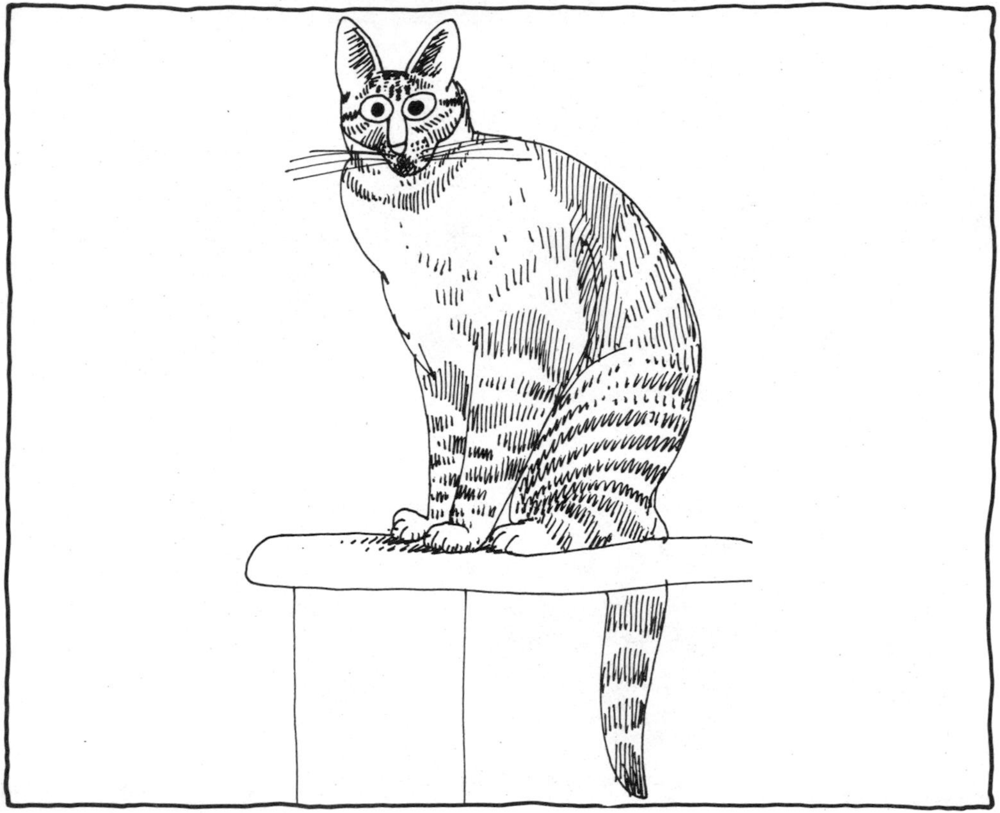

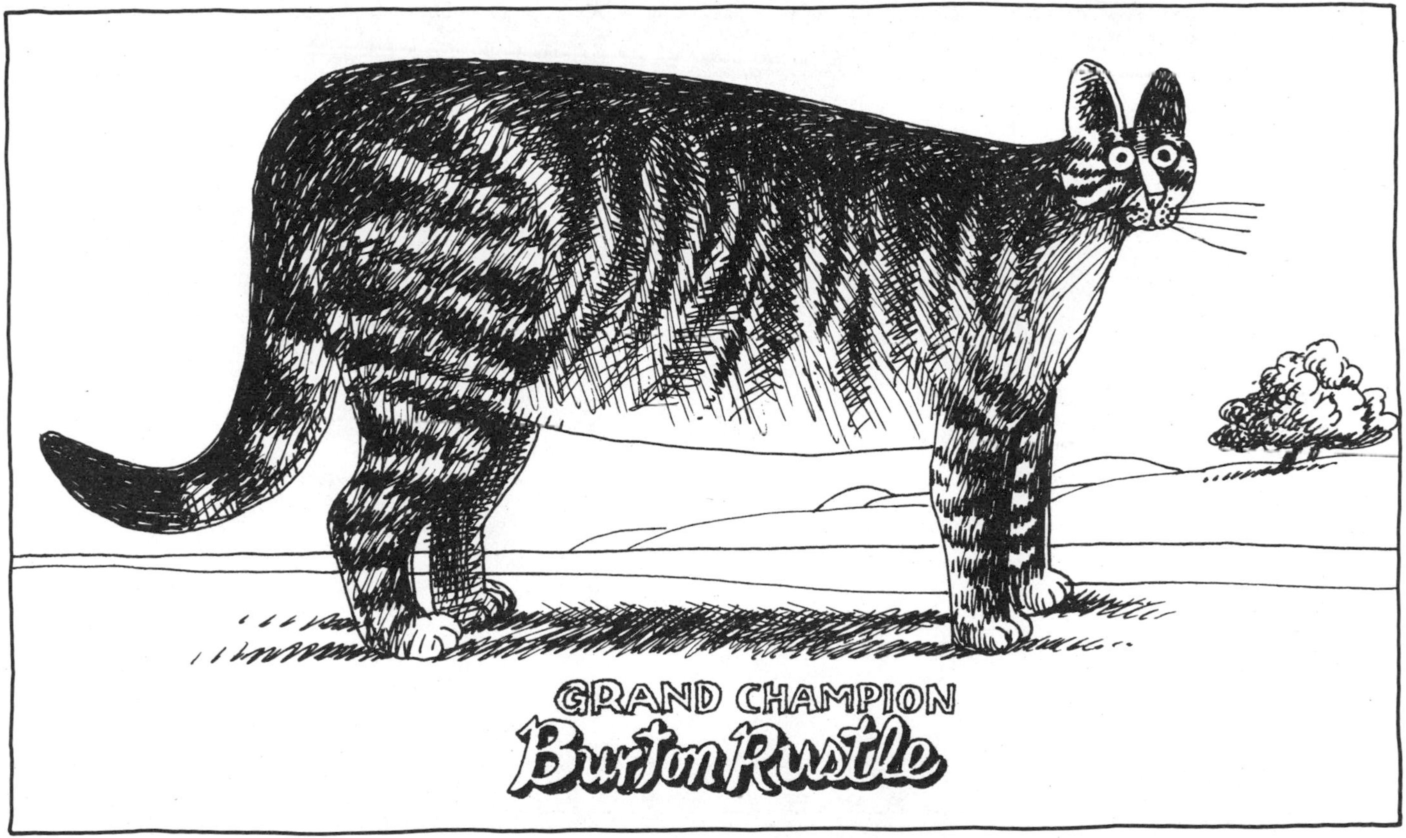
GRAND CHAMPION
Burton Rustle

Tiny Cat & Fountain Pen

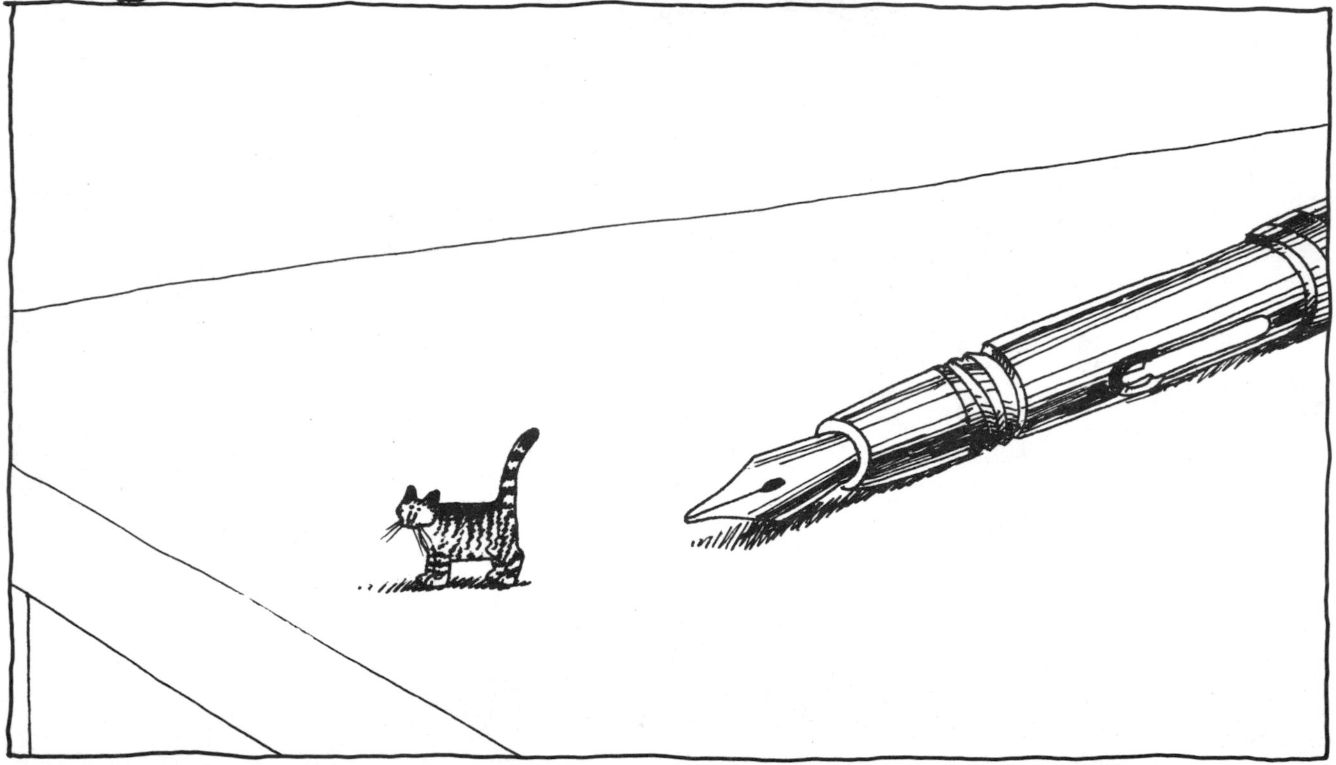

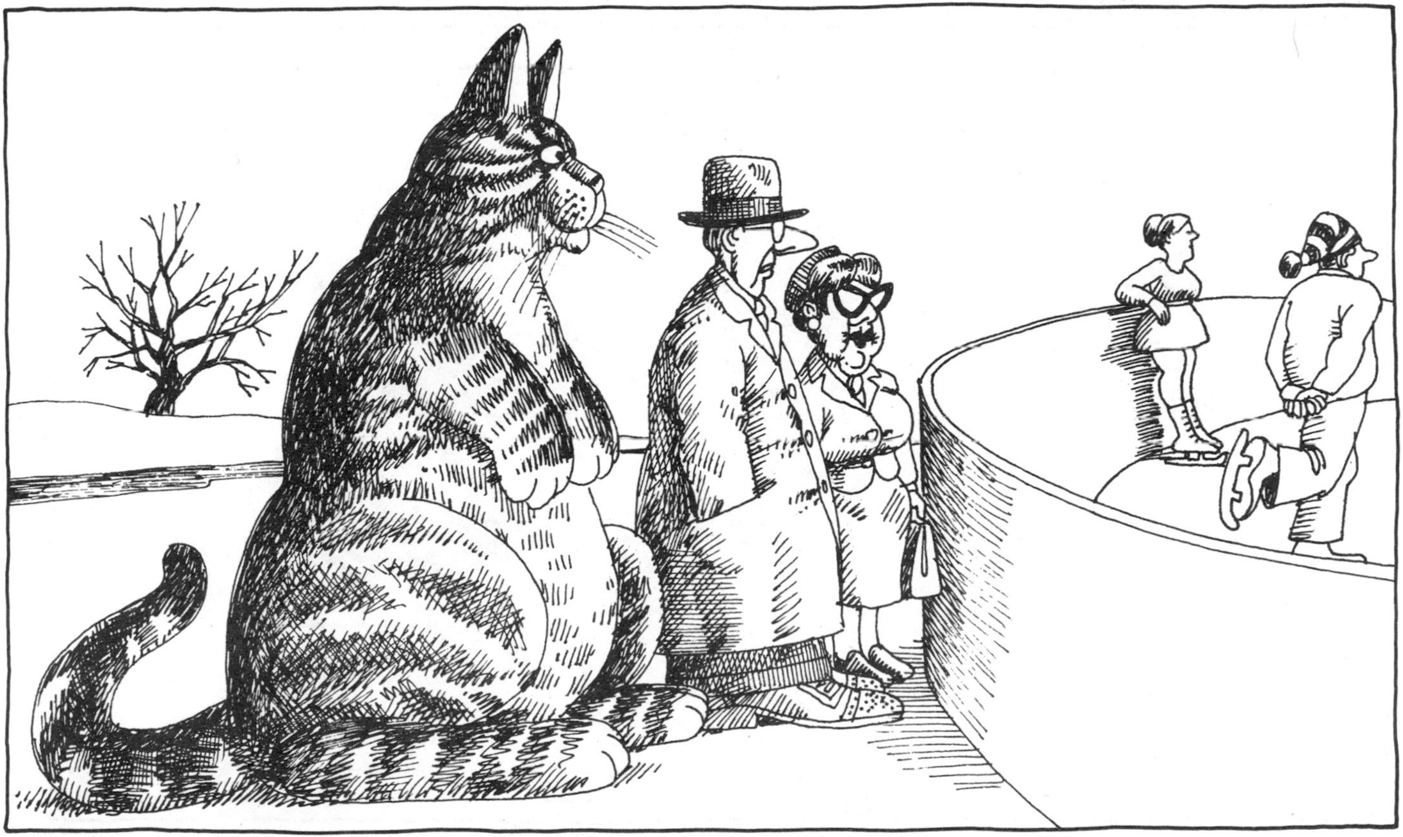

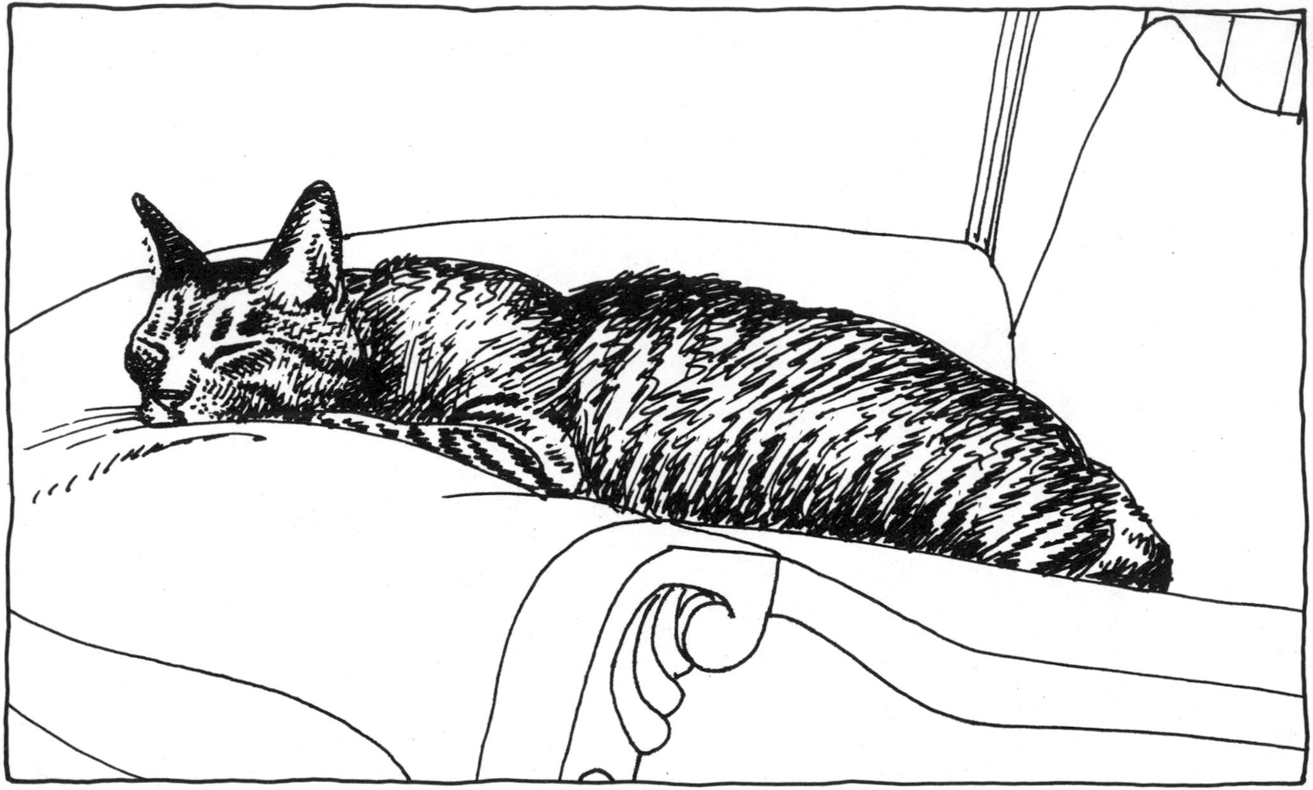

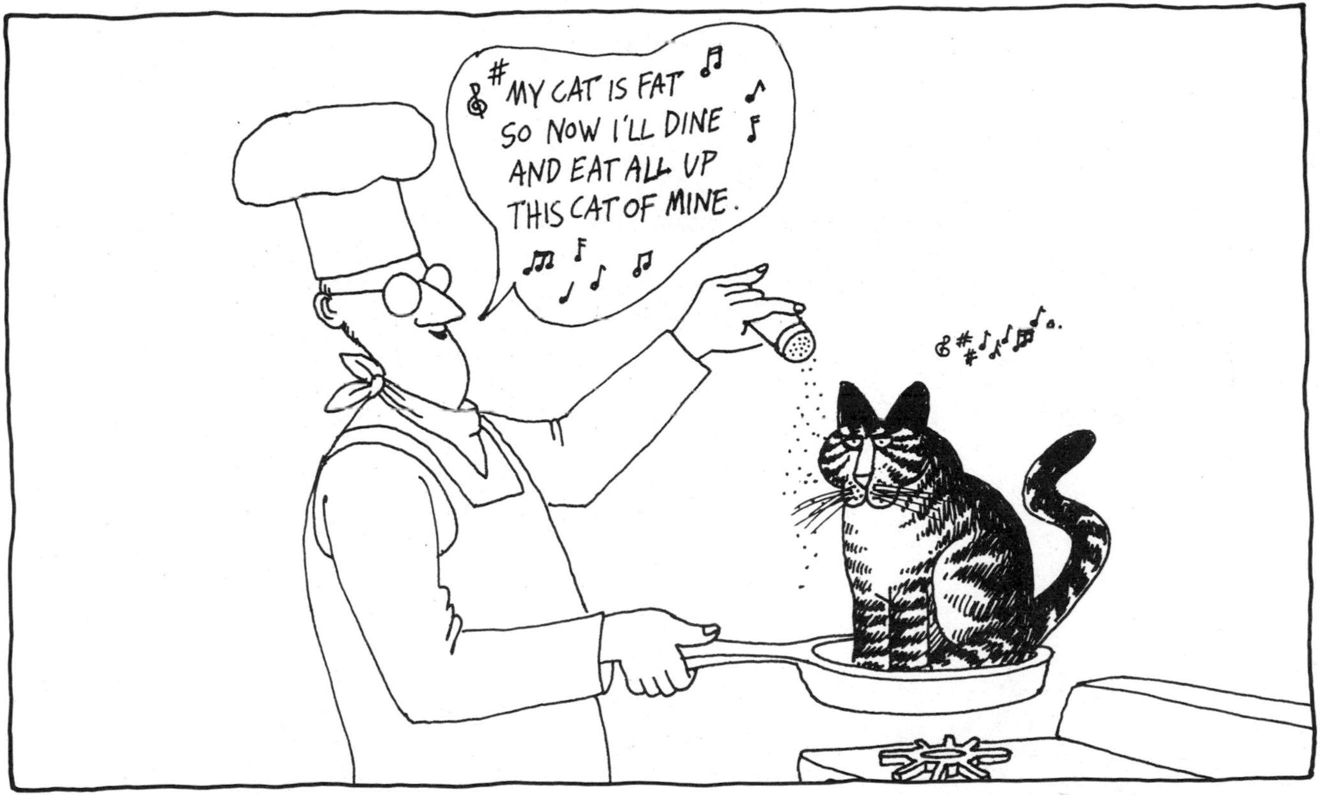
MY CAT IS FAT
SO NOW I'LL DINE
AND EAT ALL UP
THIS CAT OF MINE.

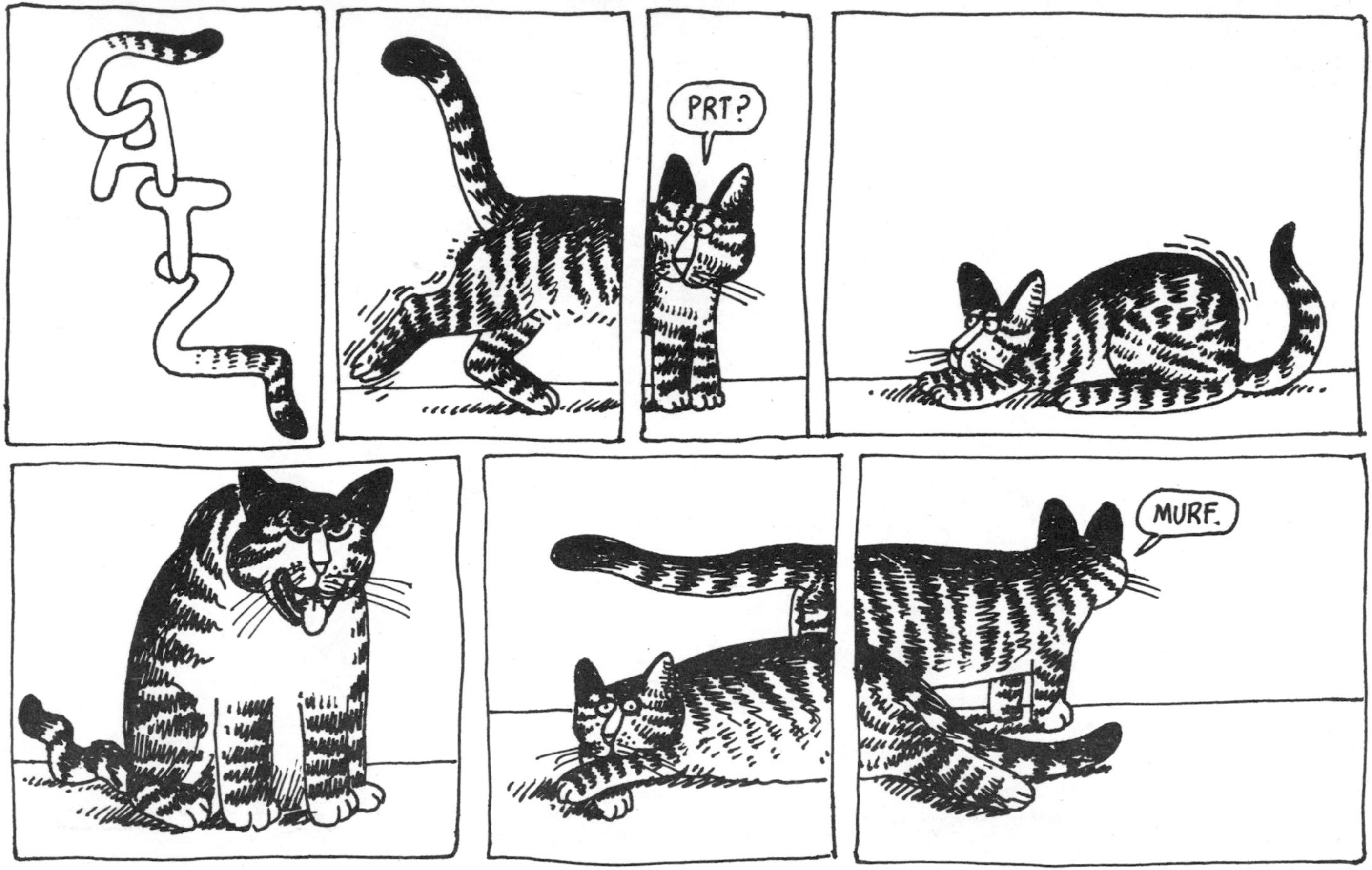
CATZ
PRT?
MURF.

Cat gun

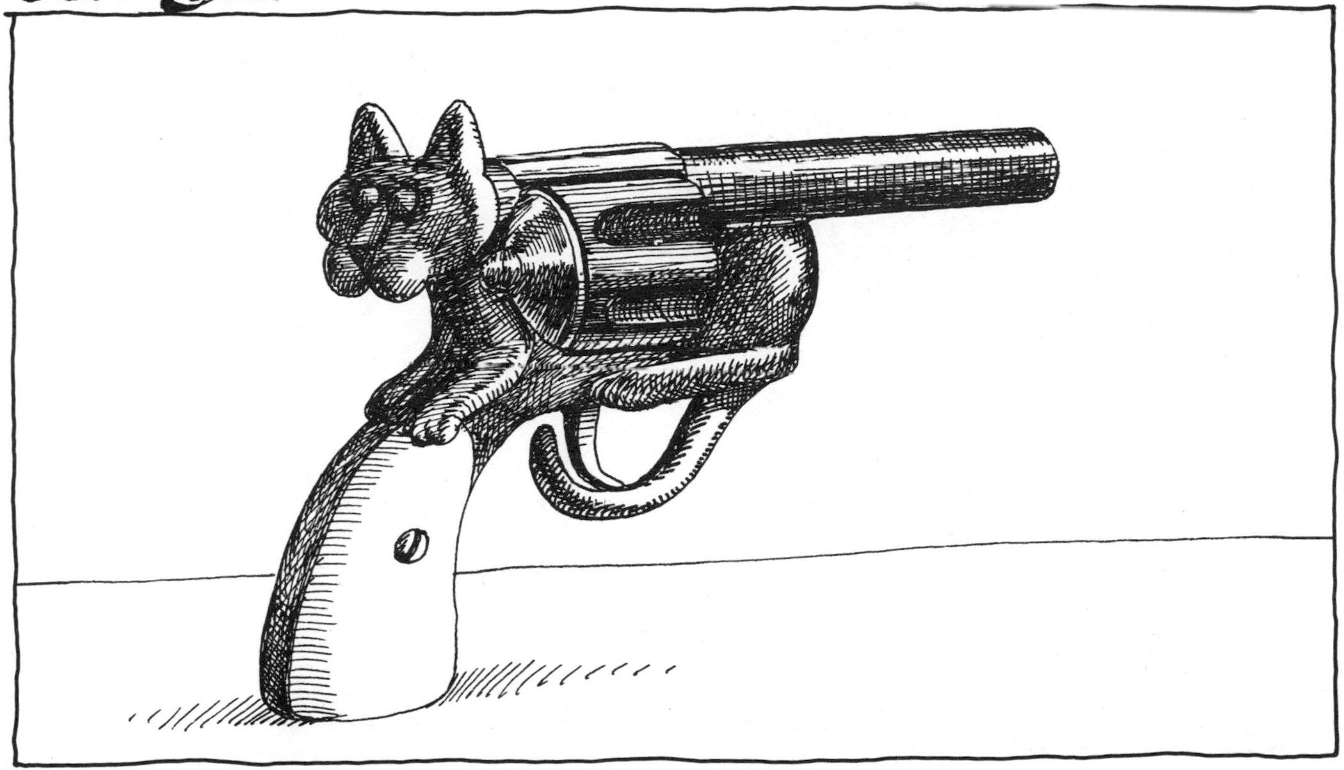

Noko Marie

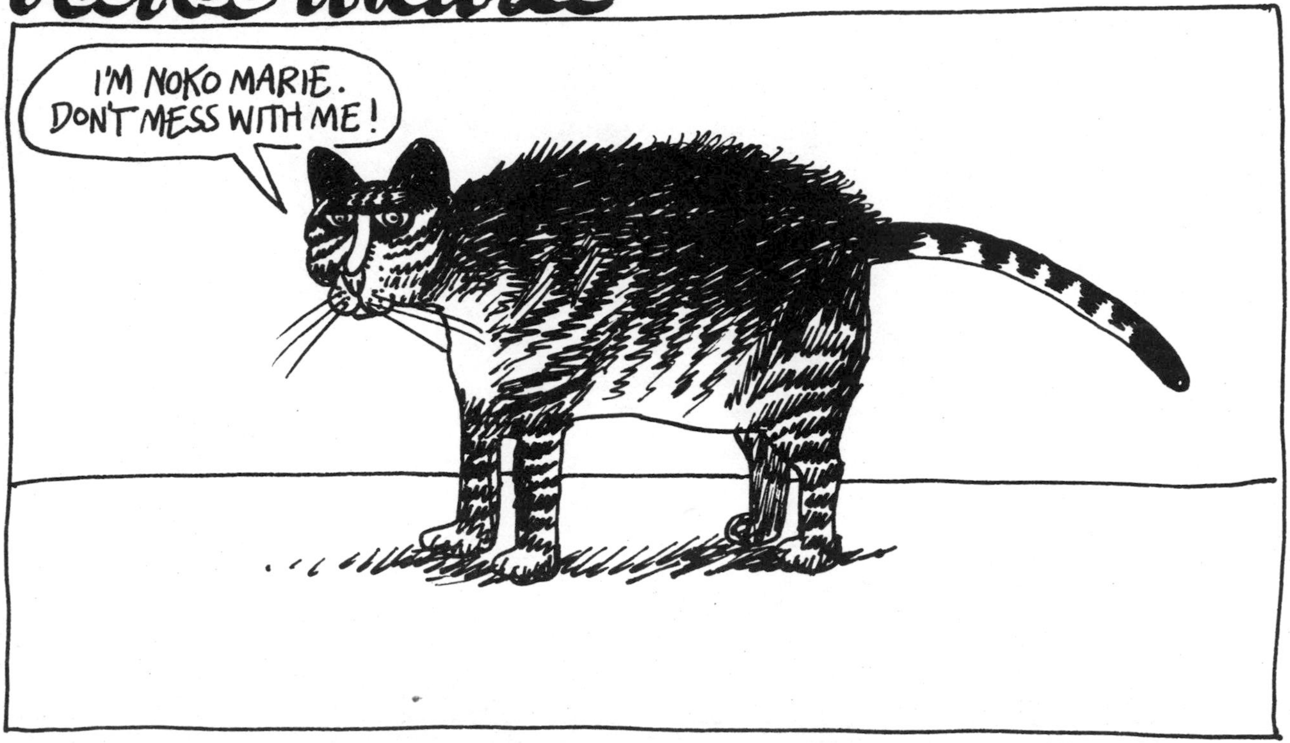
I'M NOKO MARIE. DON'T MESS WITH ME!

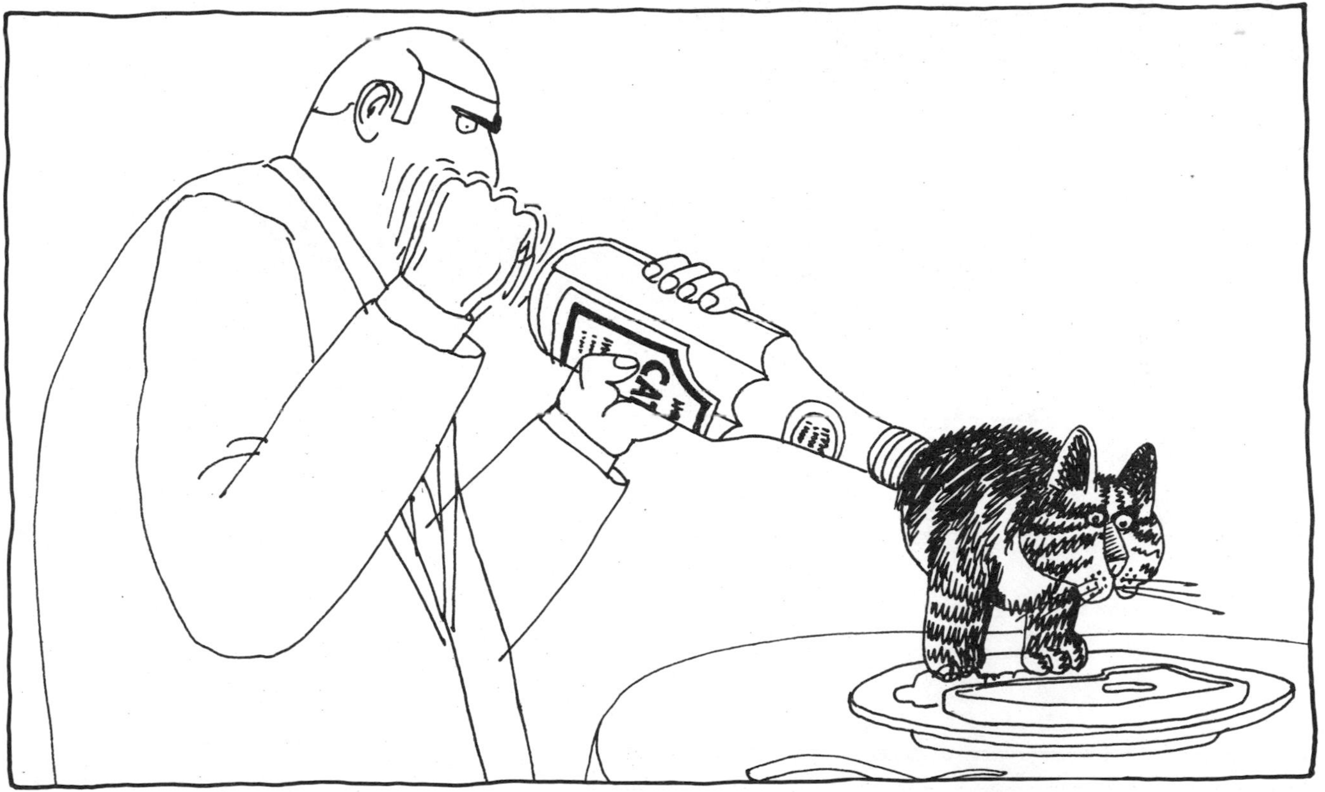

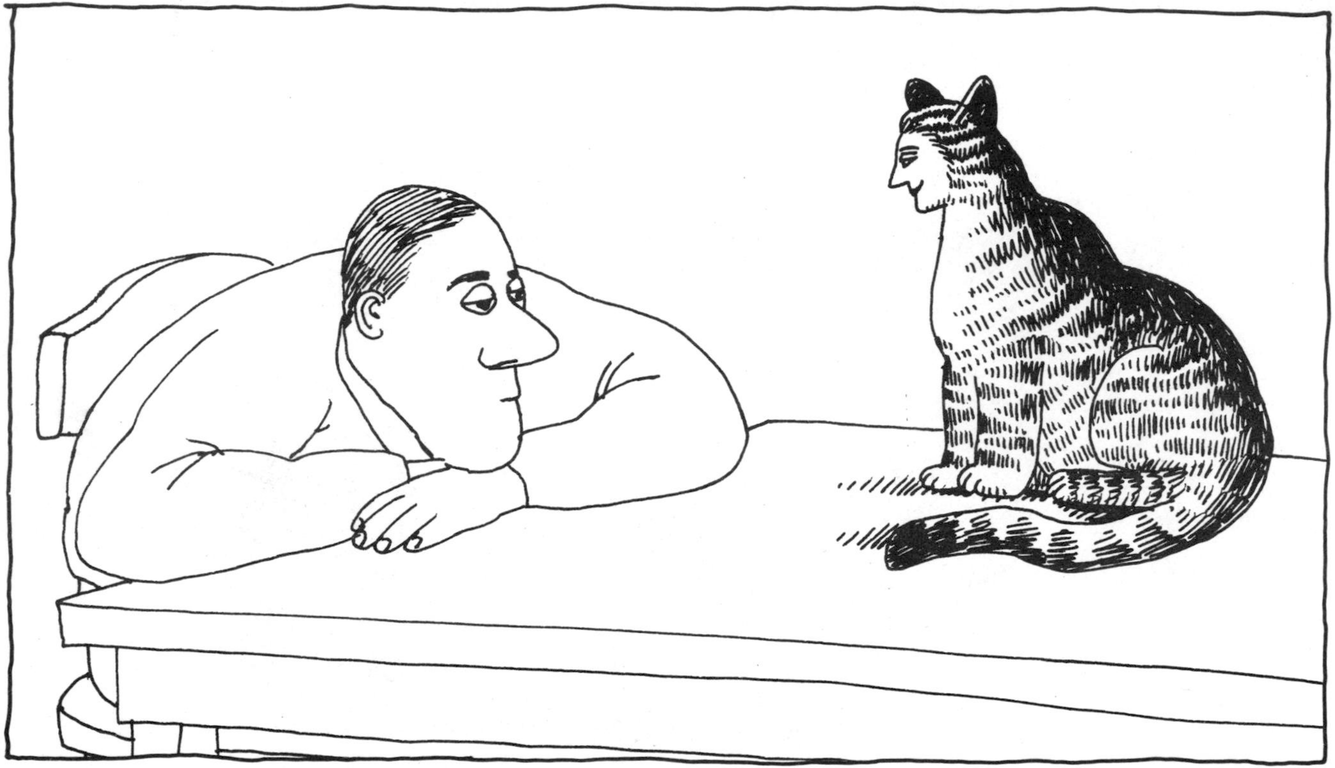

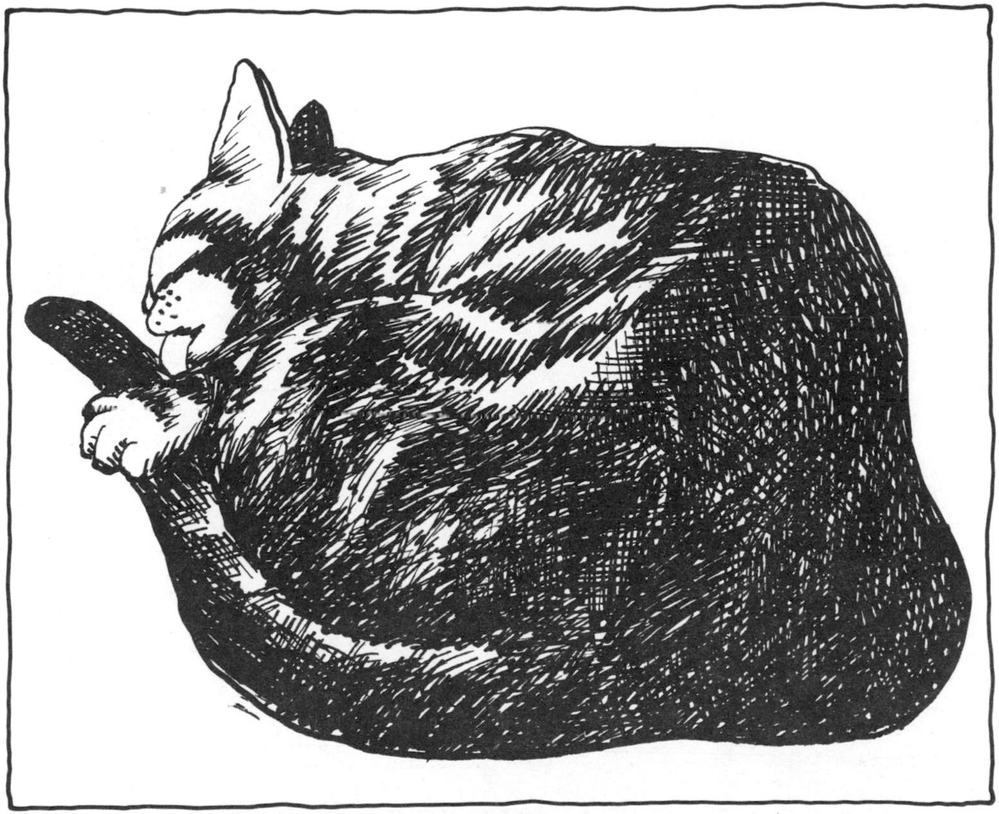

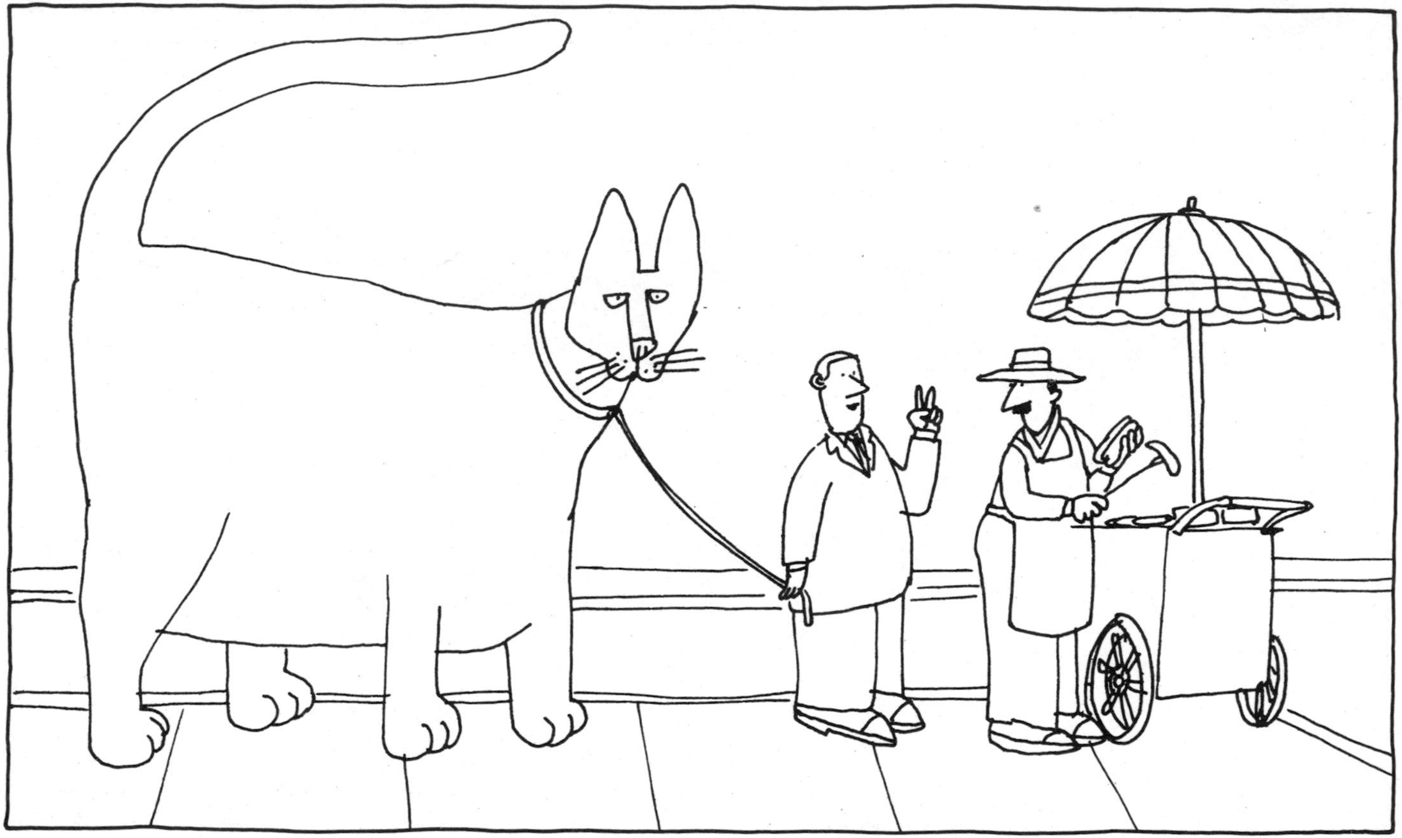

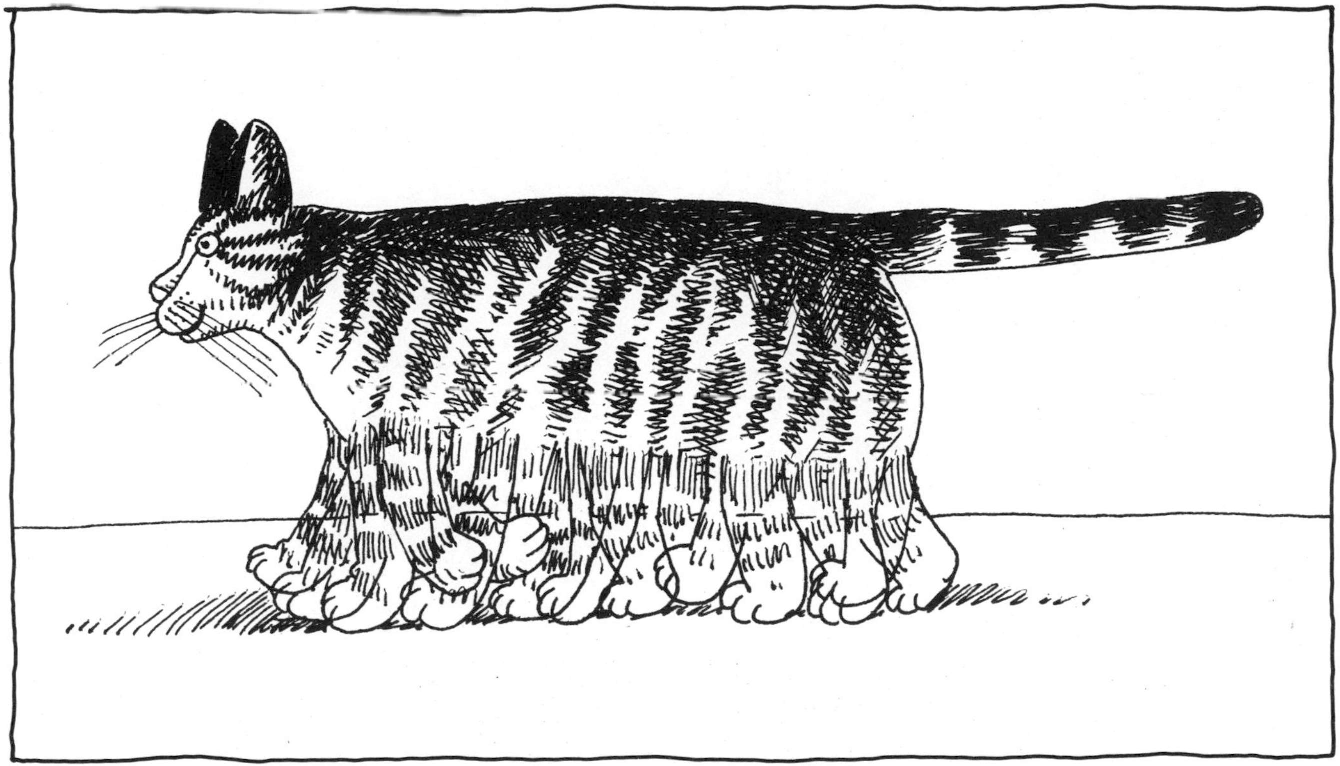

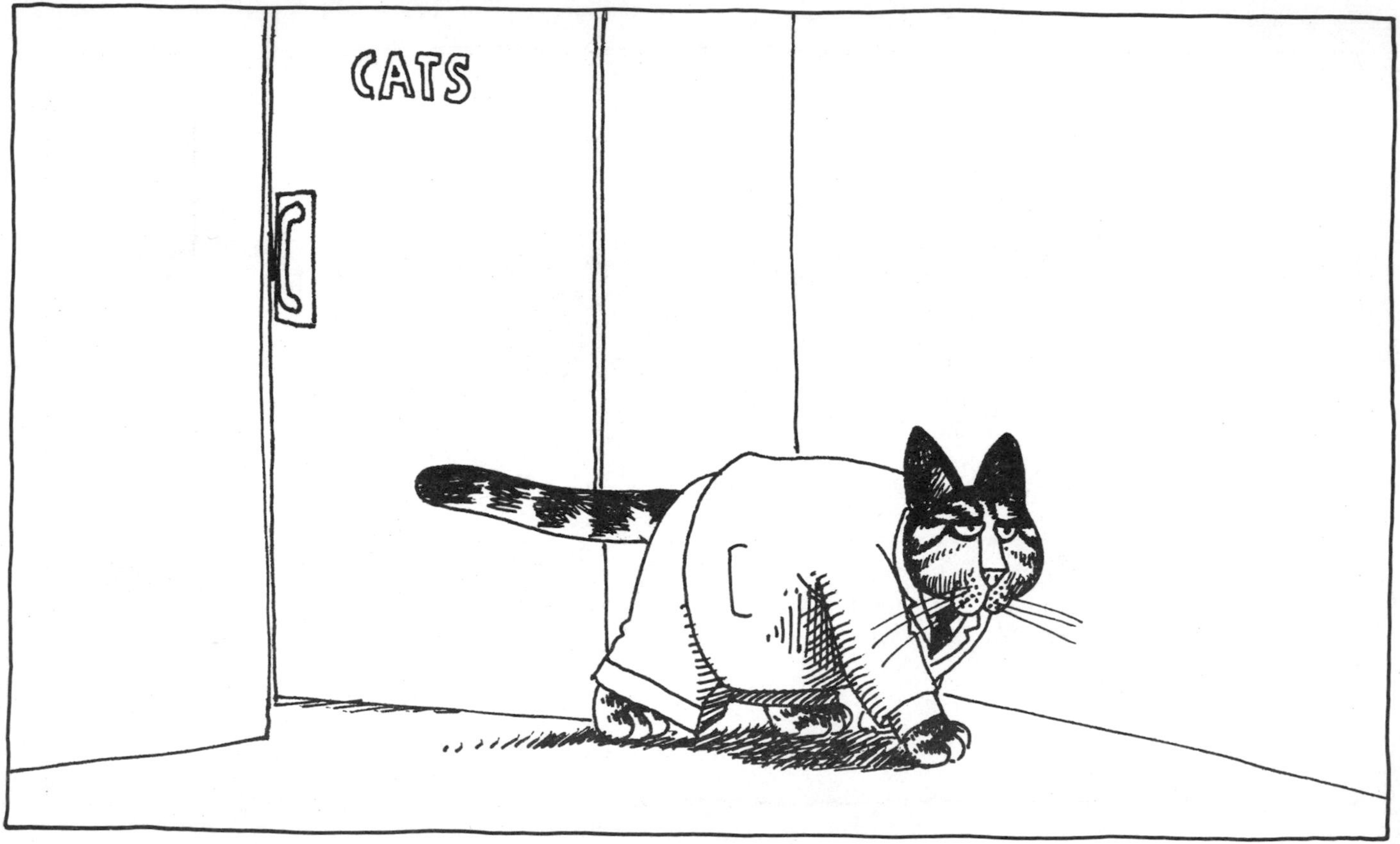
CATS

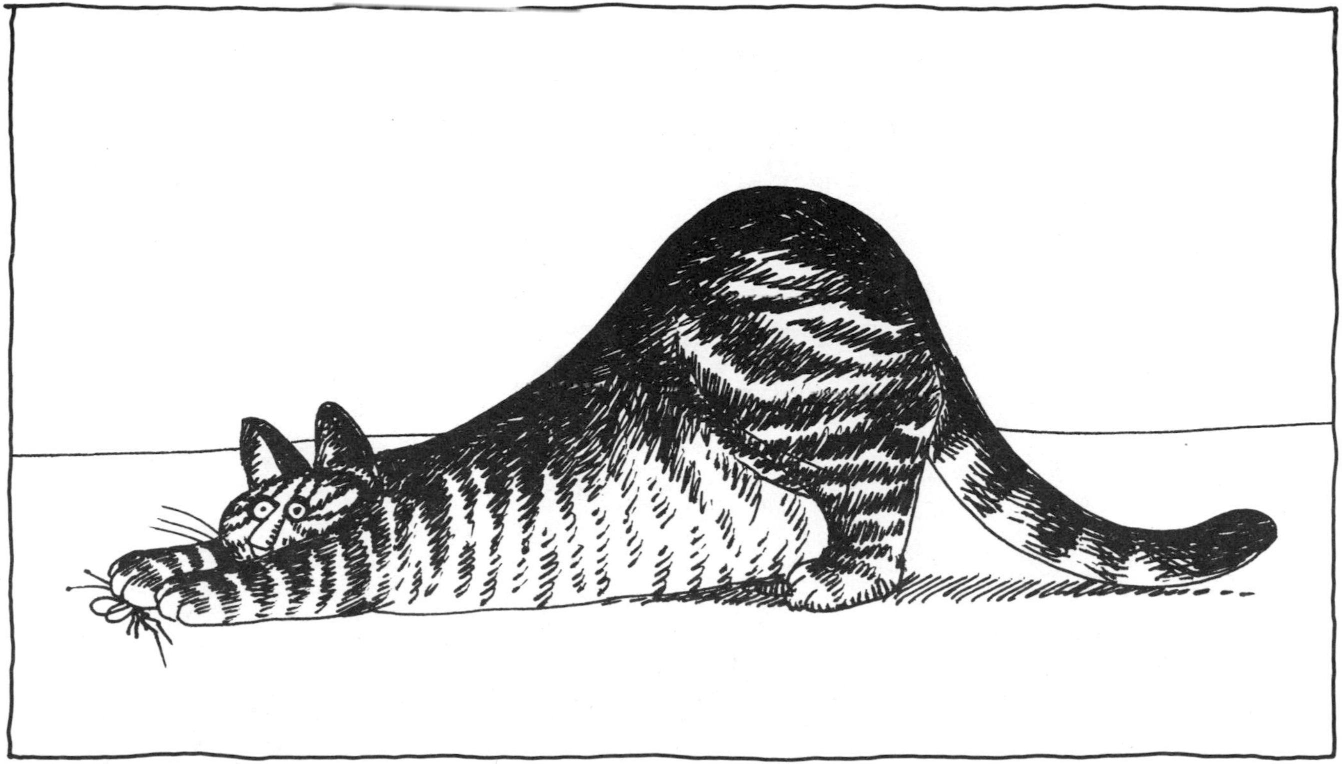

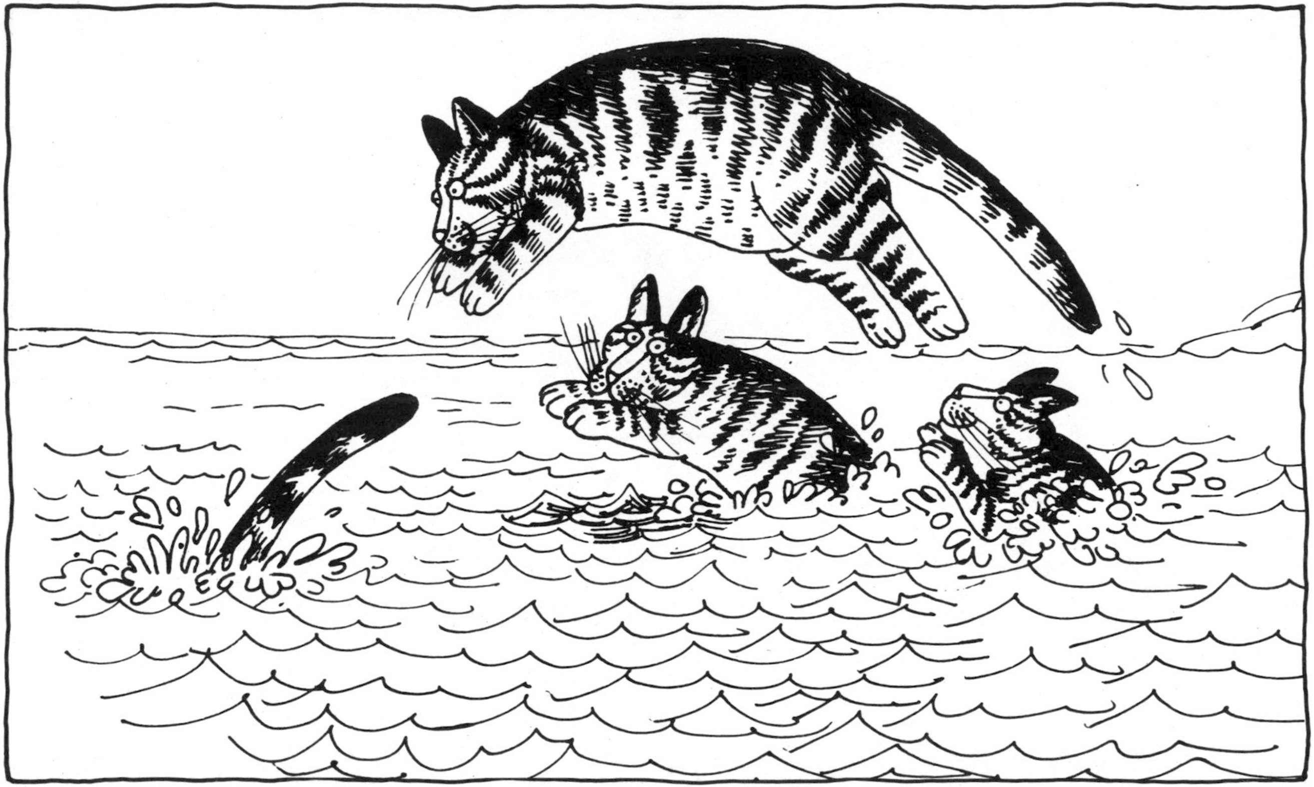

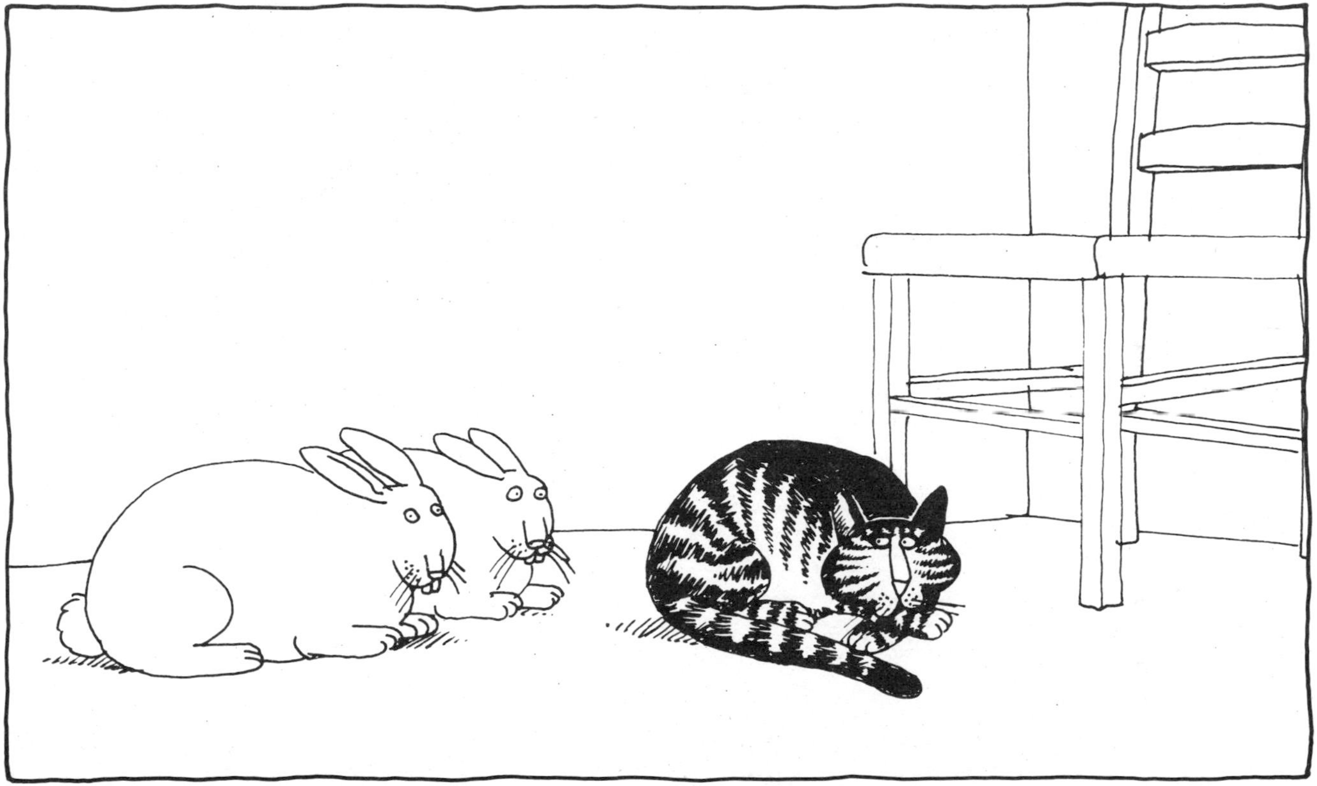

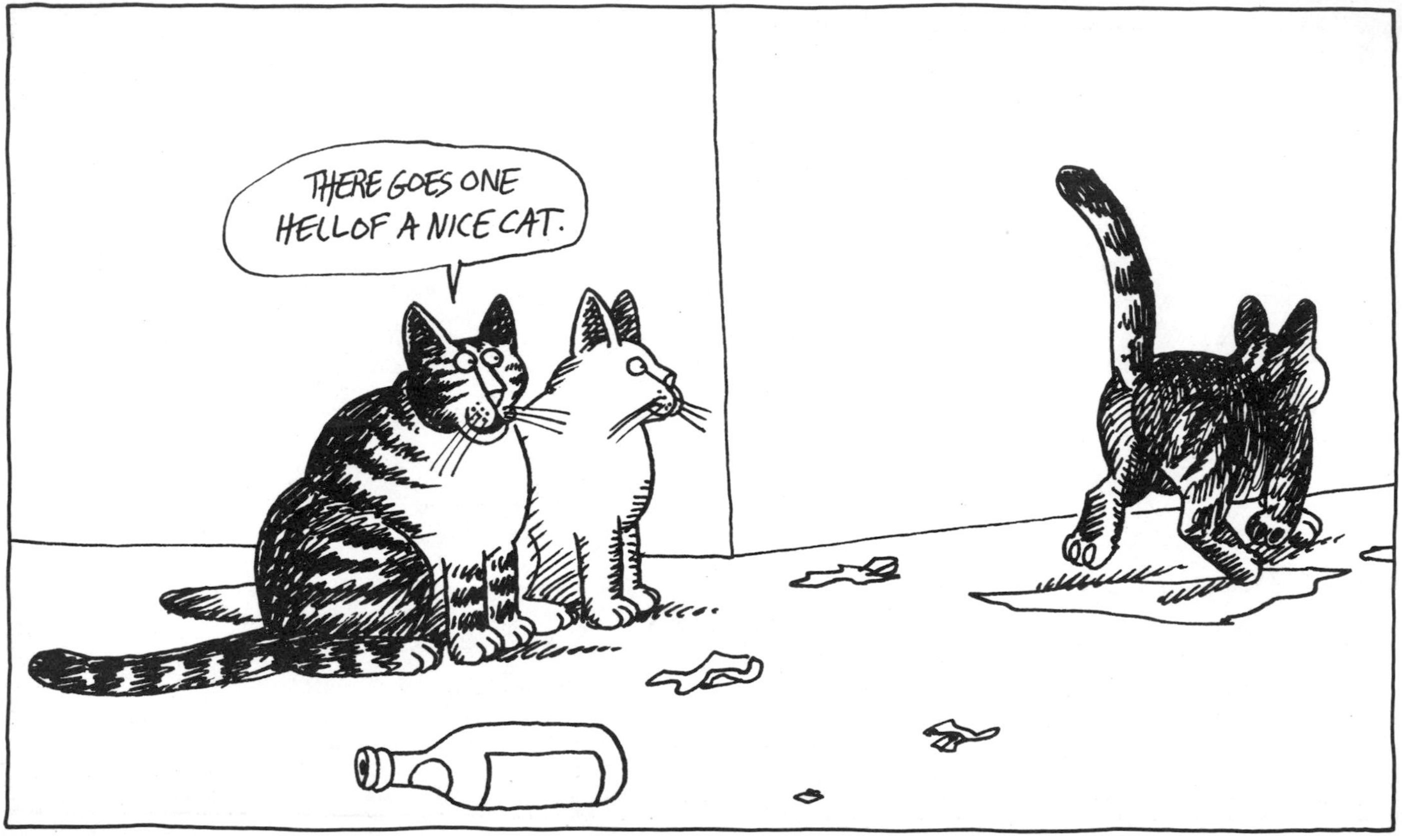
THERE GOES ONE HELL OF A NICE CAT.

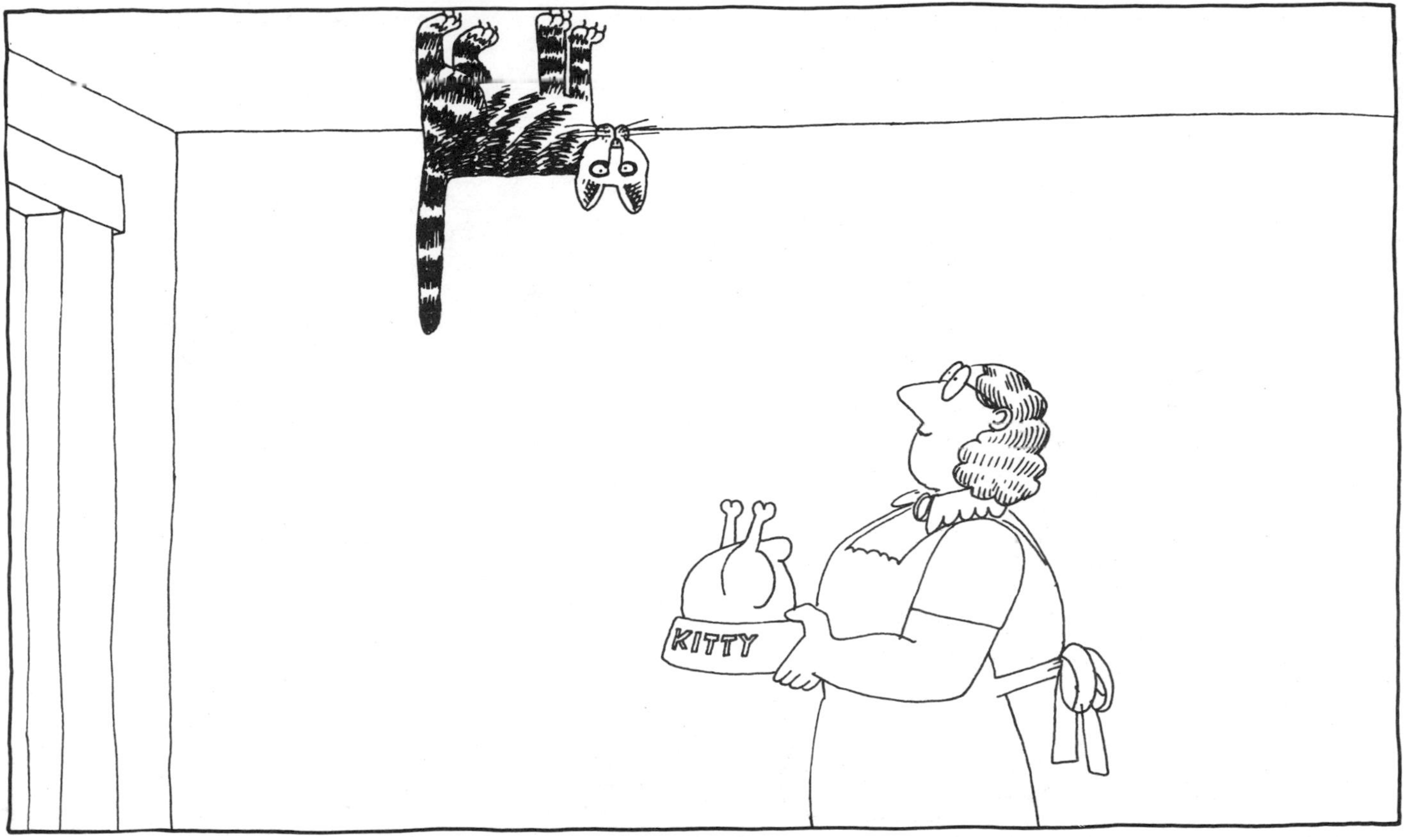
KITTY

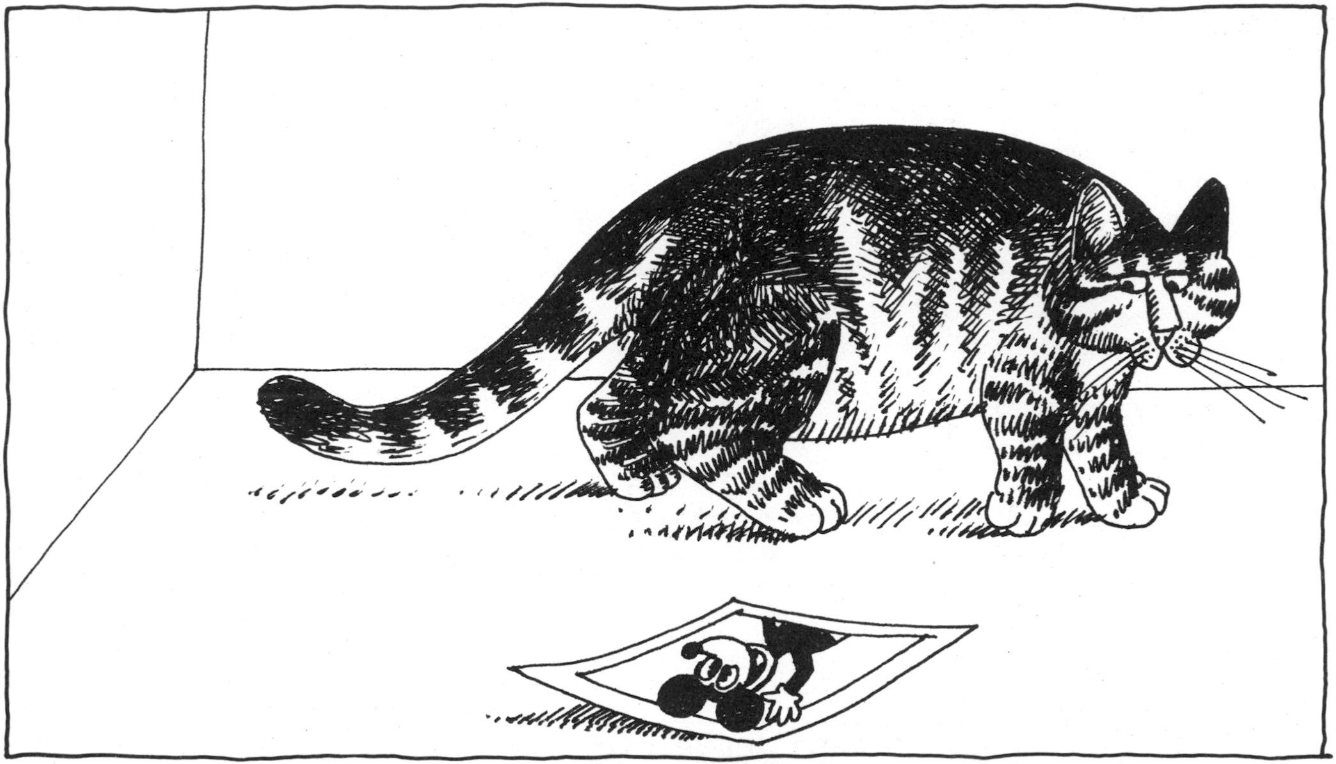

Purr Box

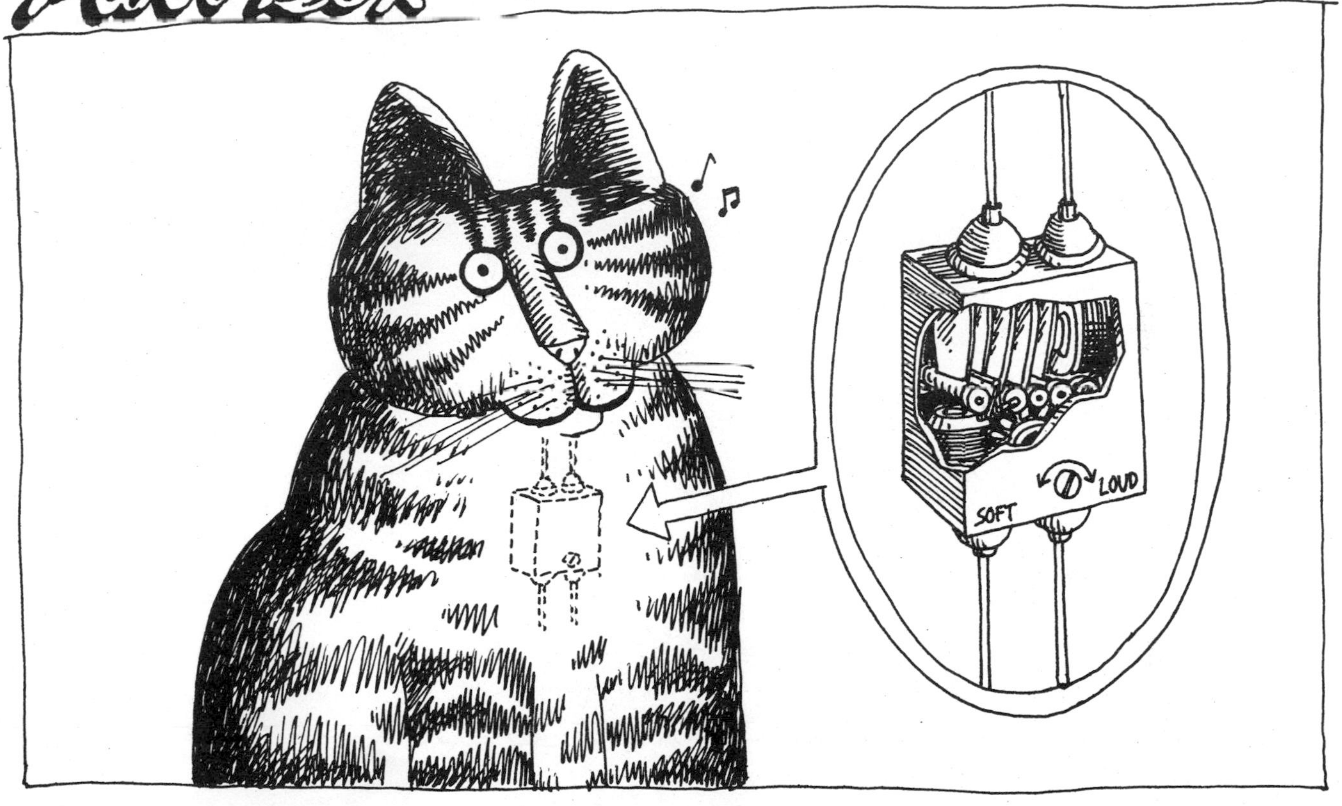
LOUD
SOFT

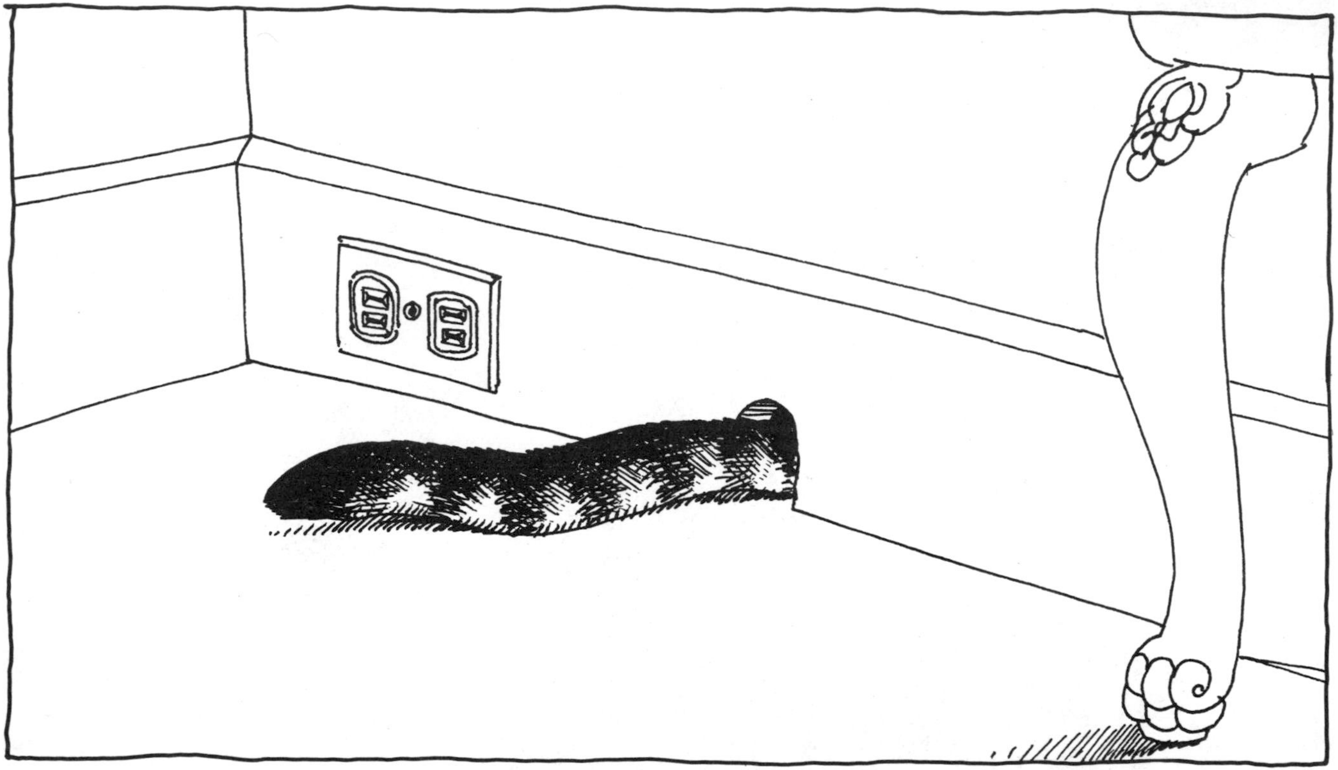

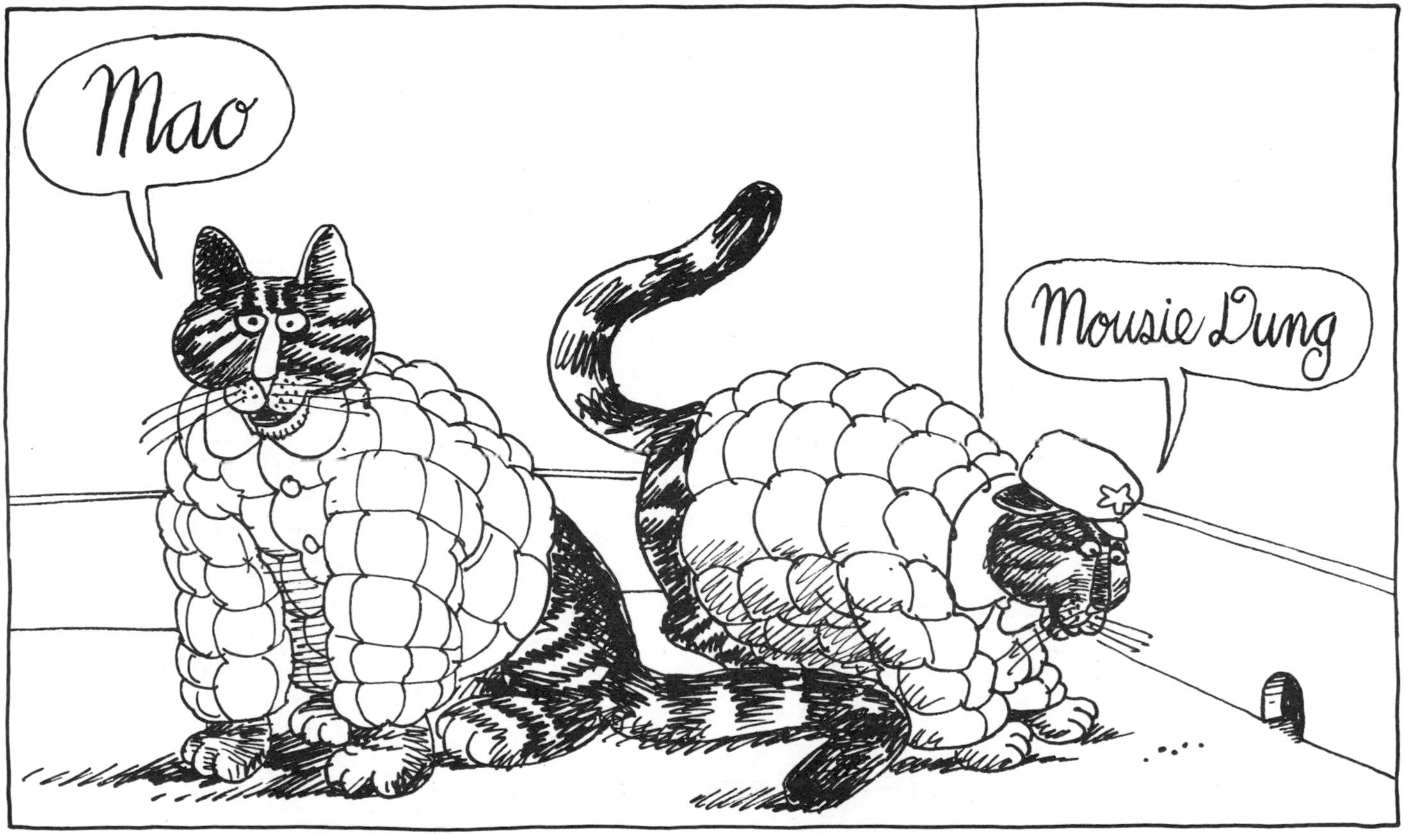
Mao
Mousie Dung

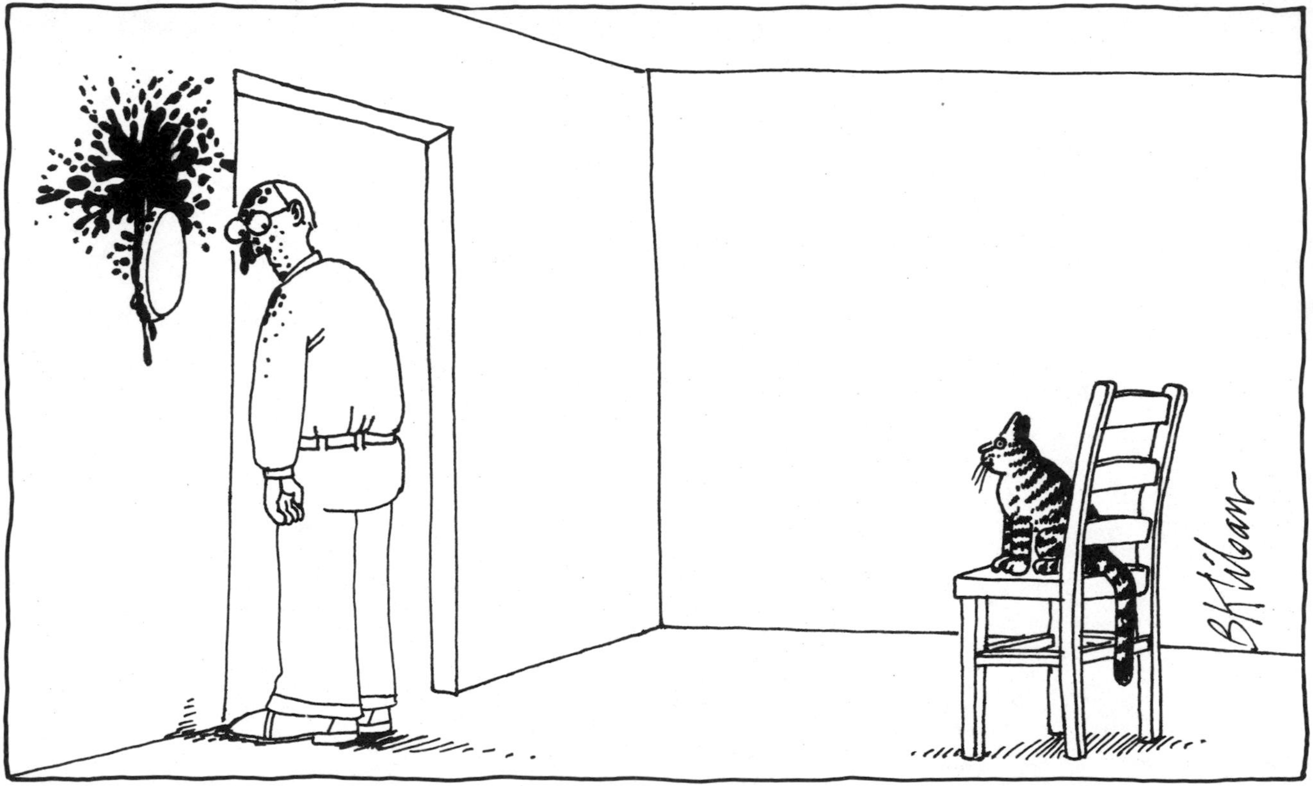
BKliban

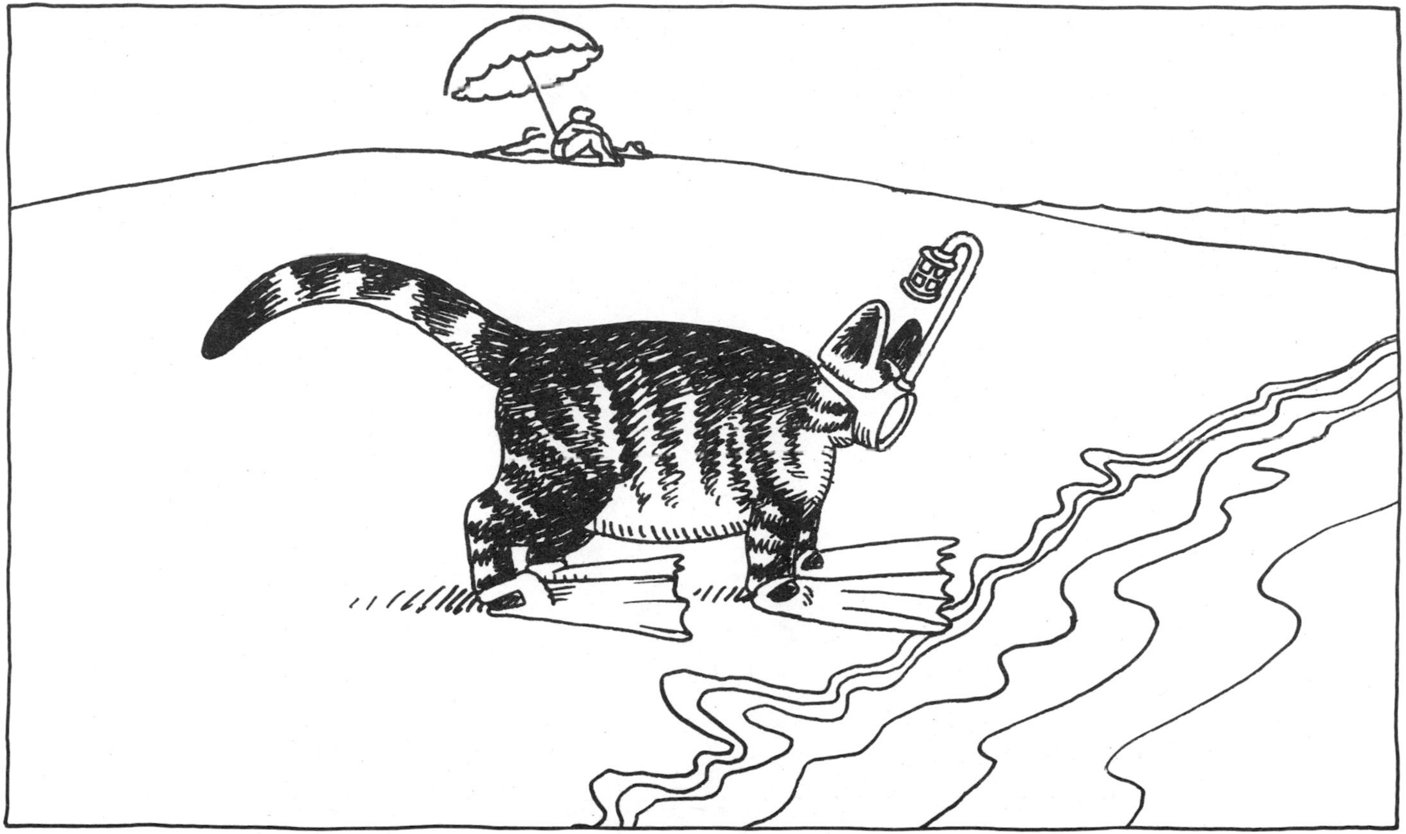

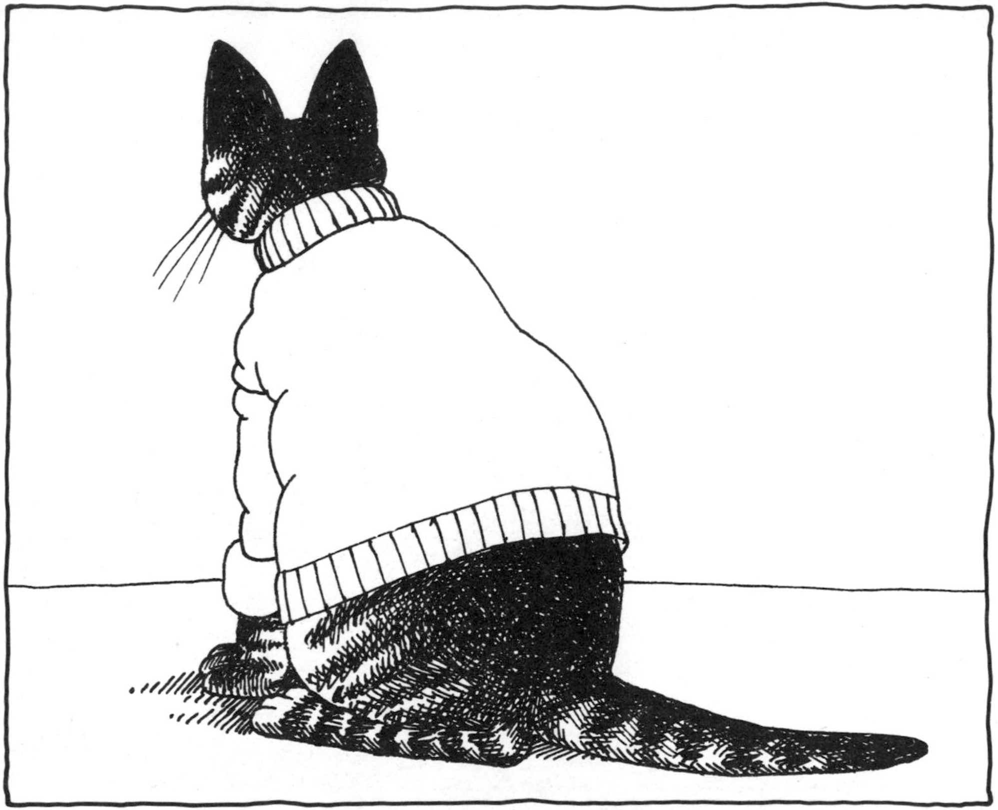

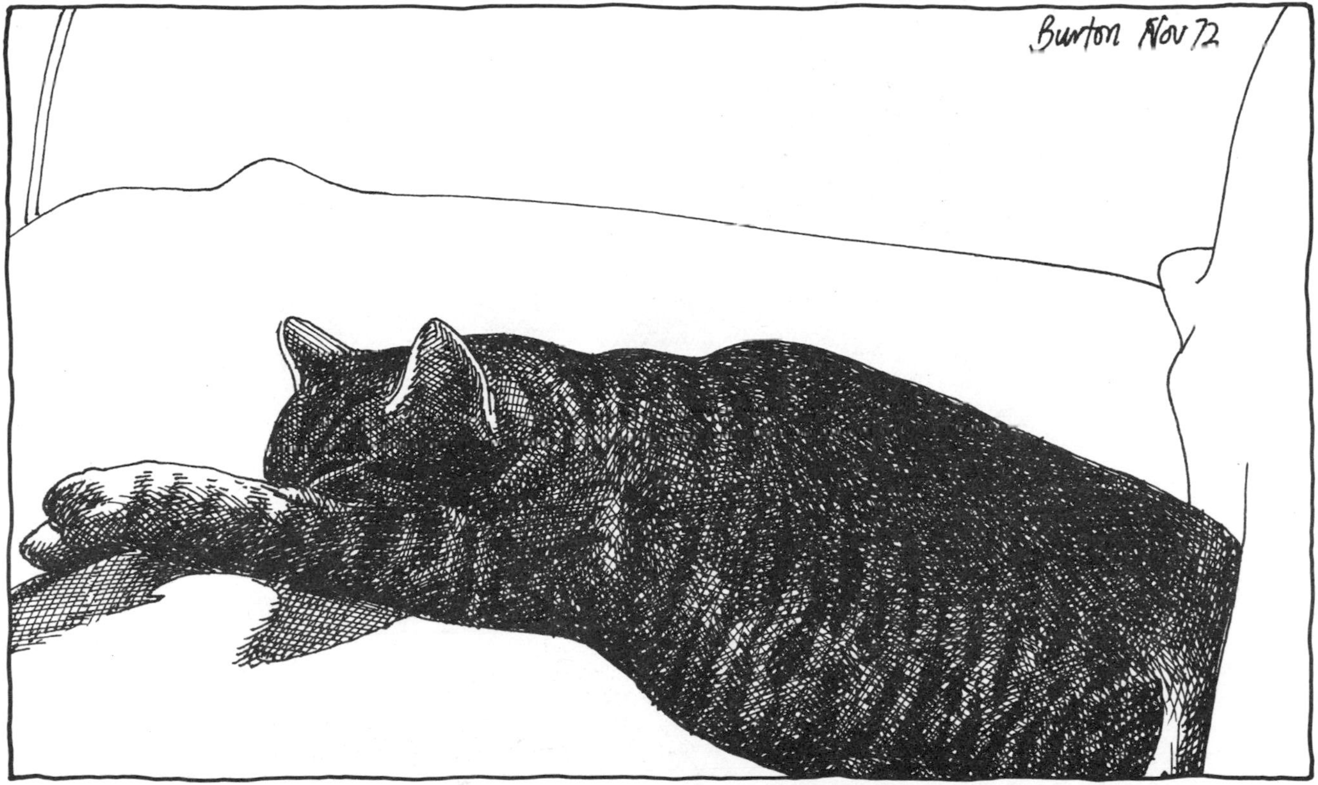
Burton Nov 72

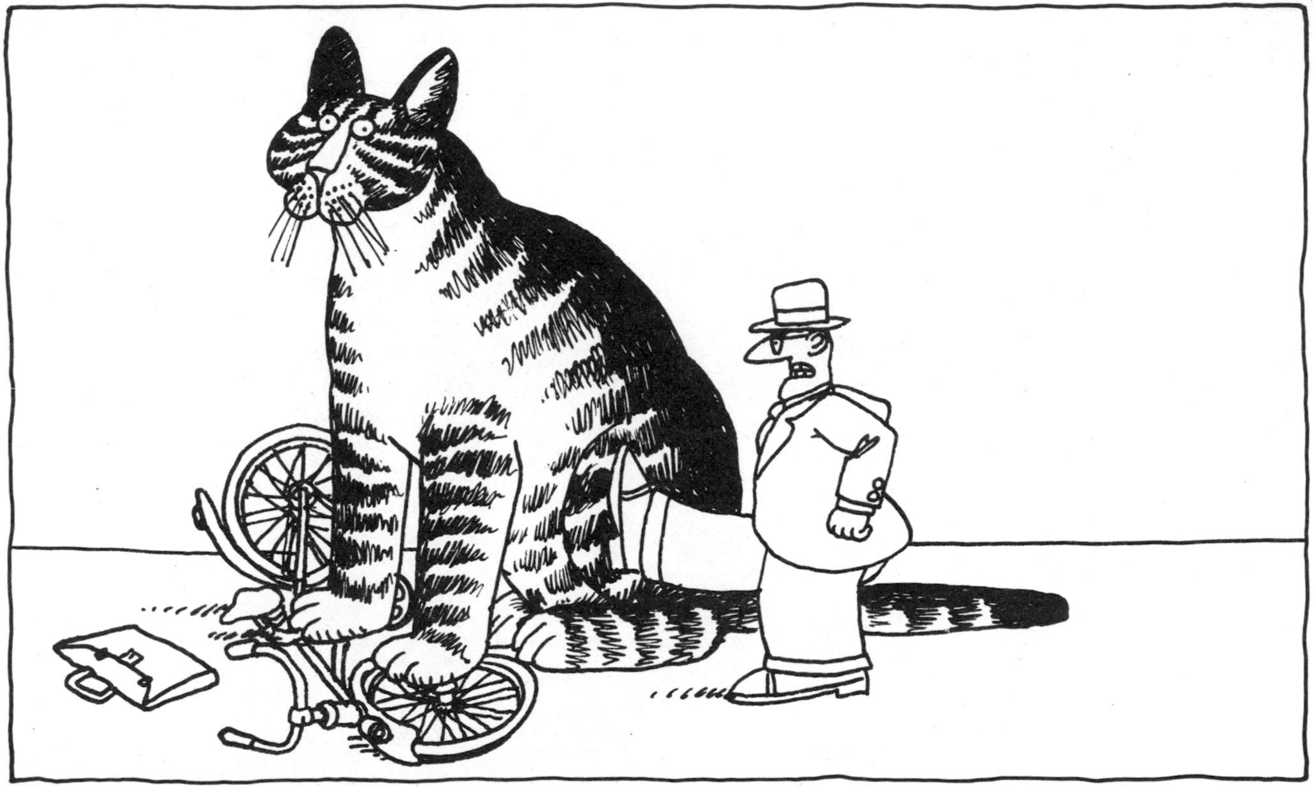

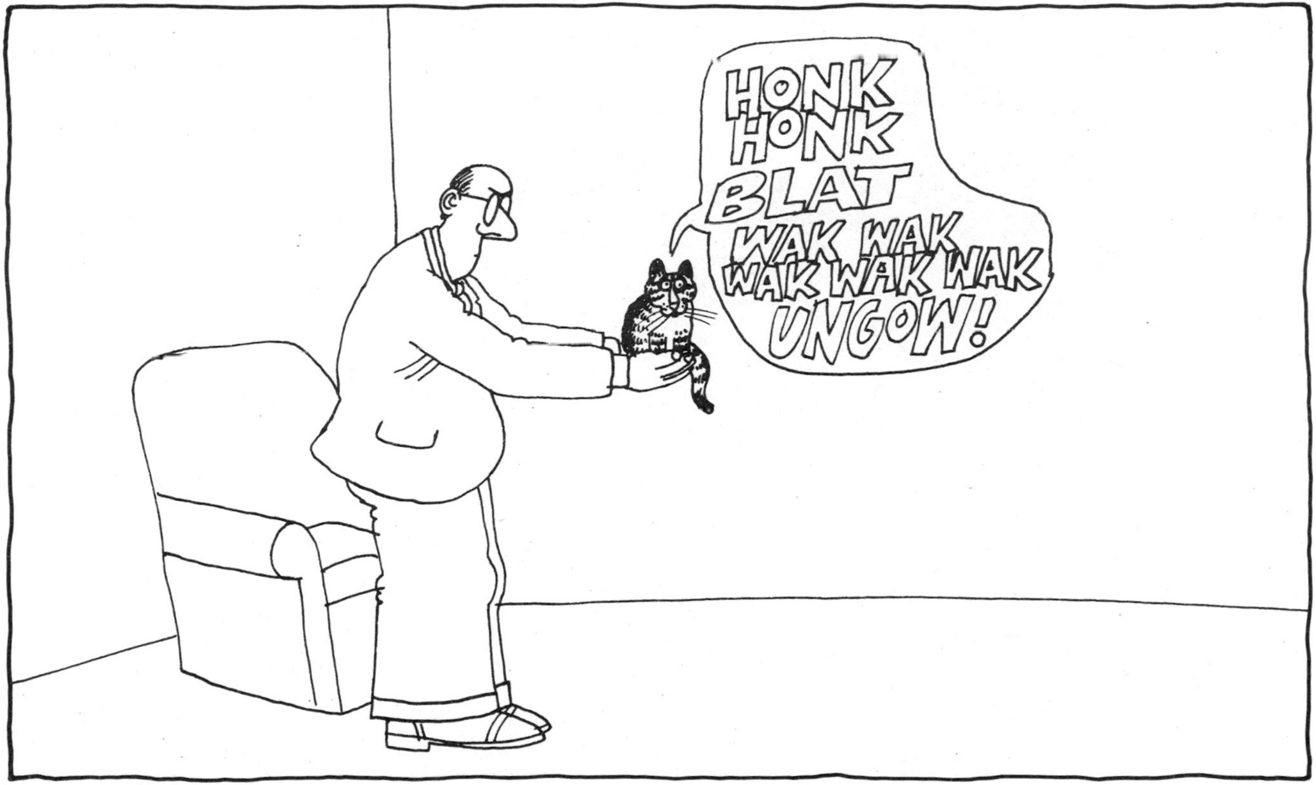
HONK
HONK
BLAT
WAK WAK
WAK WAK WAK
UNGOW!

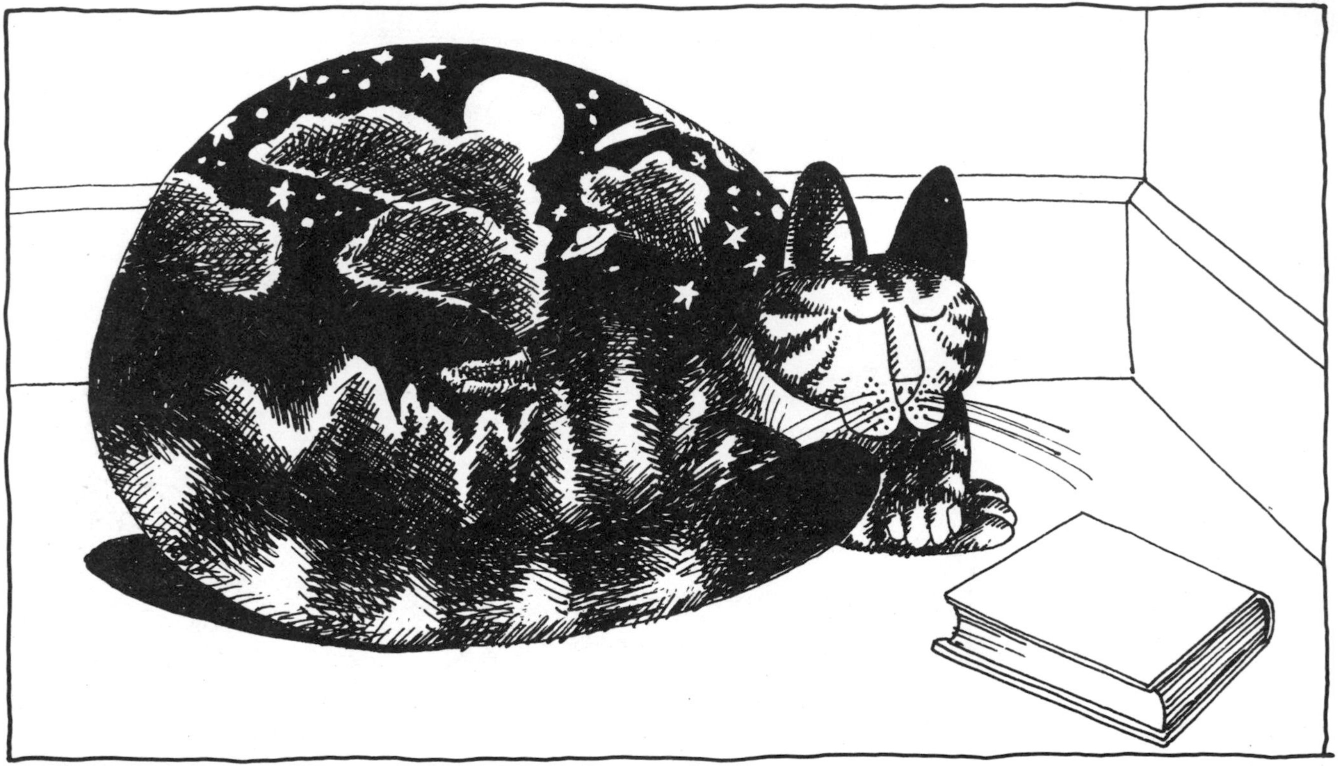

How to draw a Qat

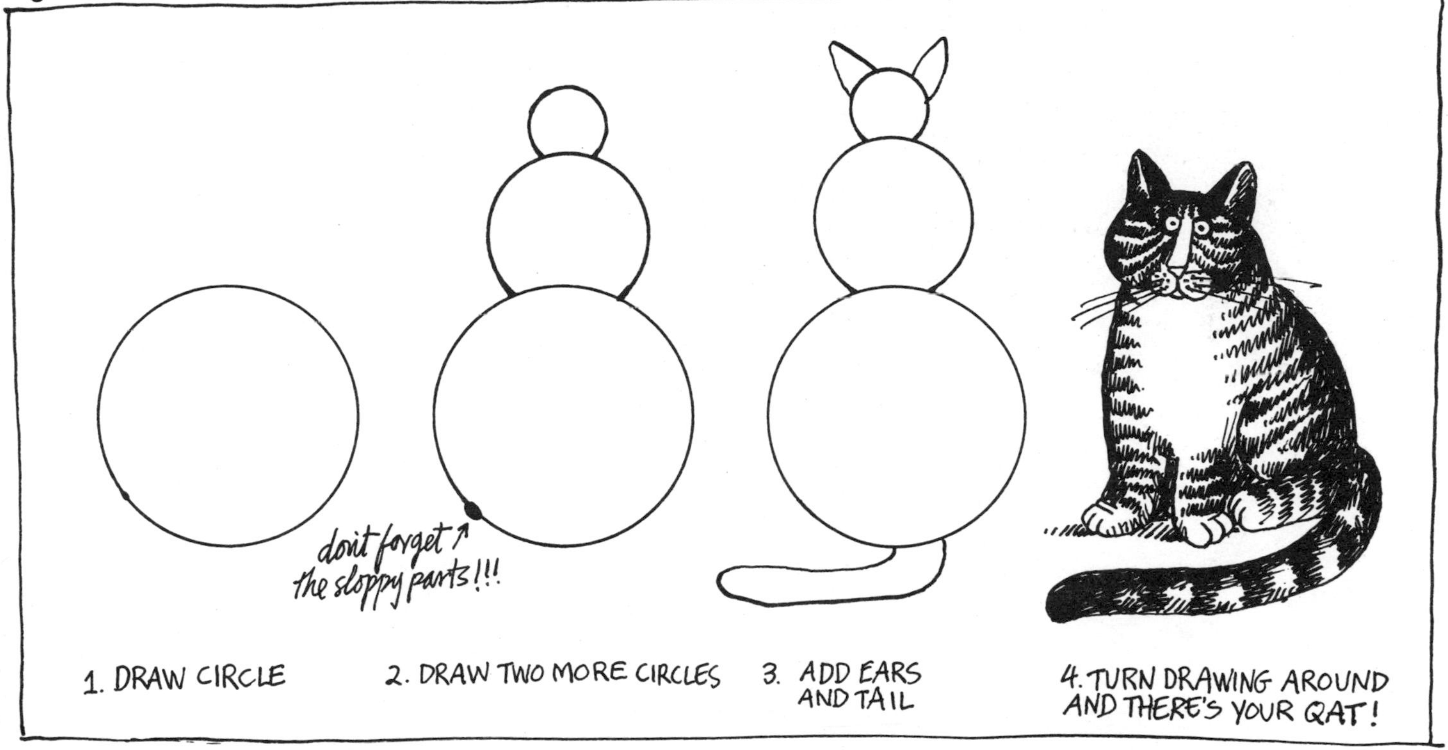
don't forget ↑
the sloppy parts!!!
1. DRAW CIRCLE
2. DRAW TWO MORE CIRCLES
3. ADD EARS AND TAIL
4. TURN DRAWING AROUND AND THERE'S YOUR QAT!

Fig 1.

MAN LYING TO A CAT

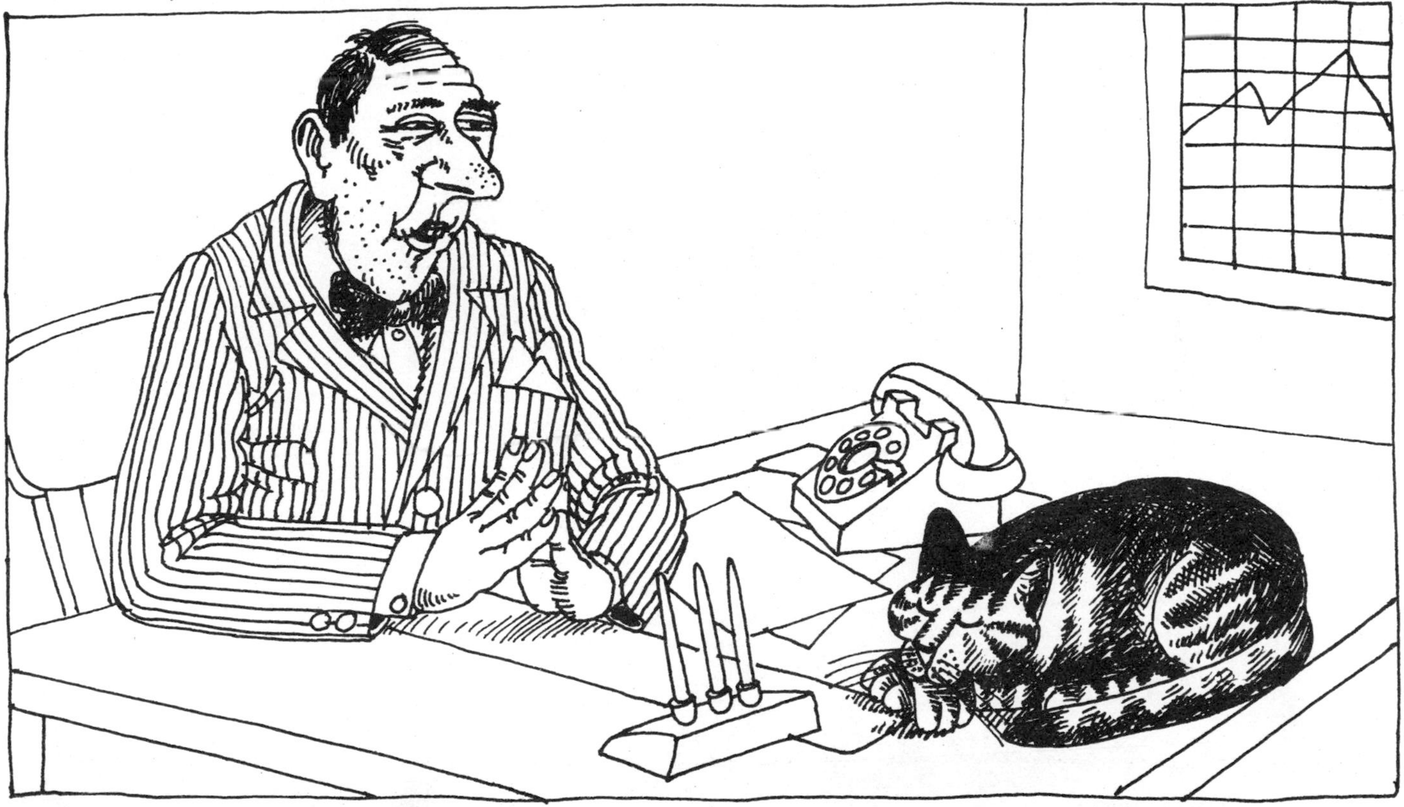

Cat Words

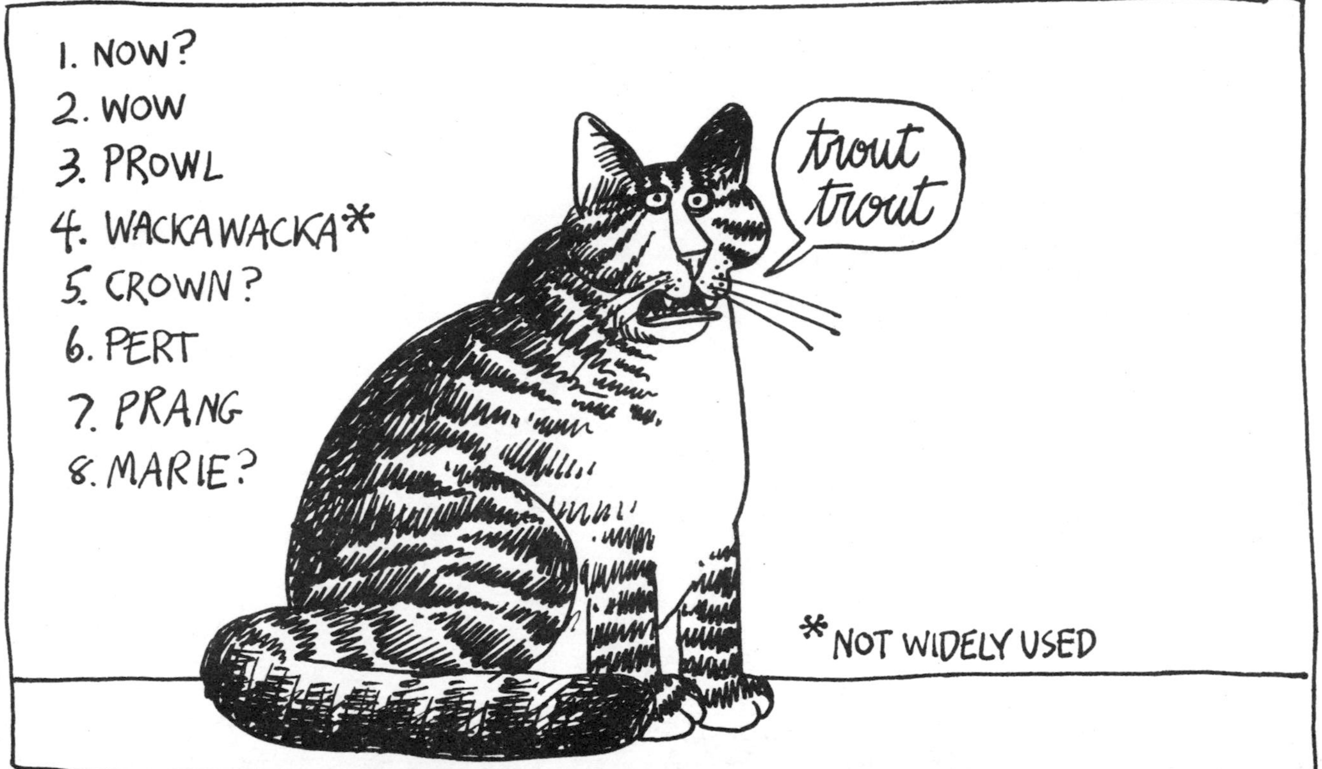
1. NOW?
2. WOW
3. PROWL
4. WACKAWACKA*
5. CROWN?
6. PERT
7. PRANG
8. MARIE?
trout trout
* NOT WIDELY USED

PURSEY CAT

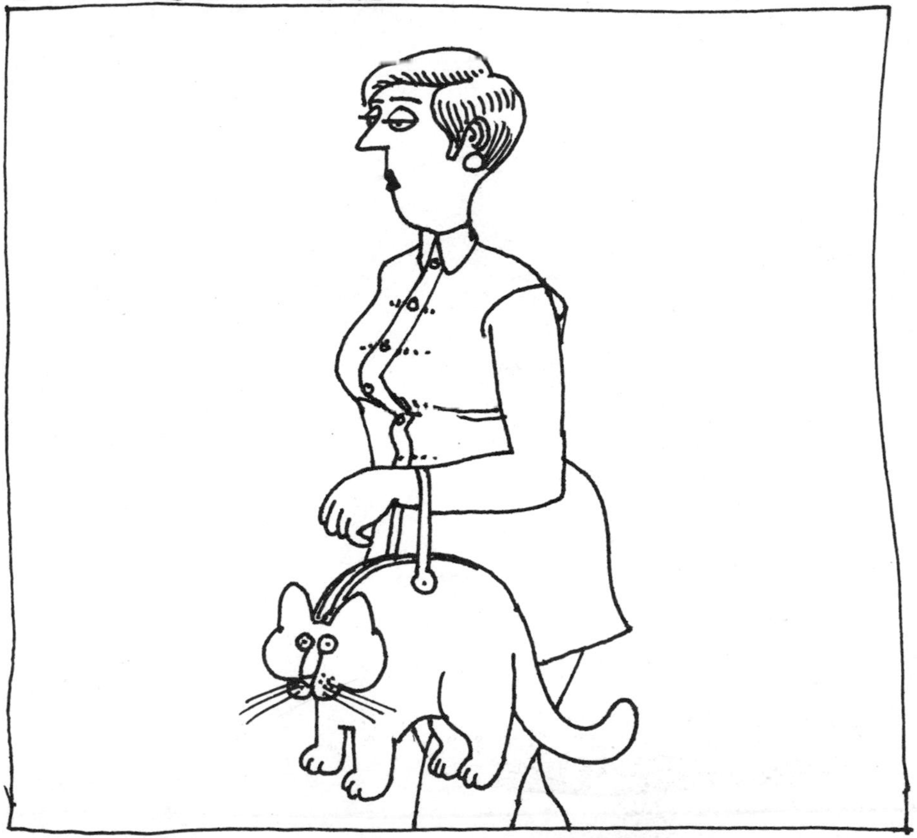

Feeding Ham to Cats

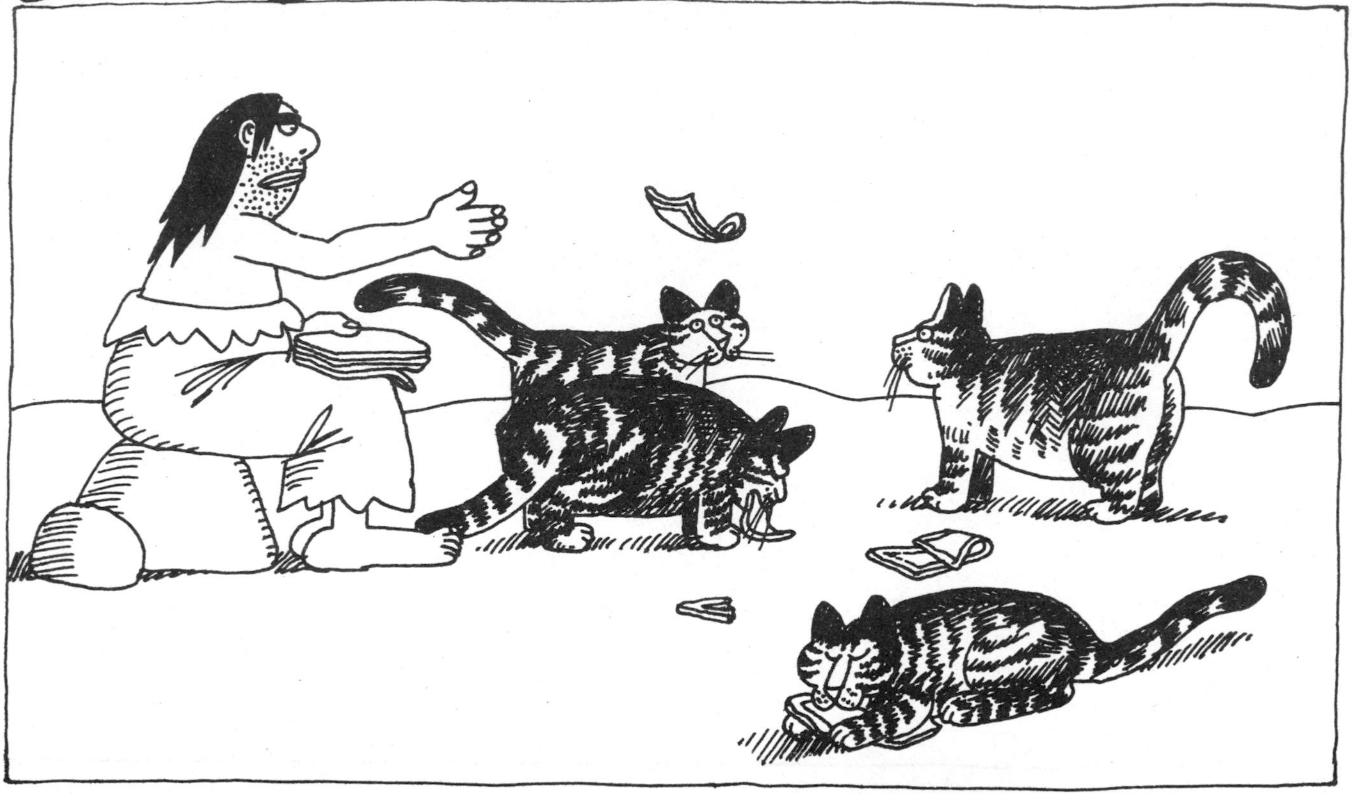

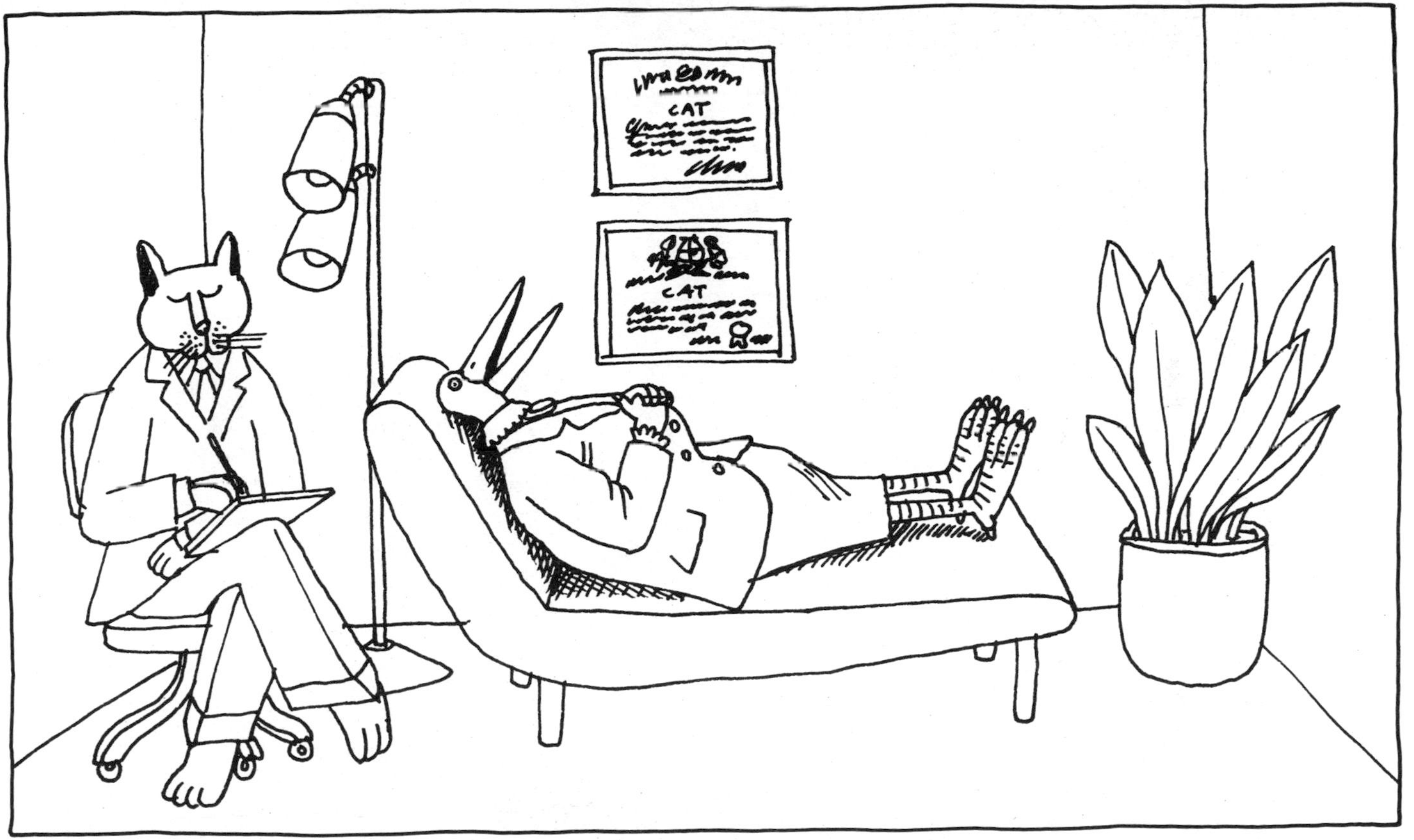
CAT
CAT

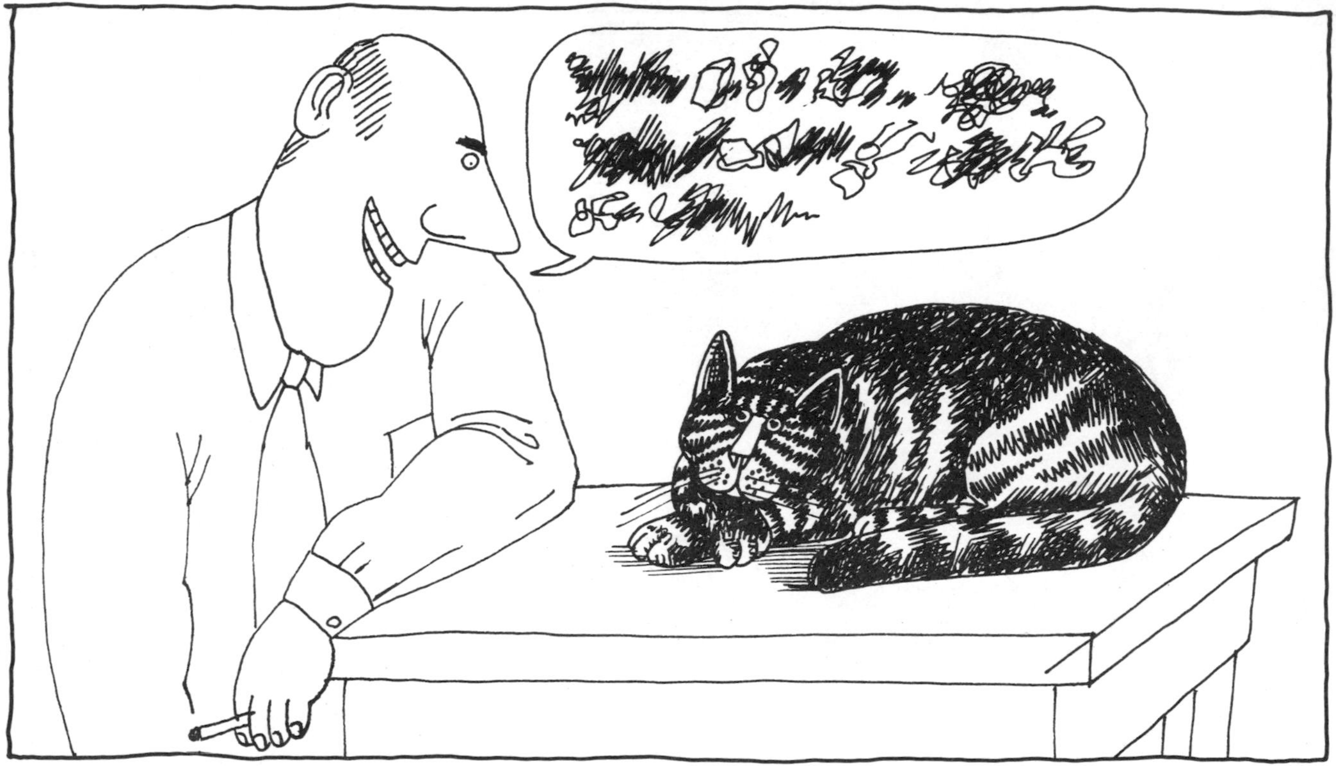

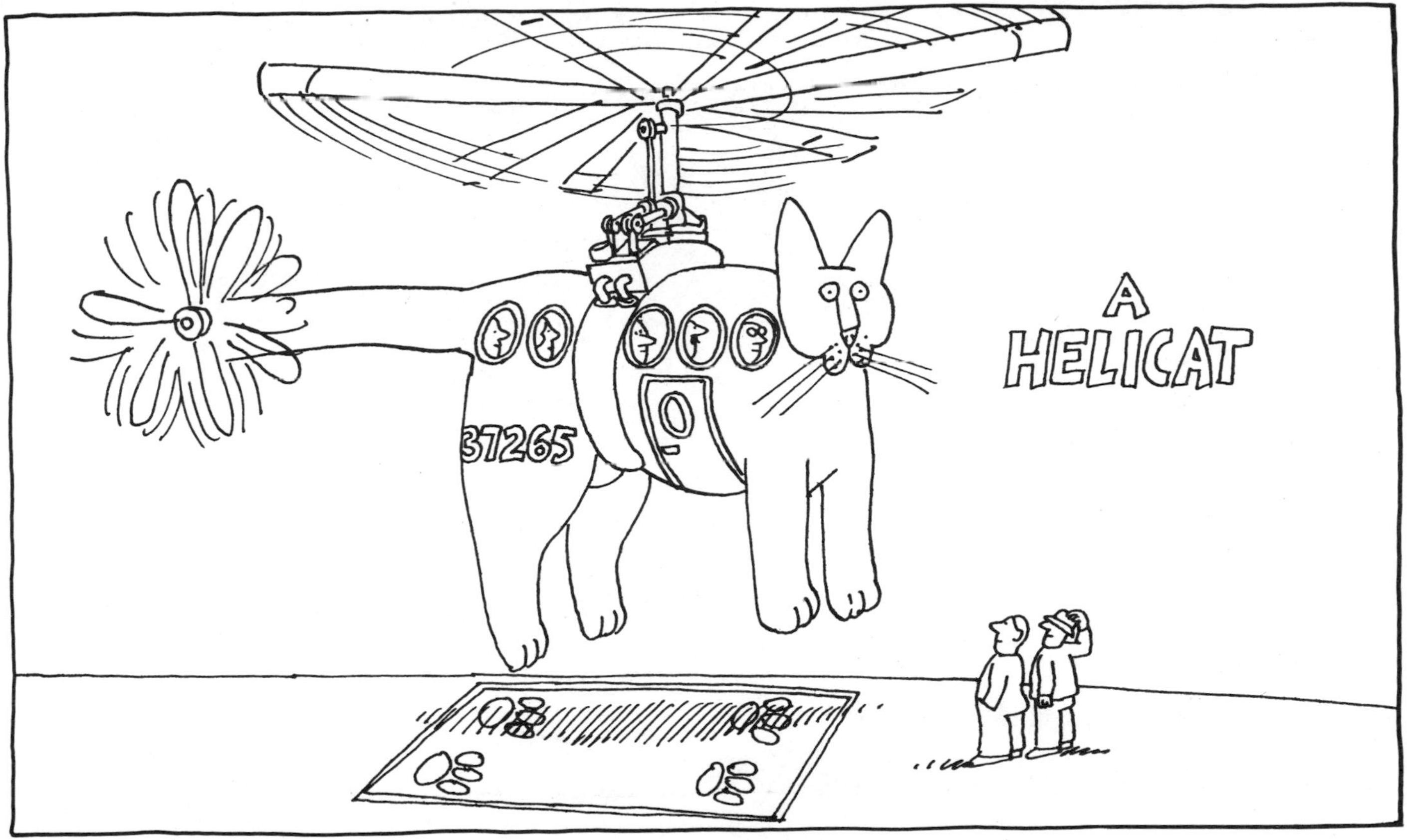
A HELICAT
37265

SUPERSTITIONS • KICK A CAT AND YOU'LL LOSE YOUR HAT.

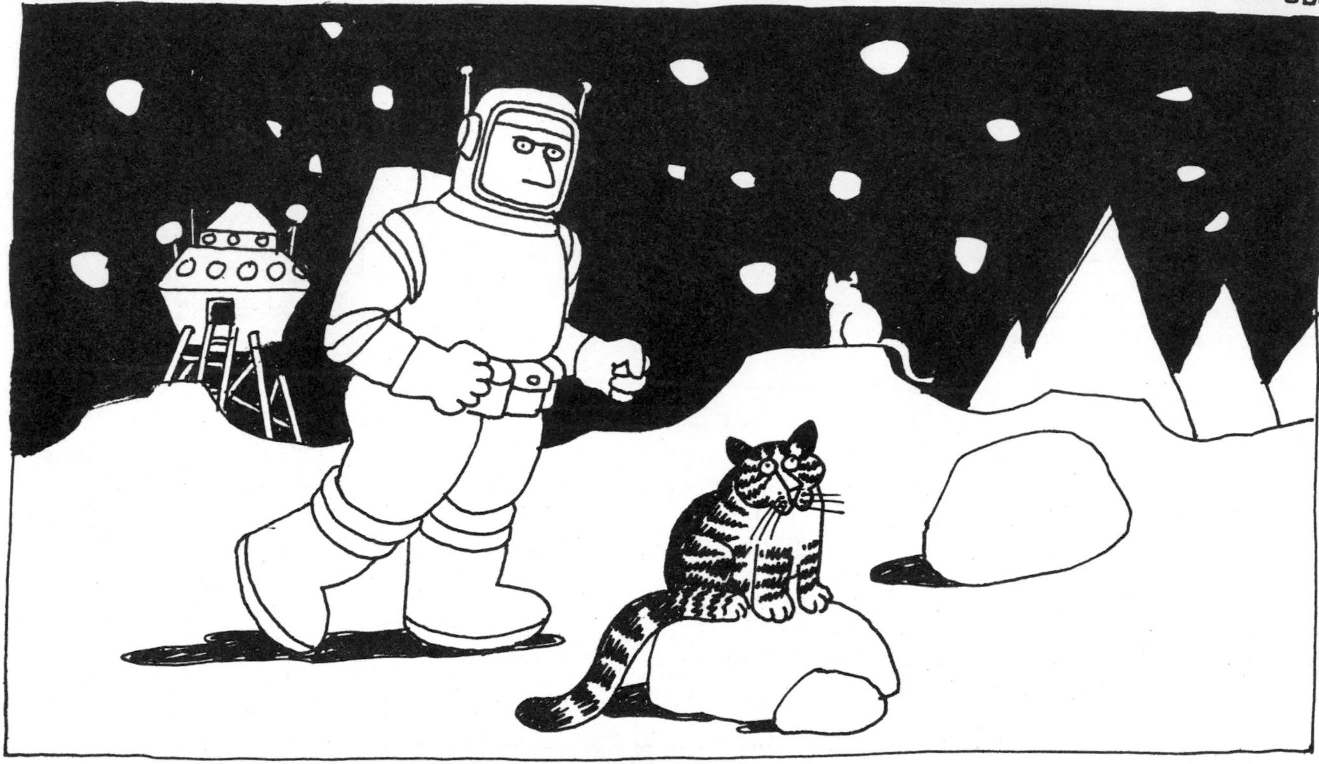

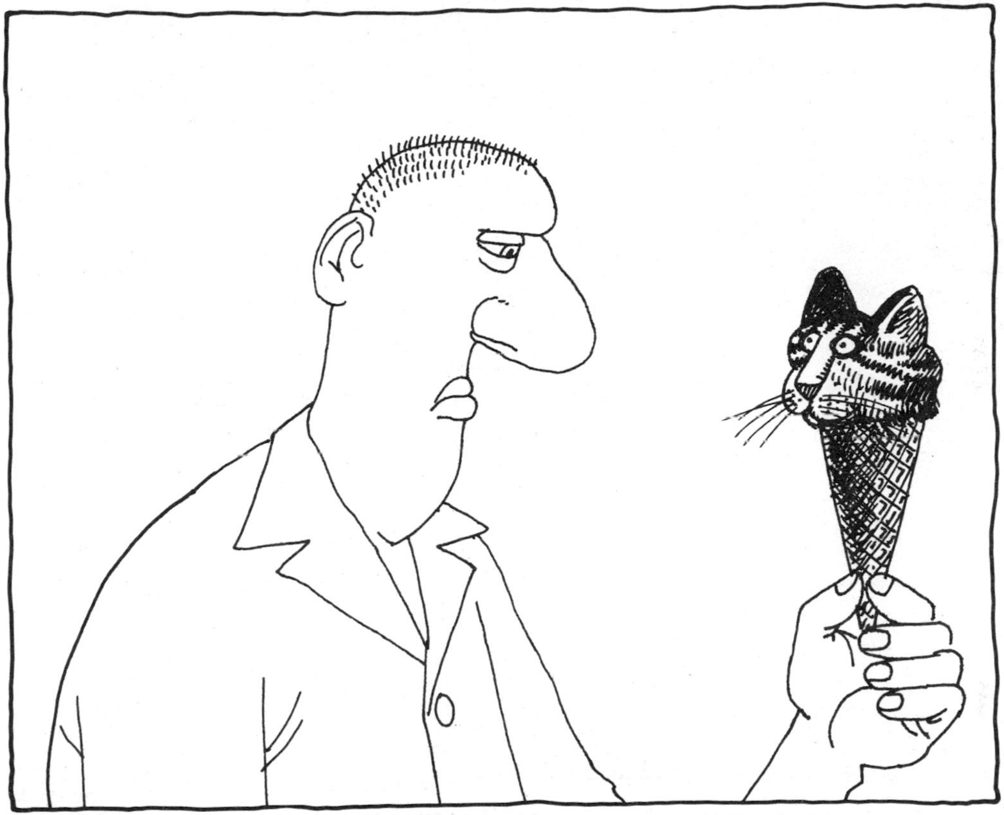

Mad

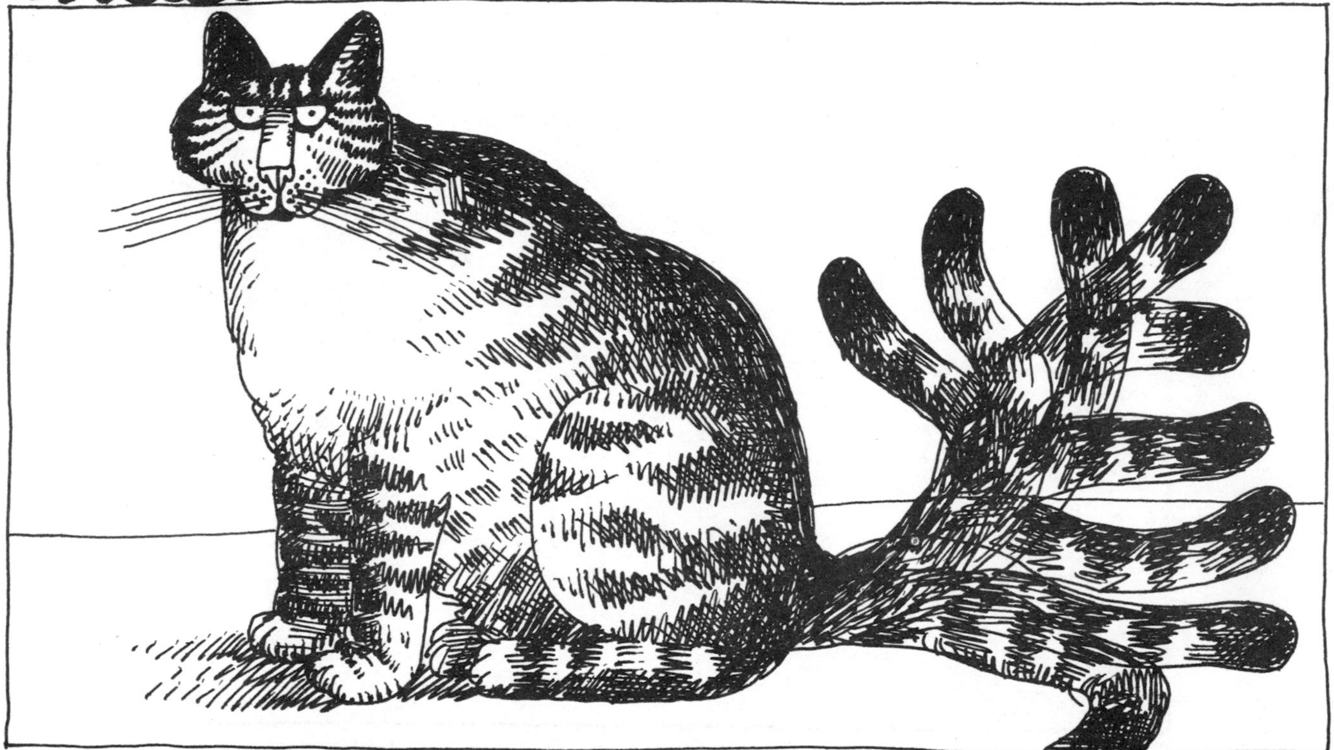

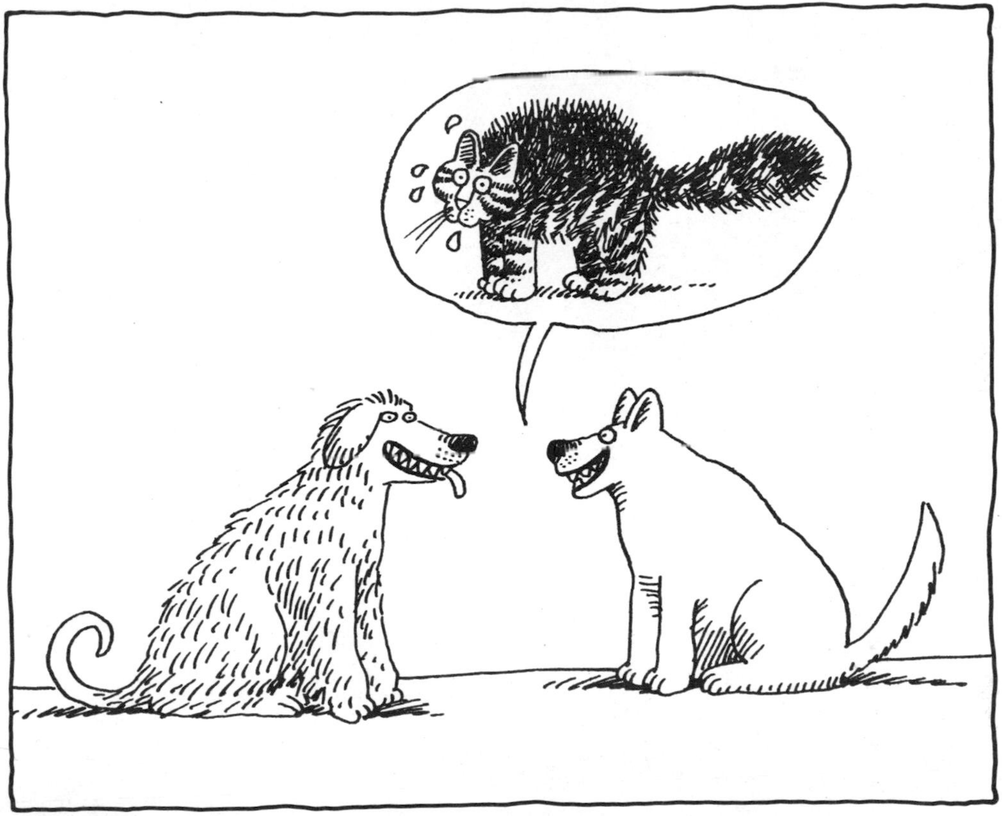

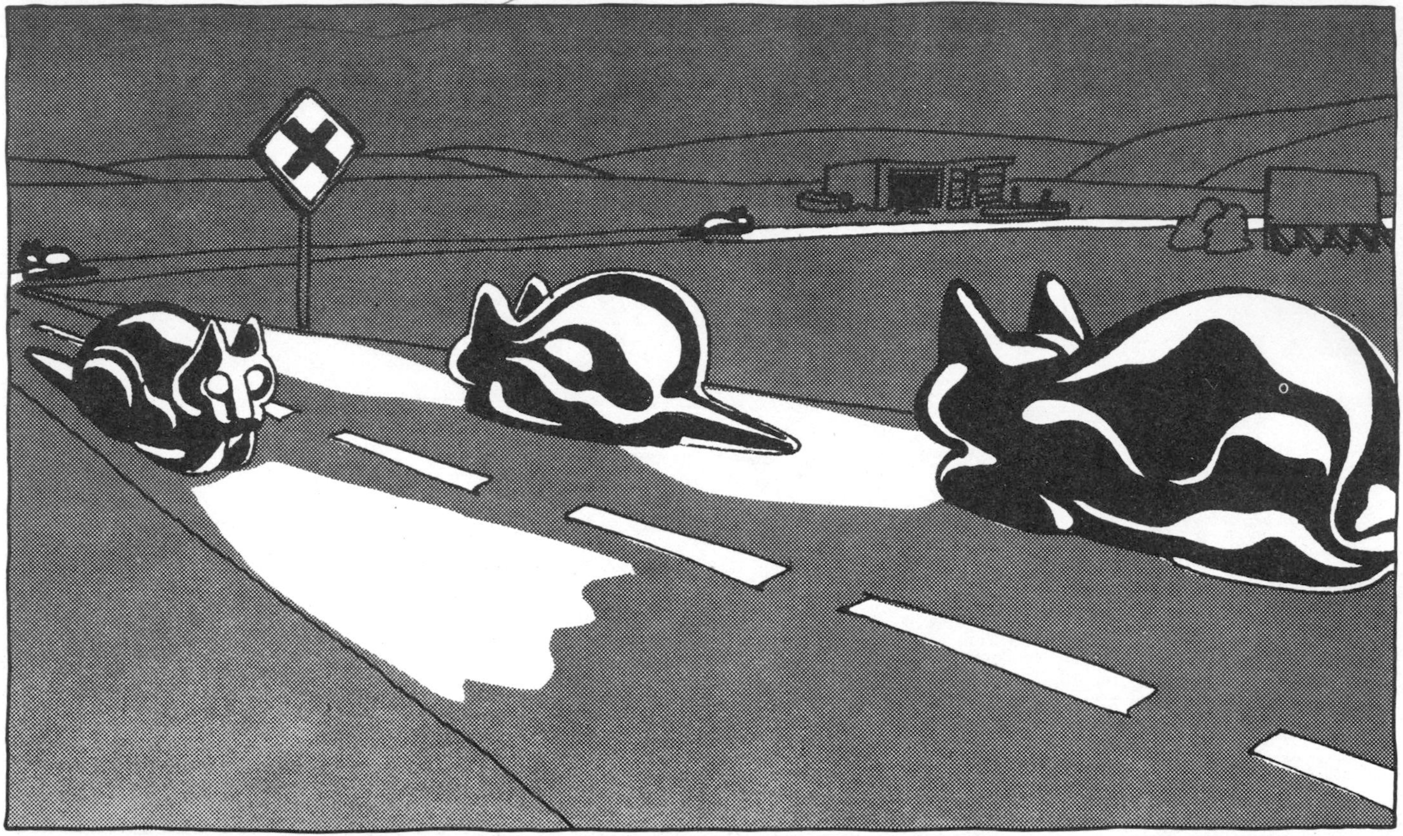

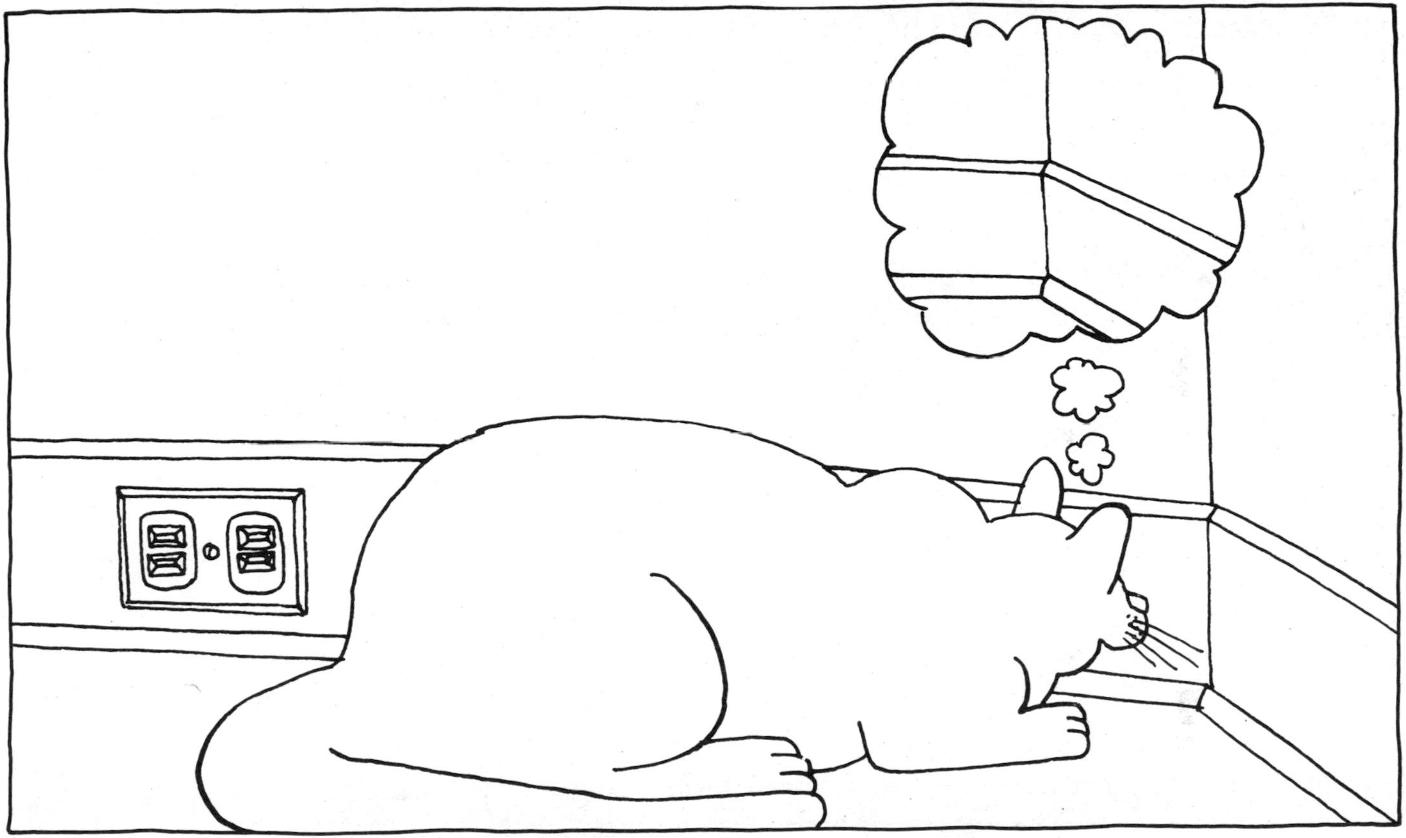

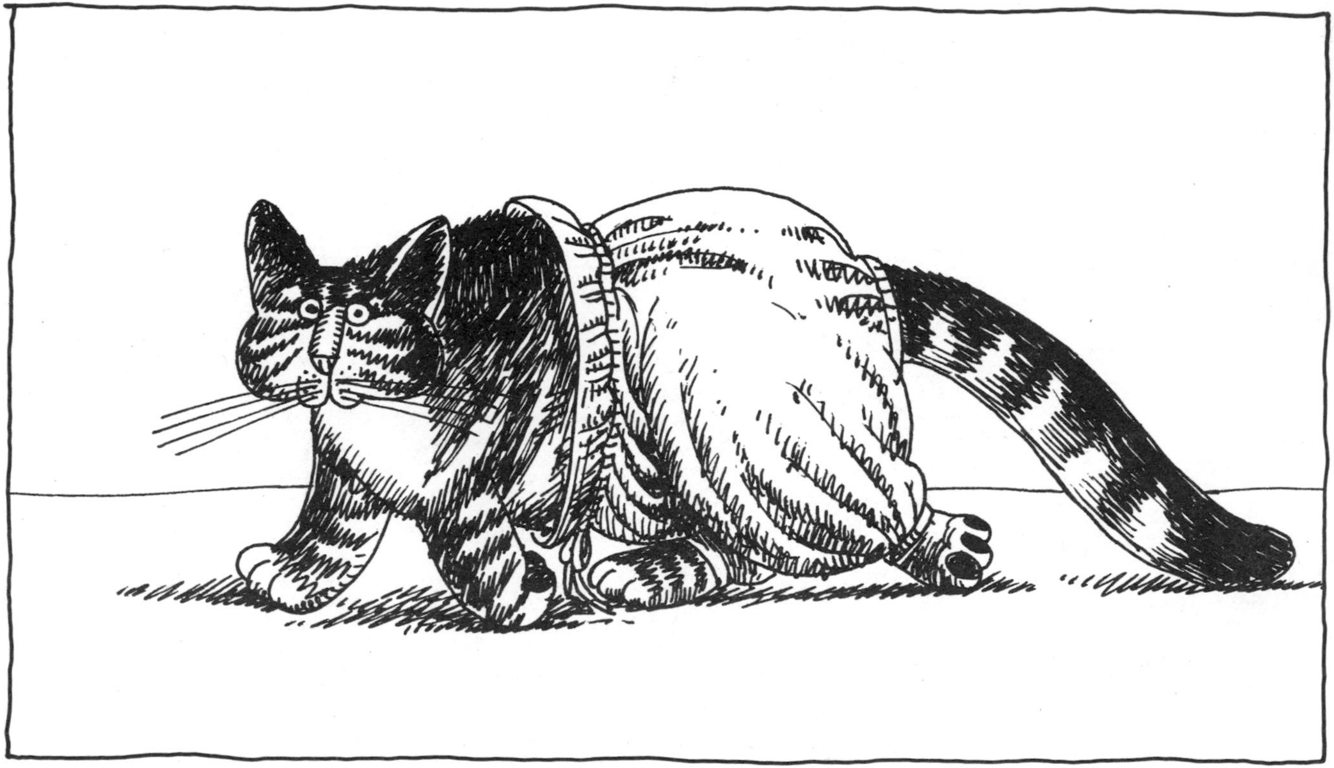

The Color Years
(A Curated Selection)

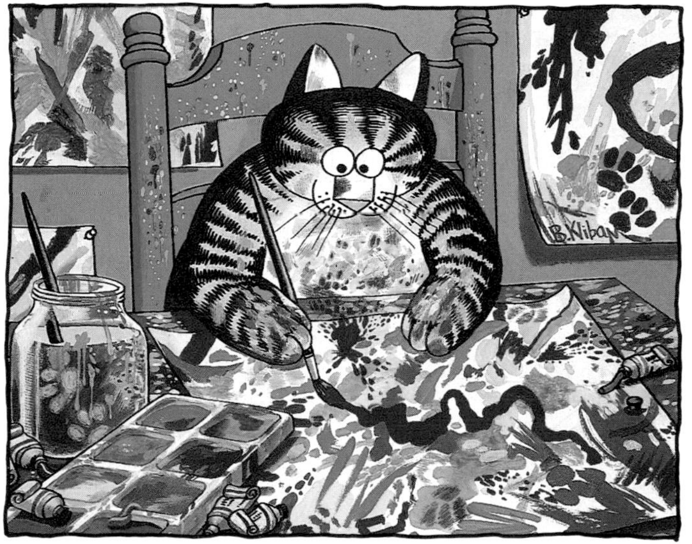
B. Kliban

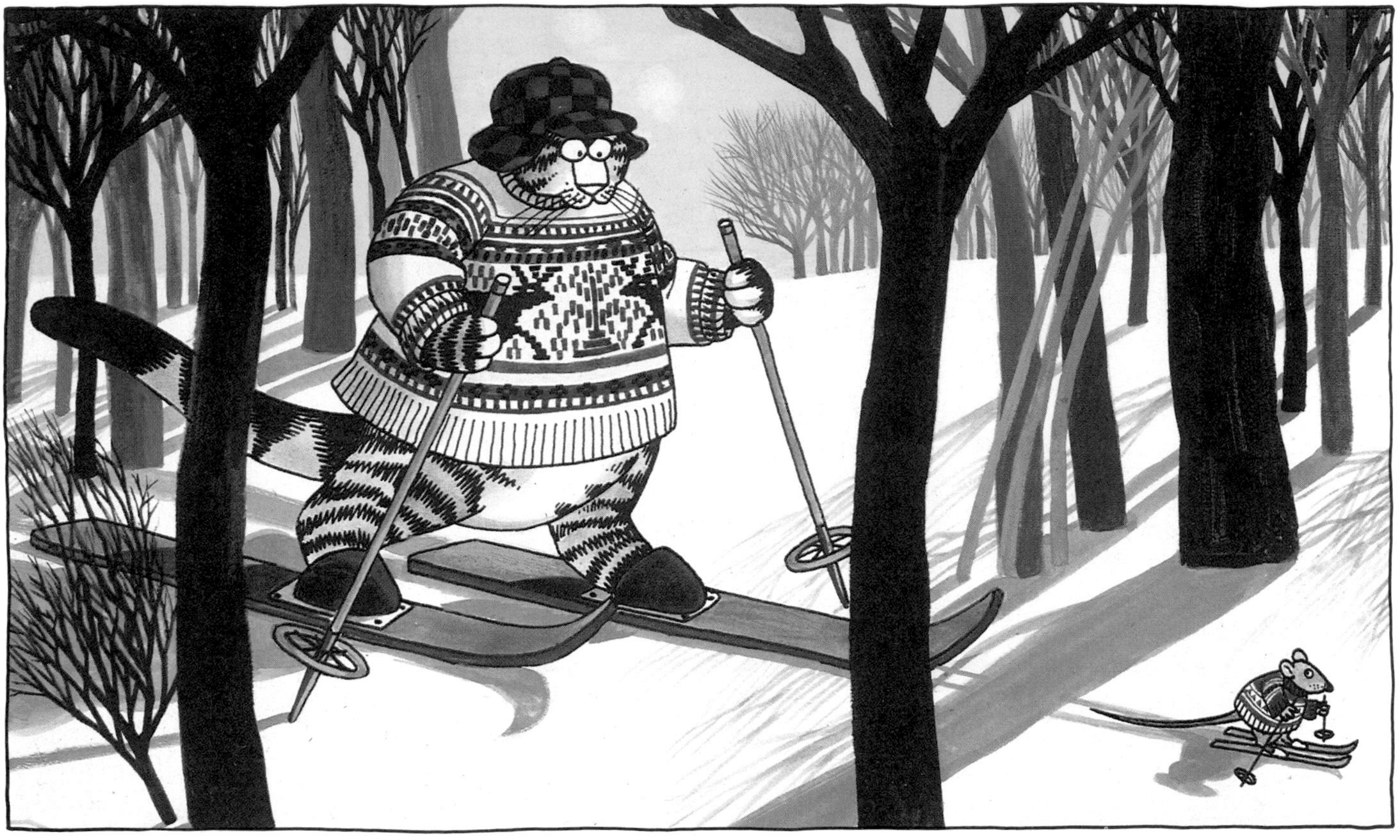

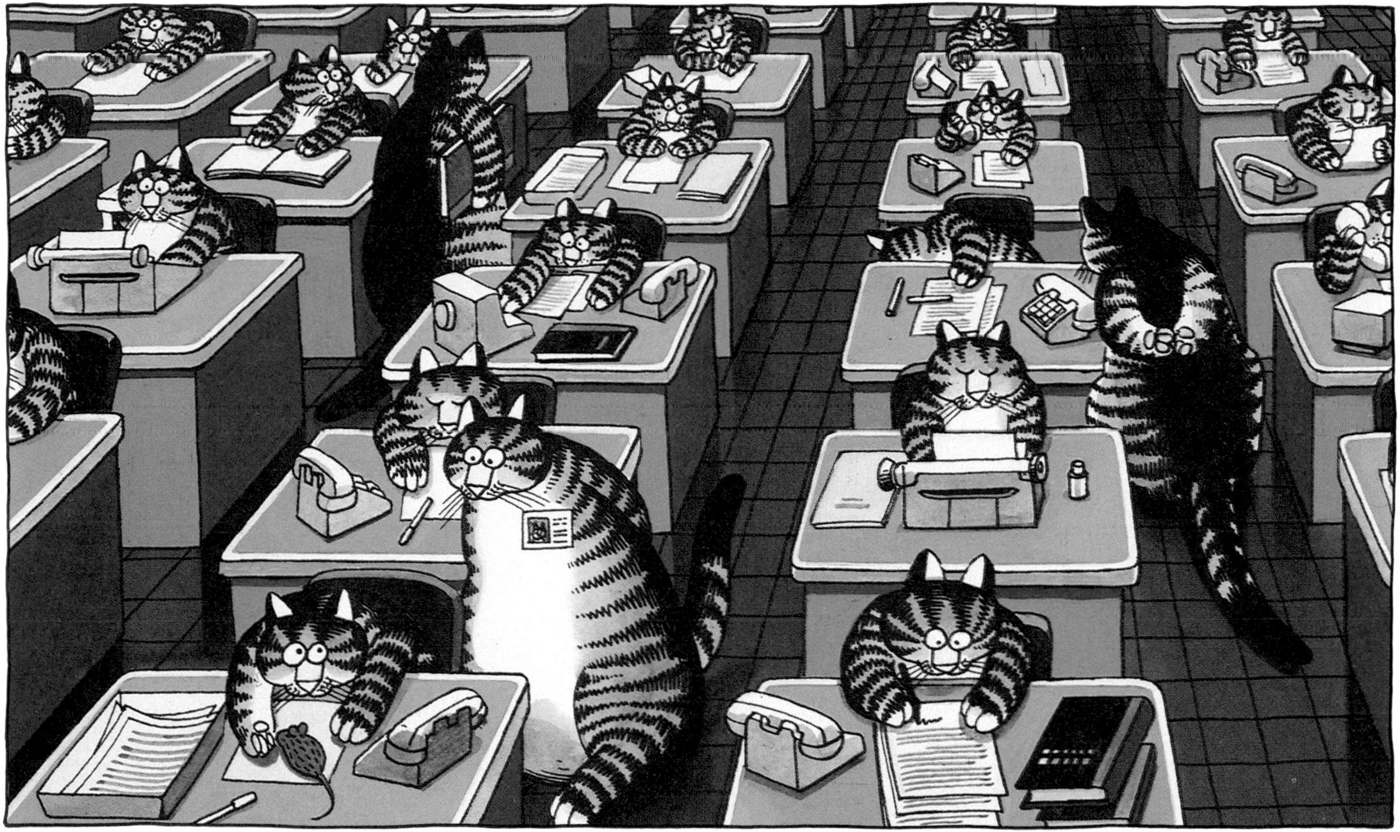

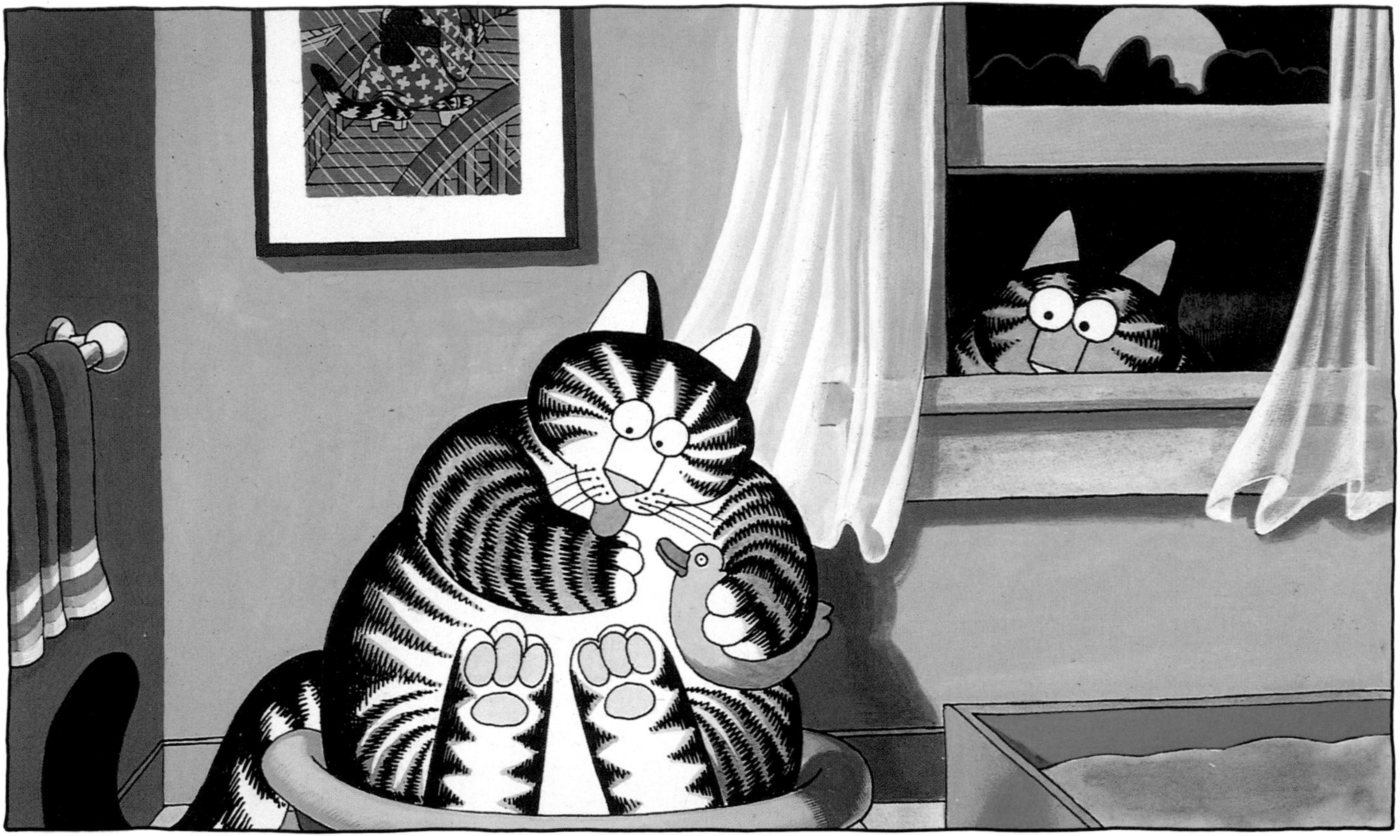

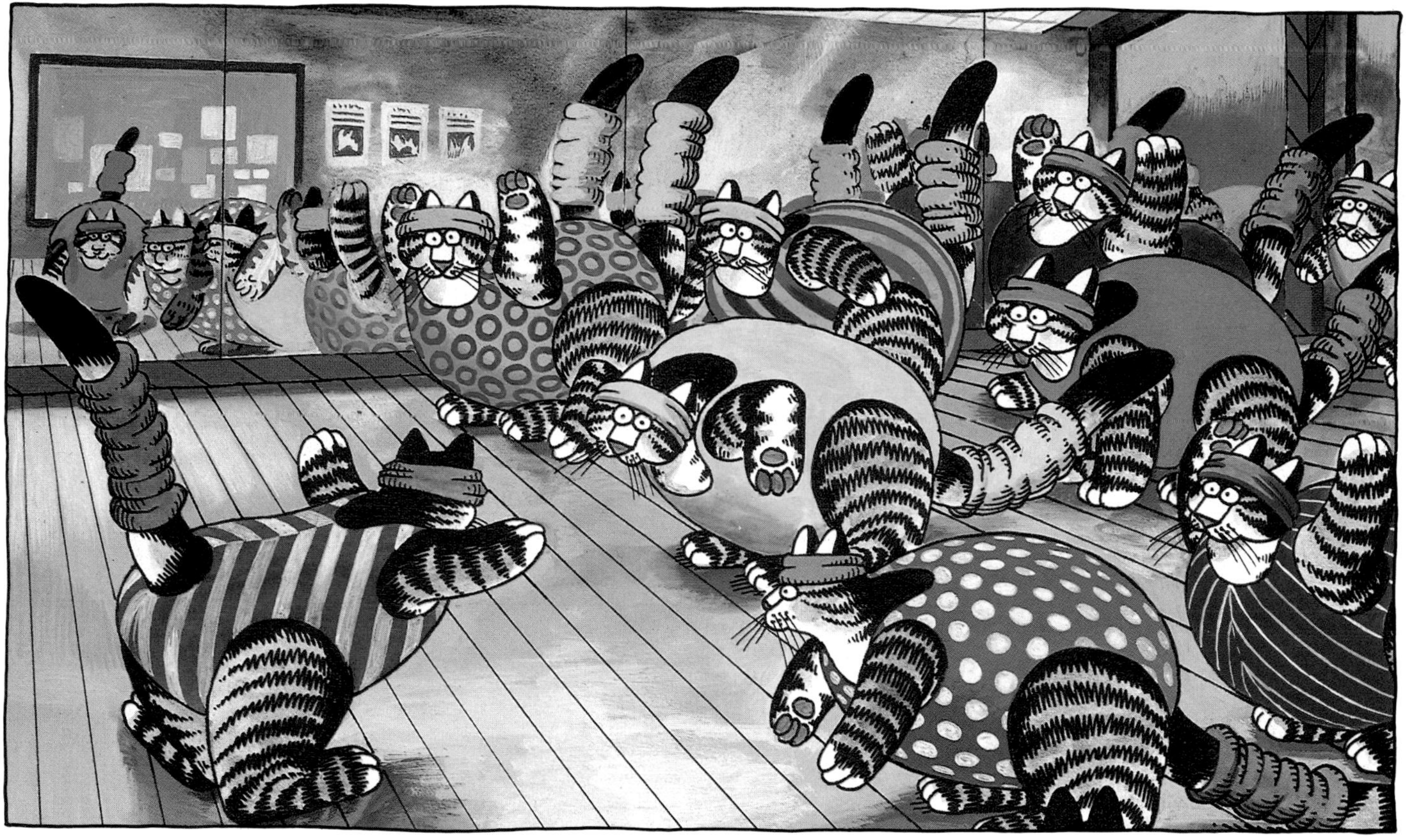

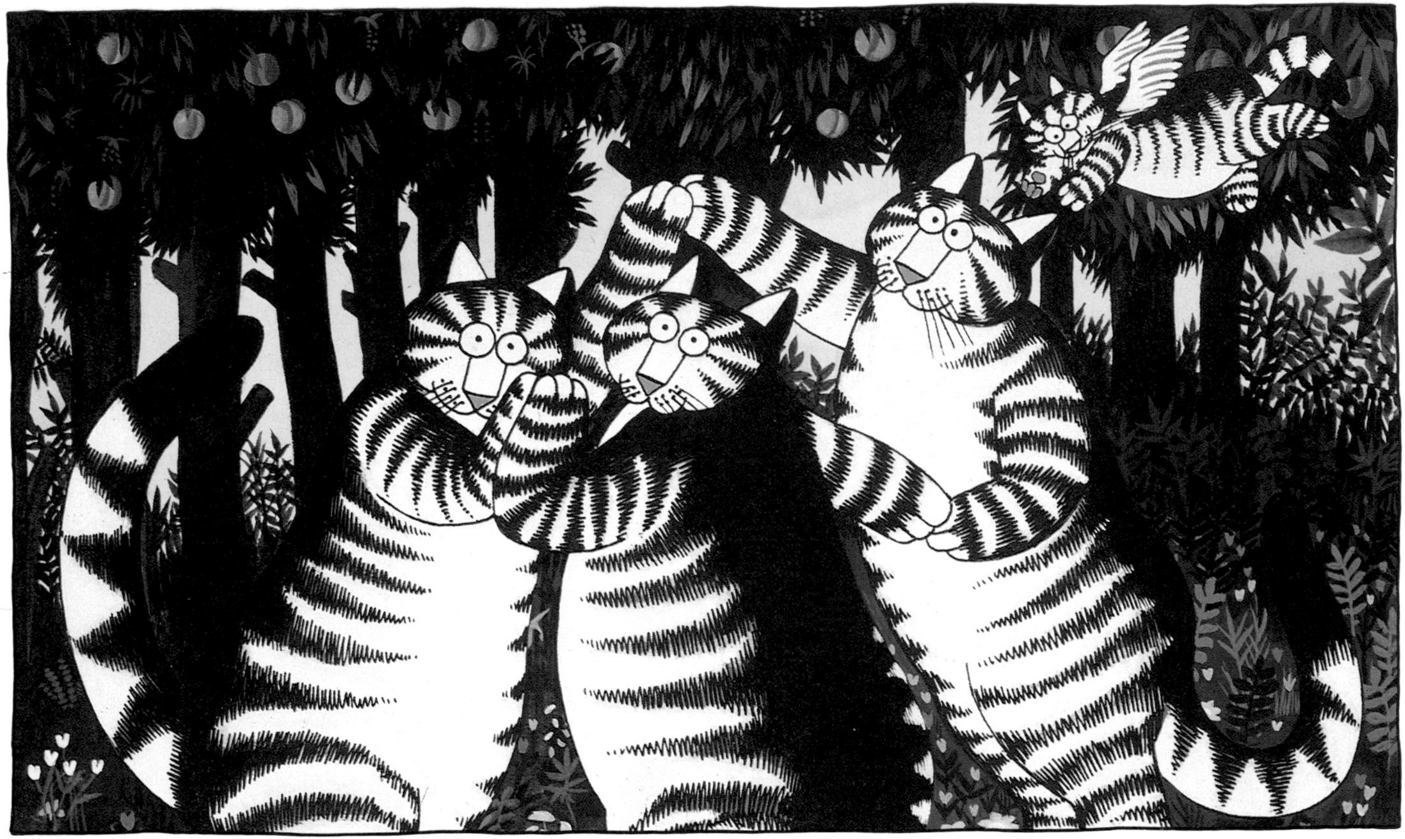

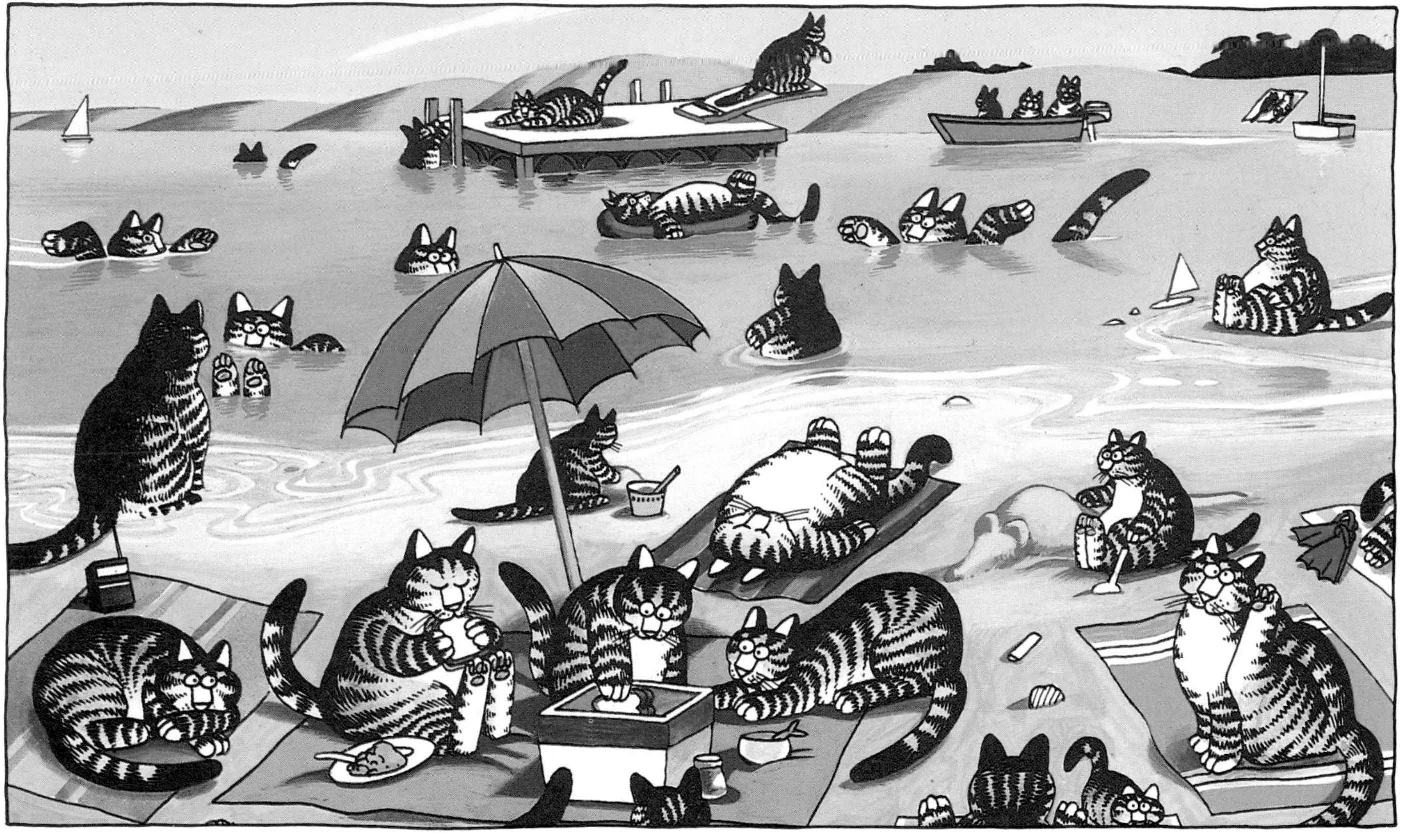

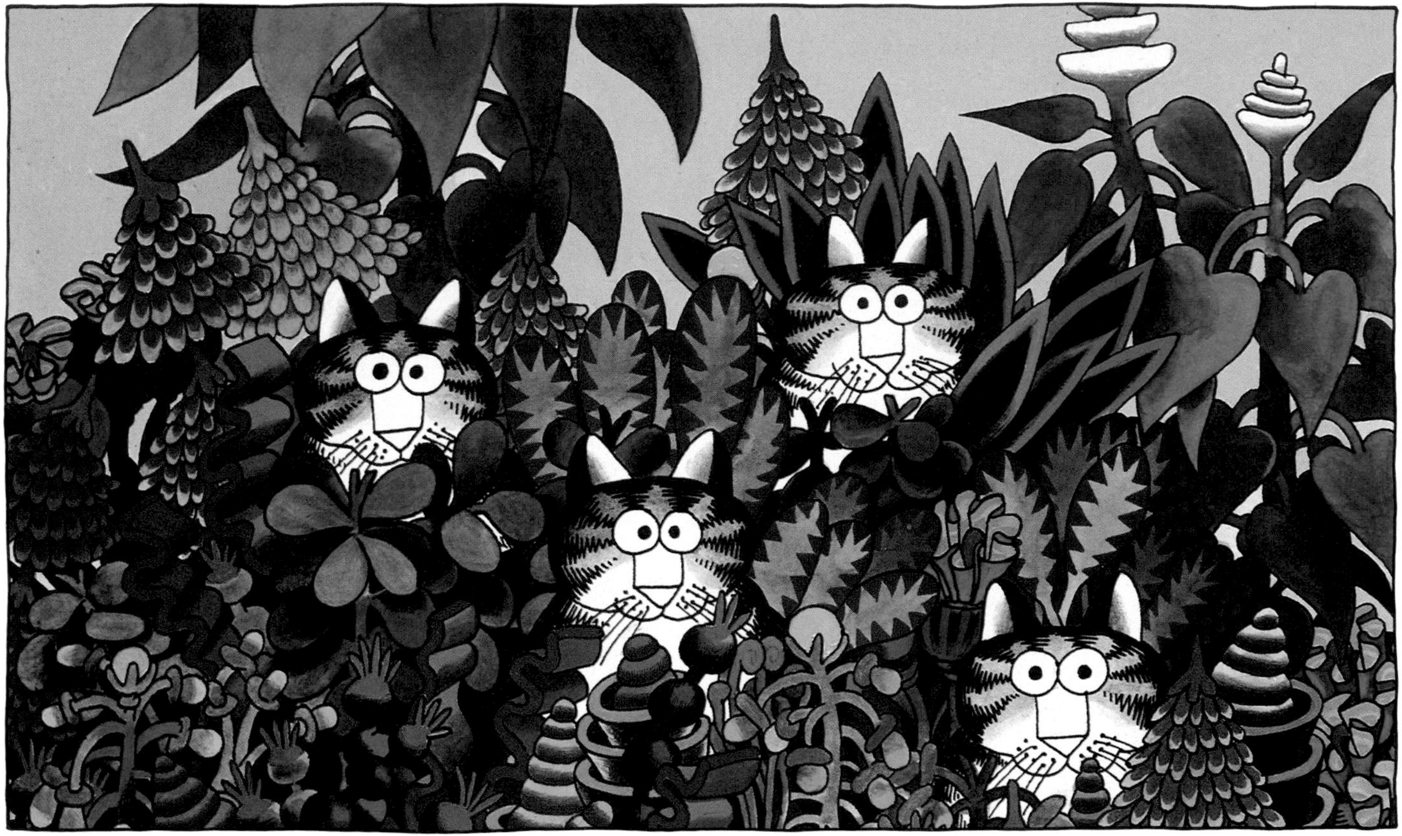

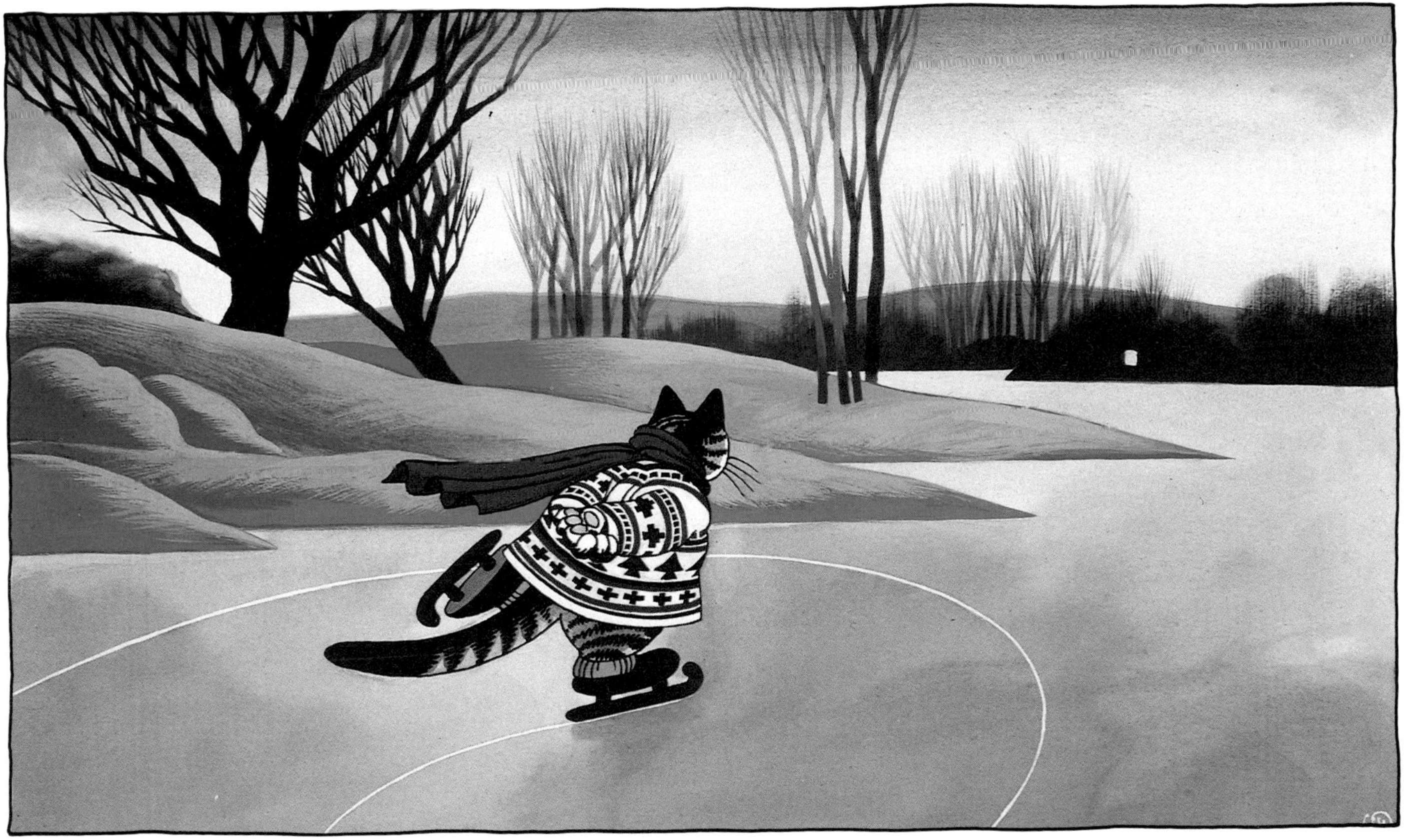

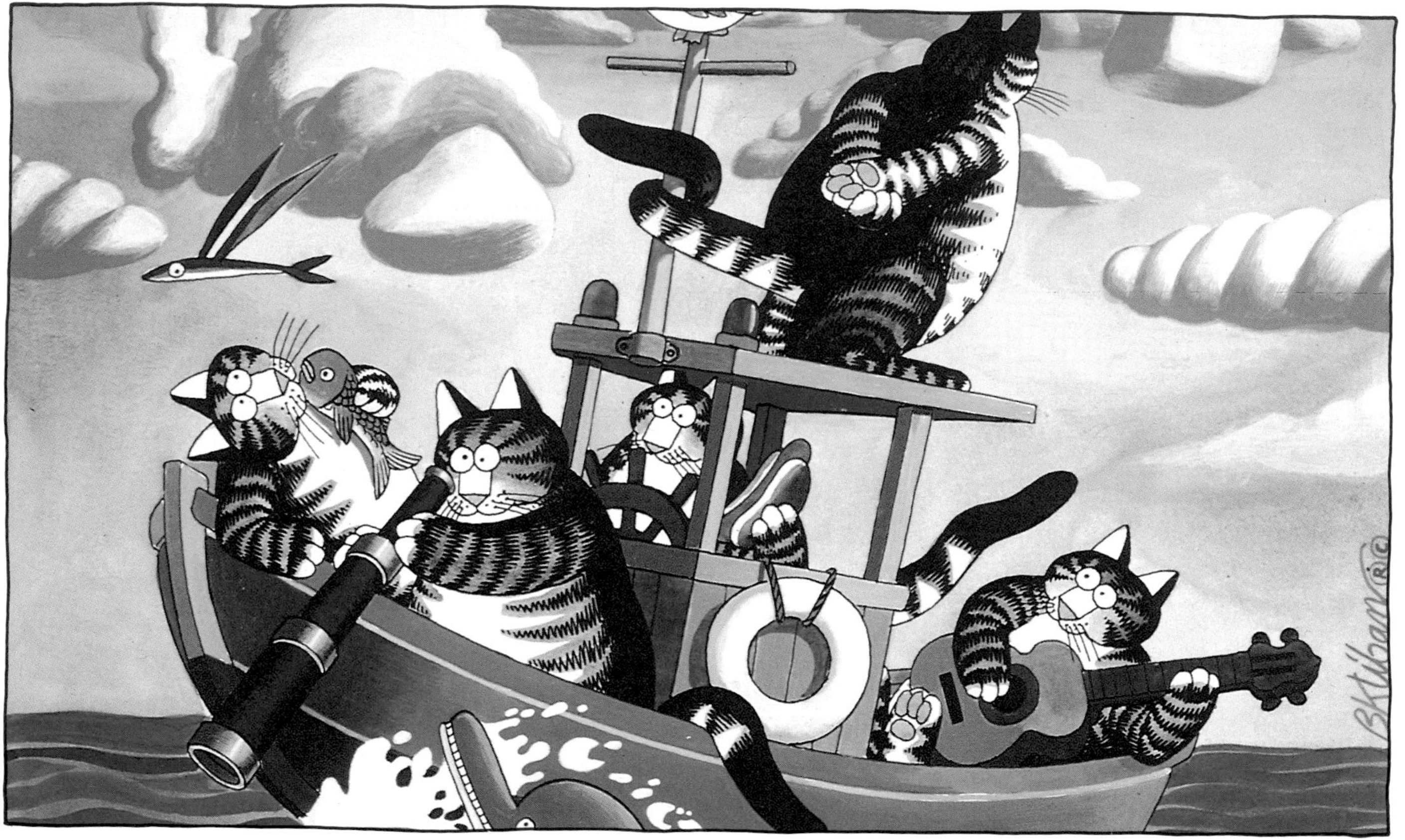
BKliban

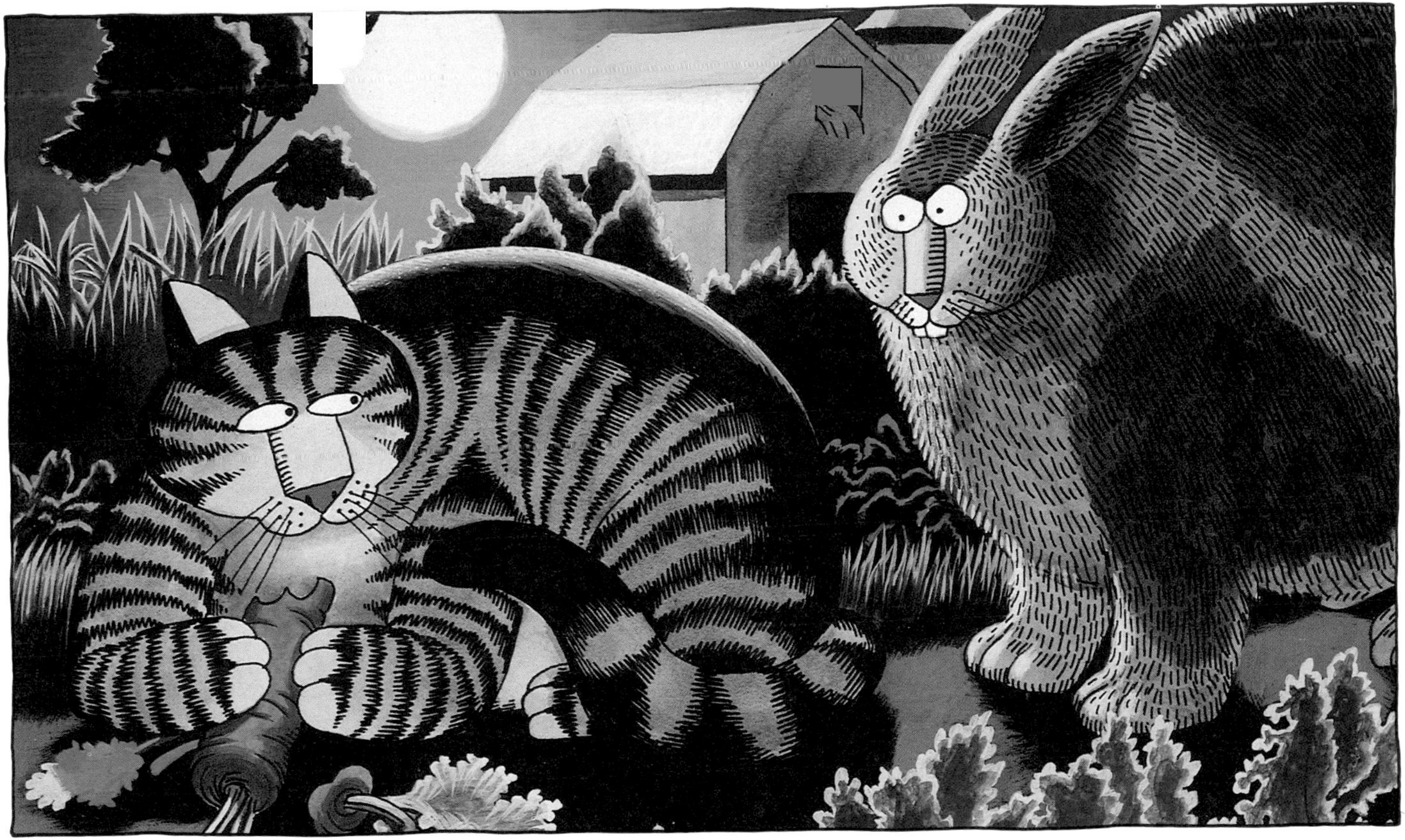

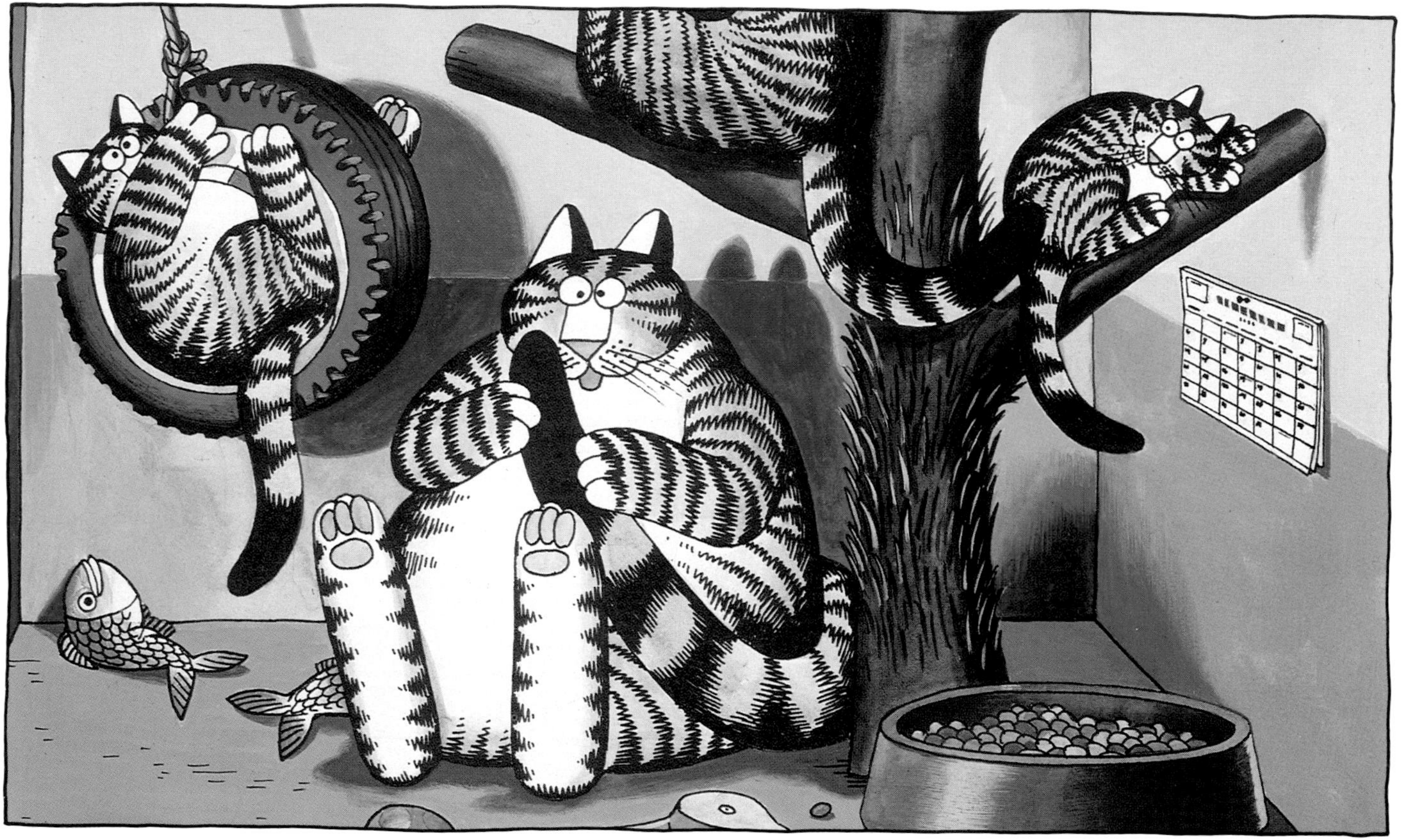

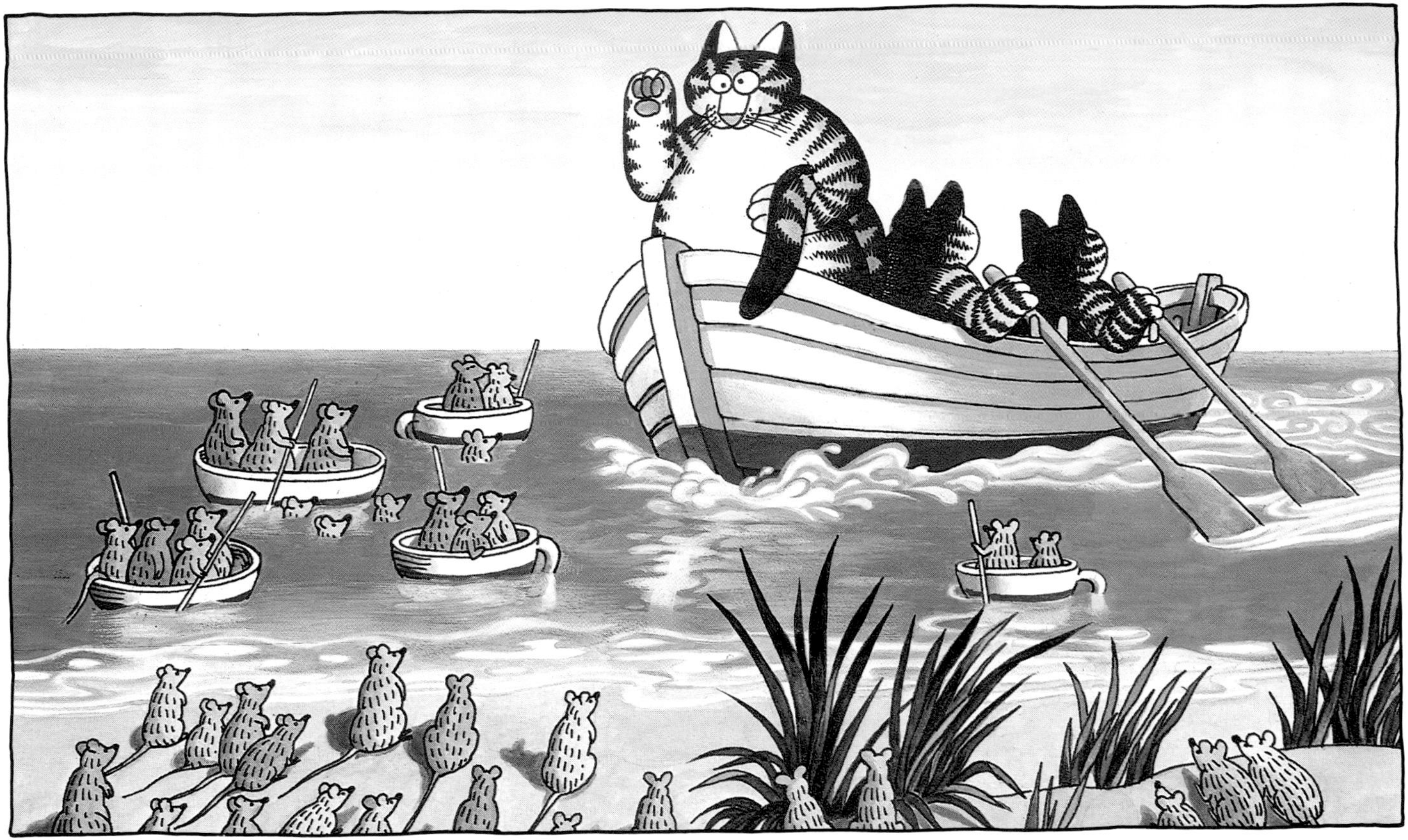

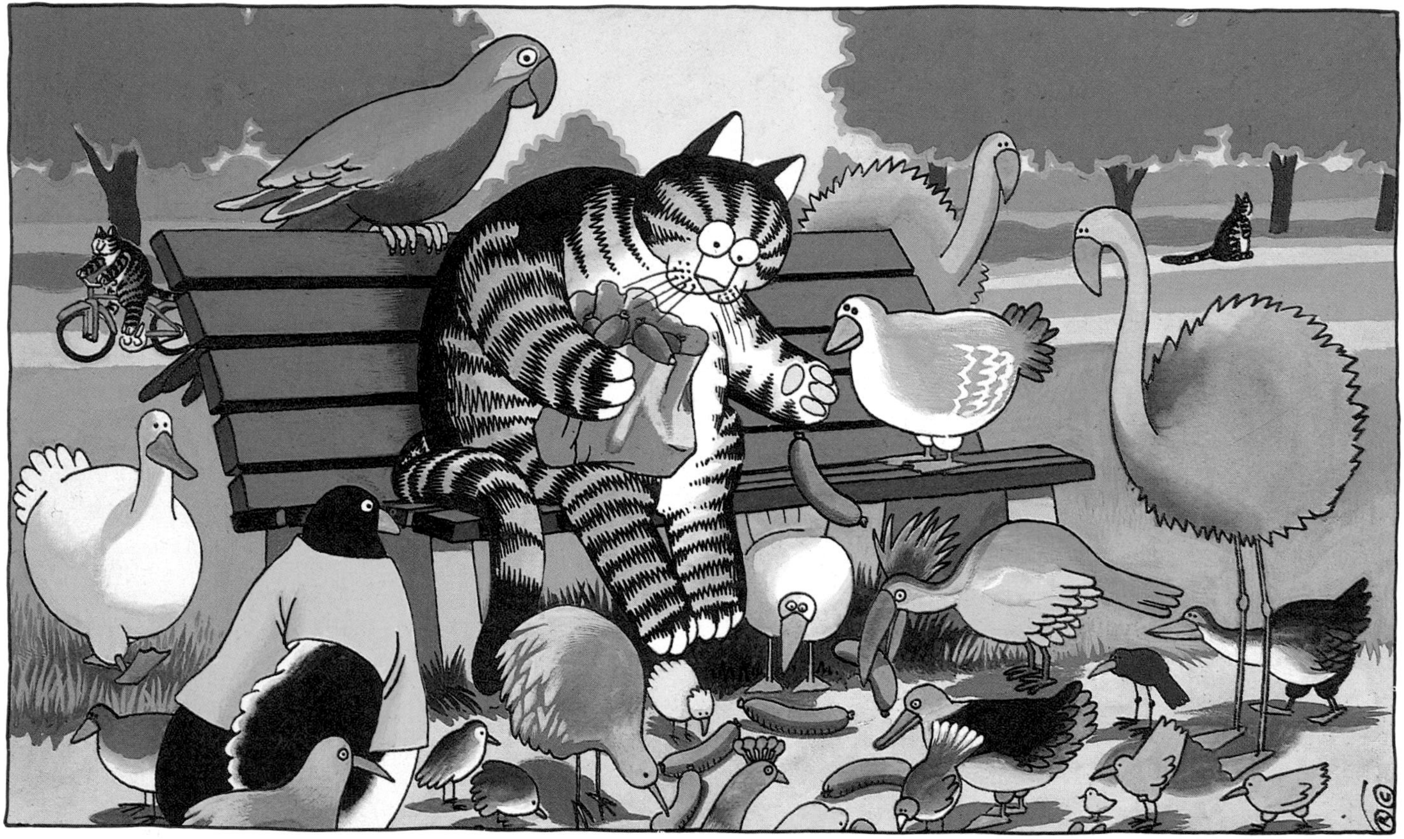

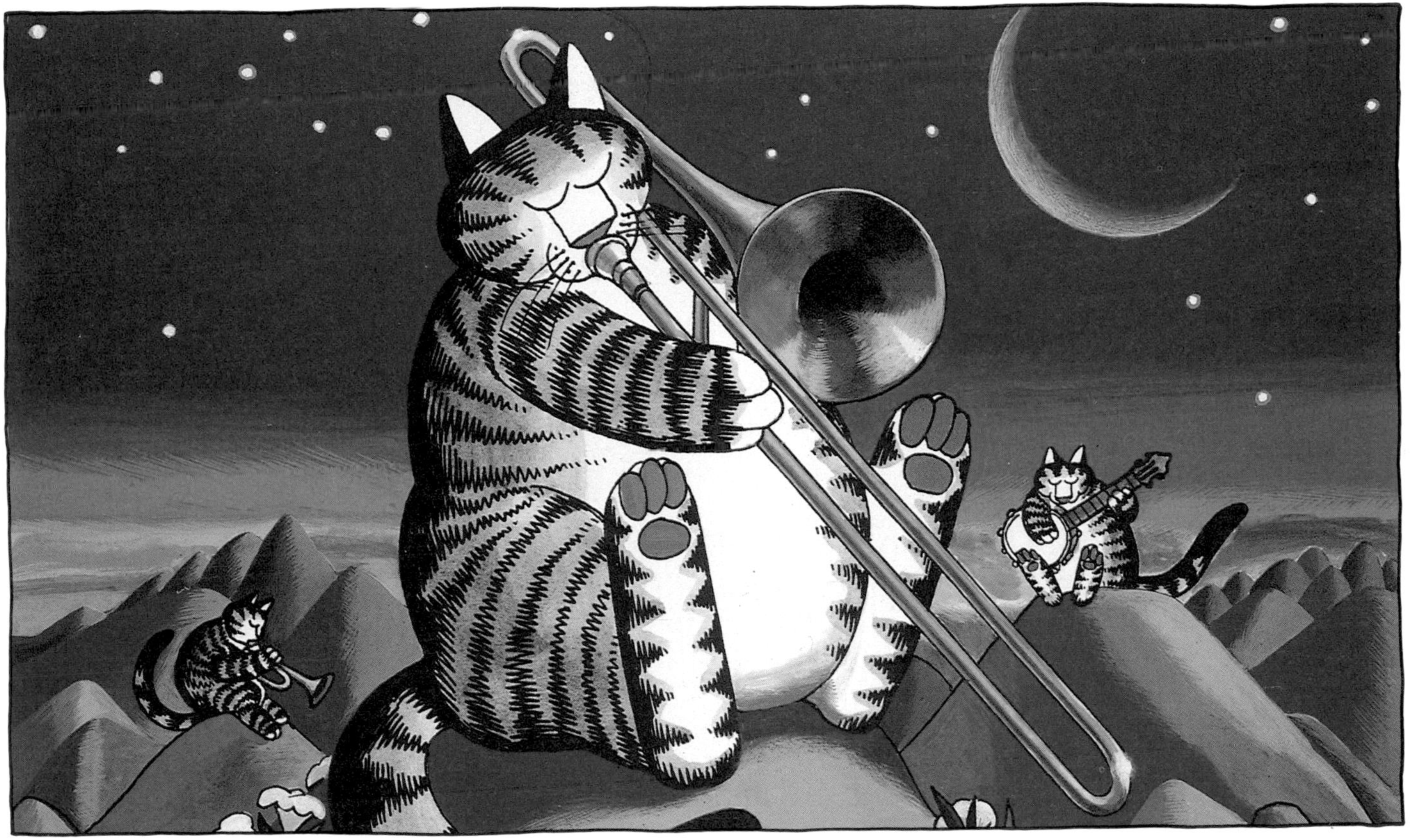

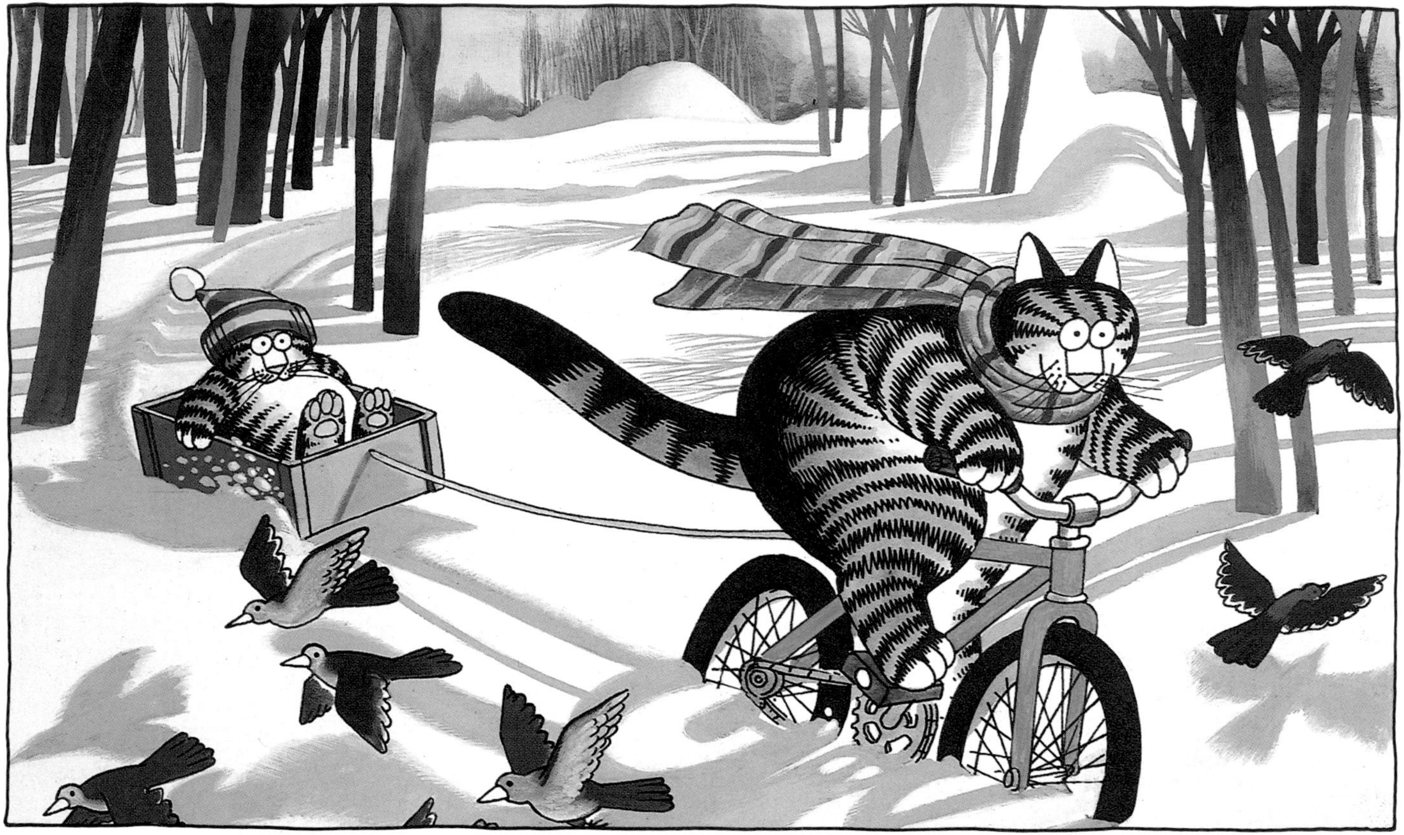

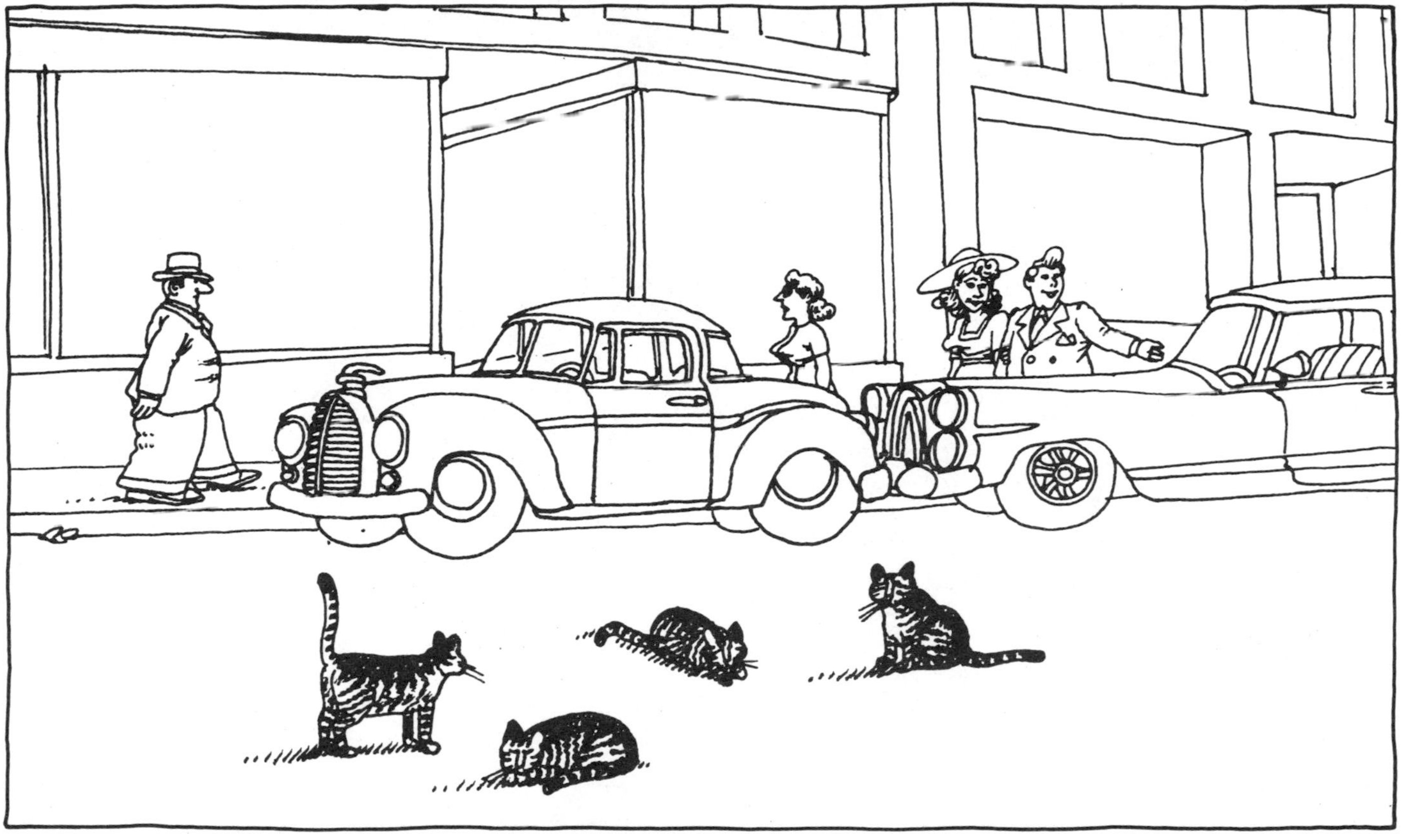

A Dreaded Hamwort

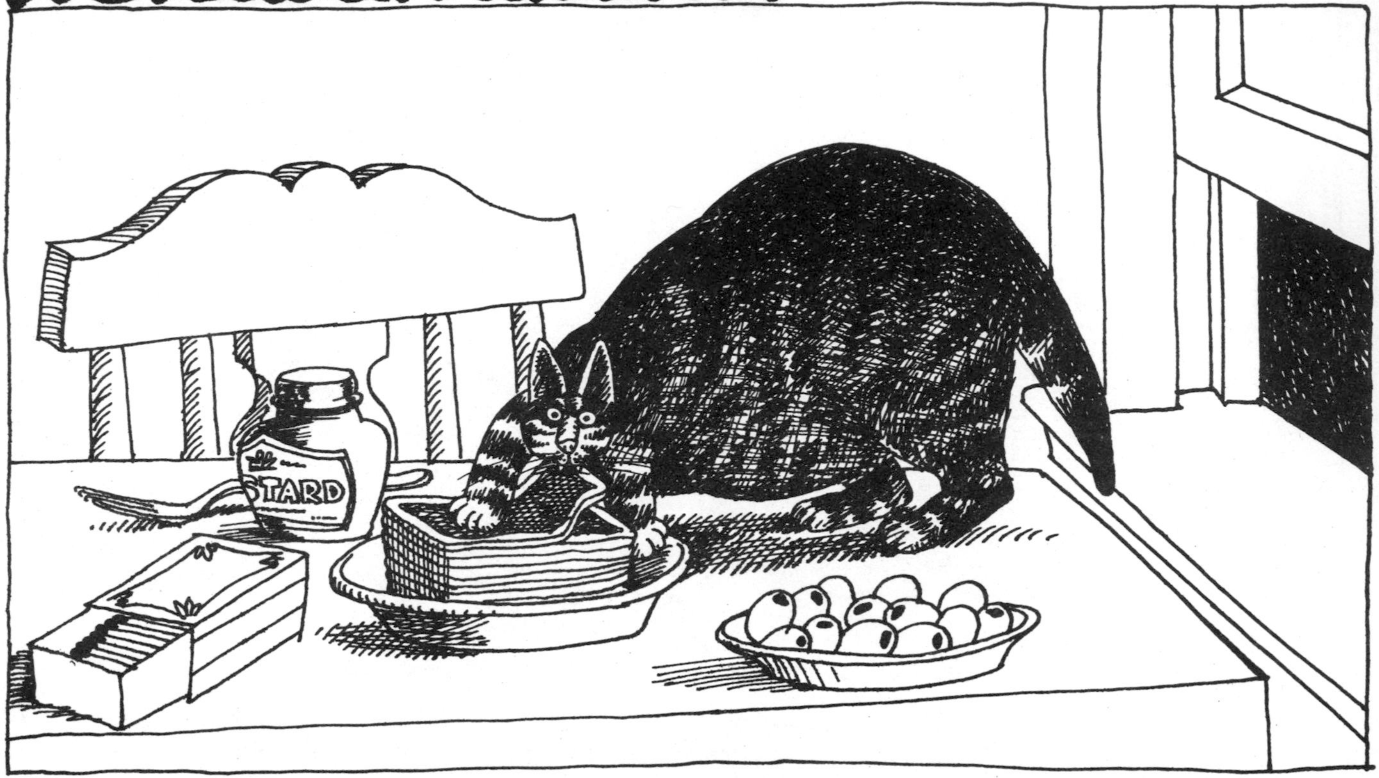
STARD

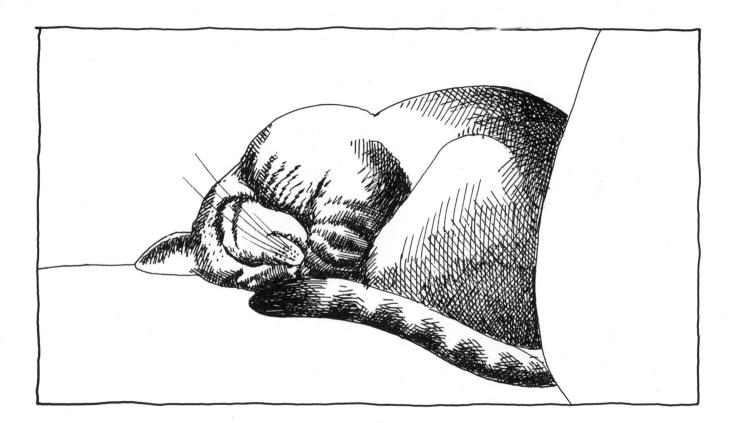

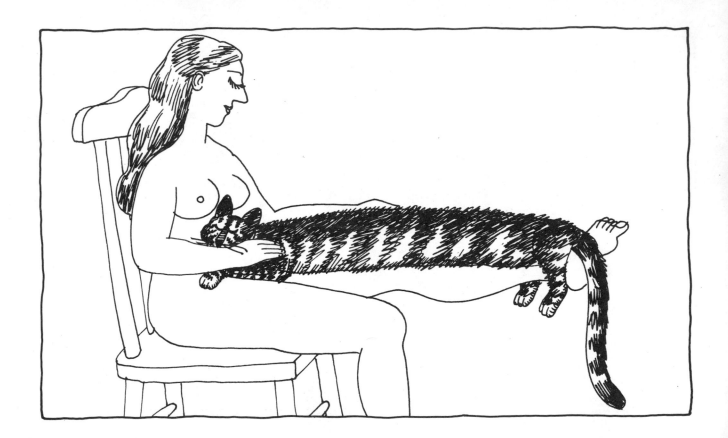

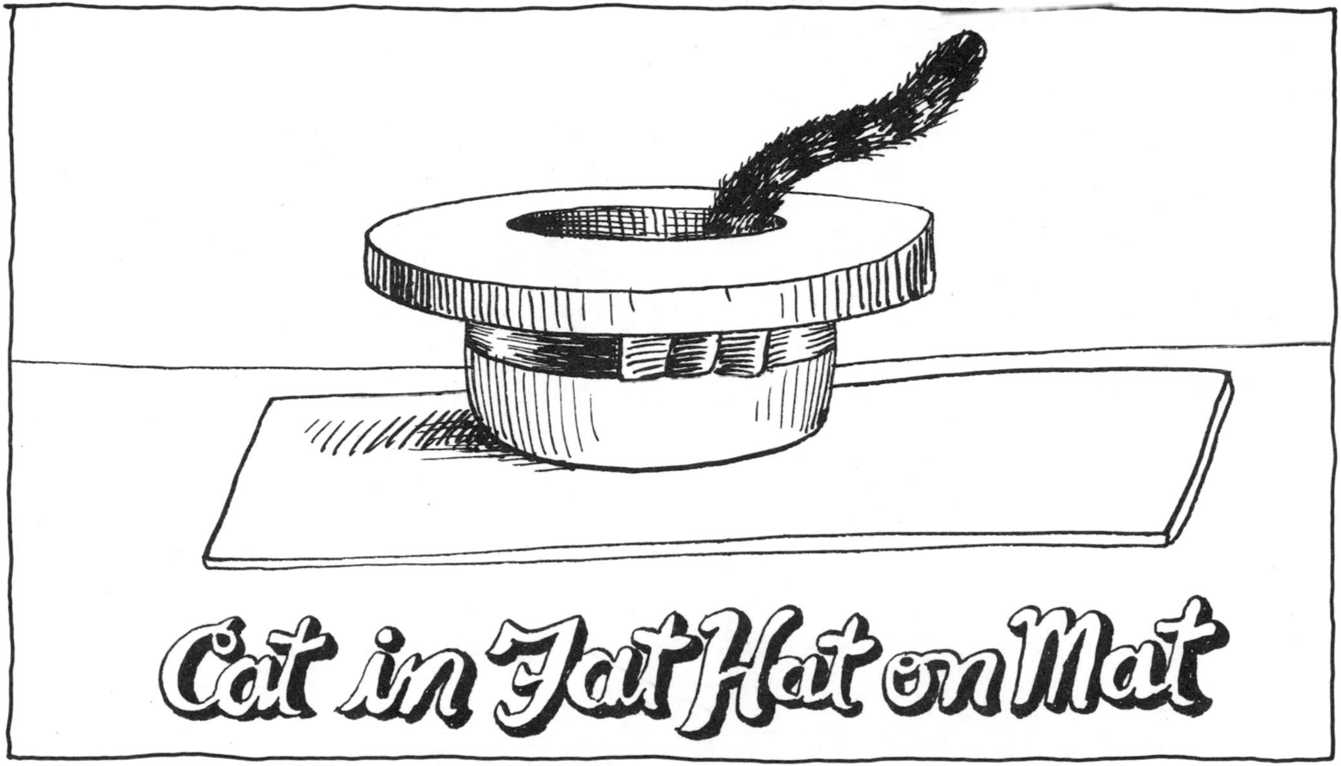
Cat in Fat Hat on Mat

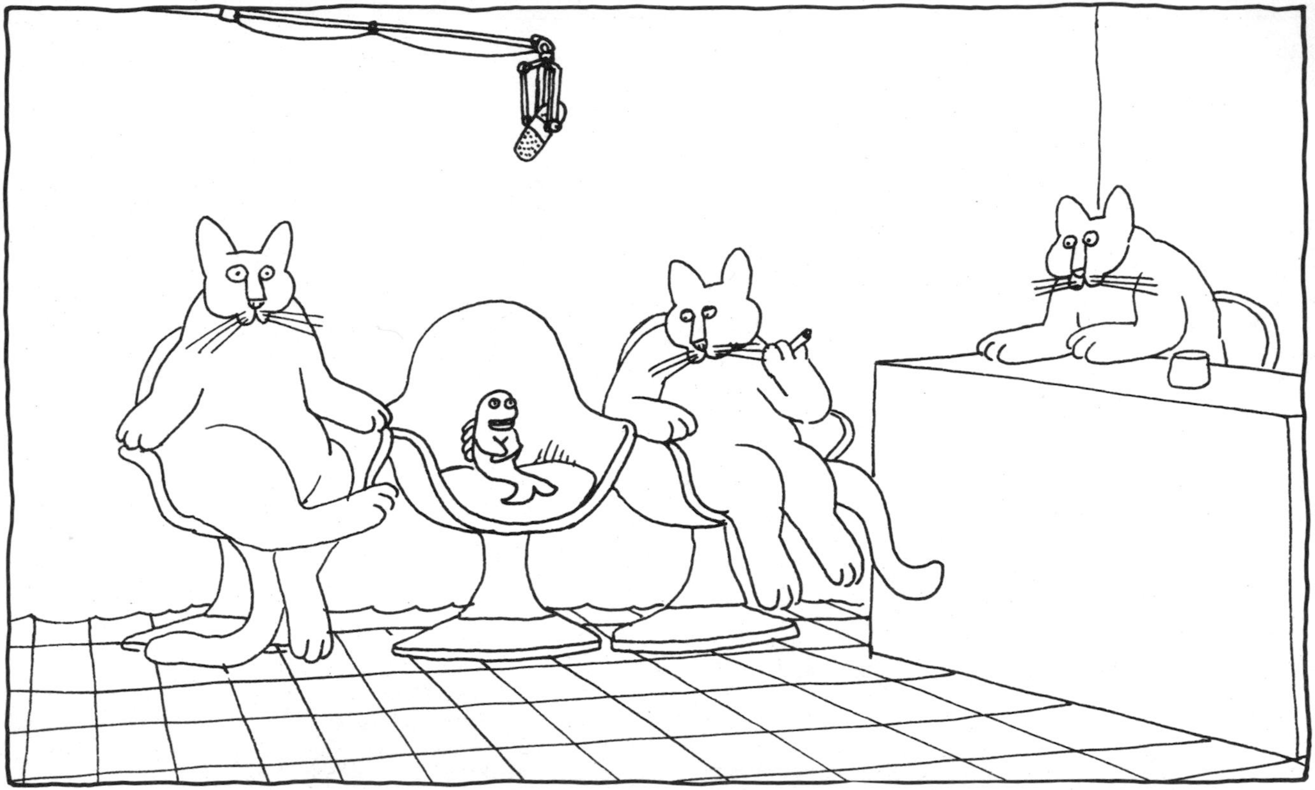

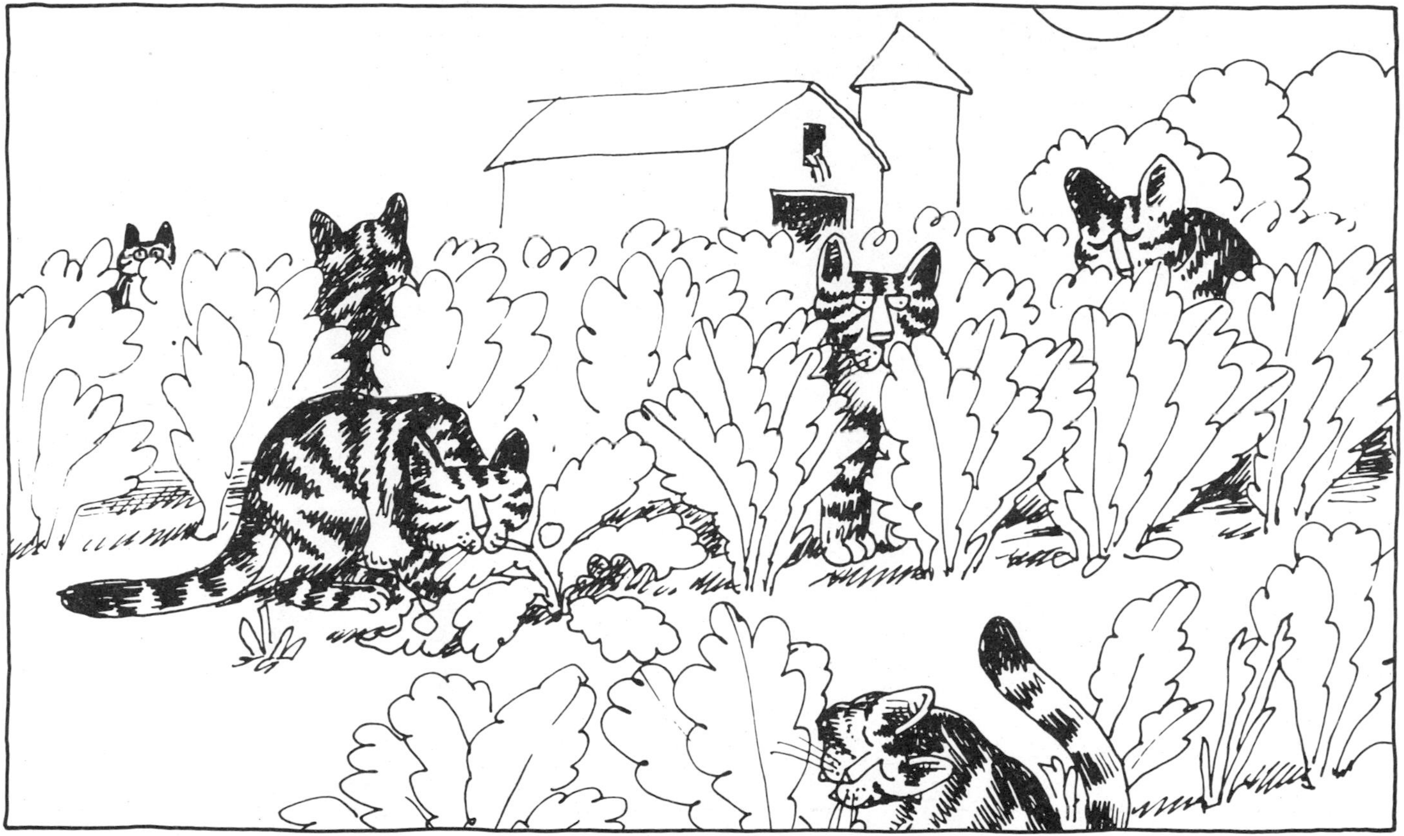

Nit & the Ham Tree

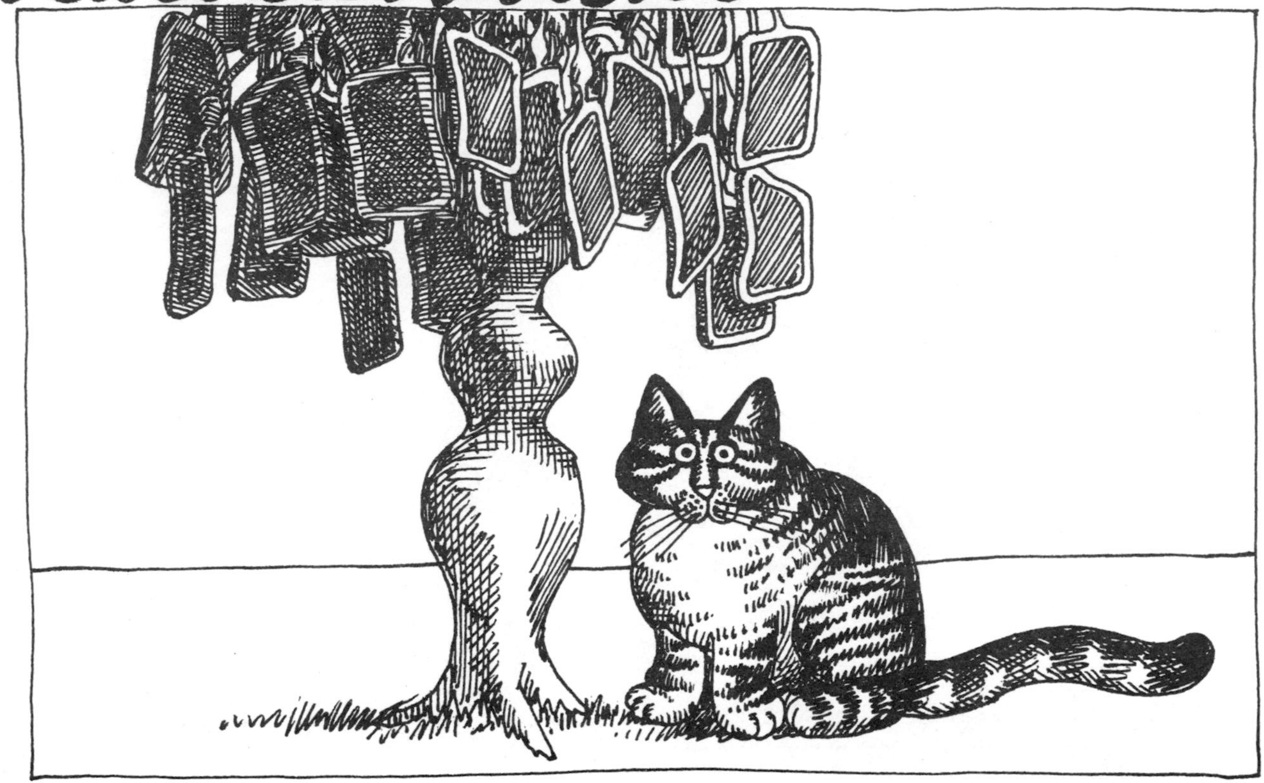

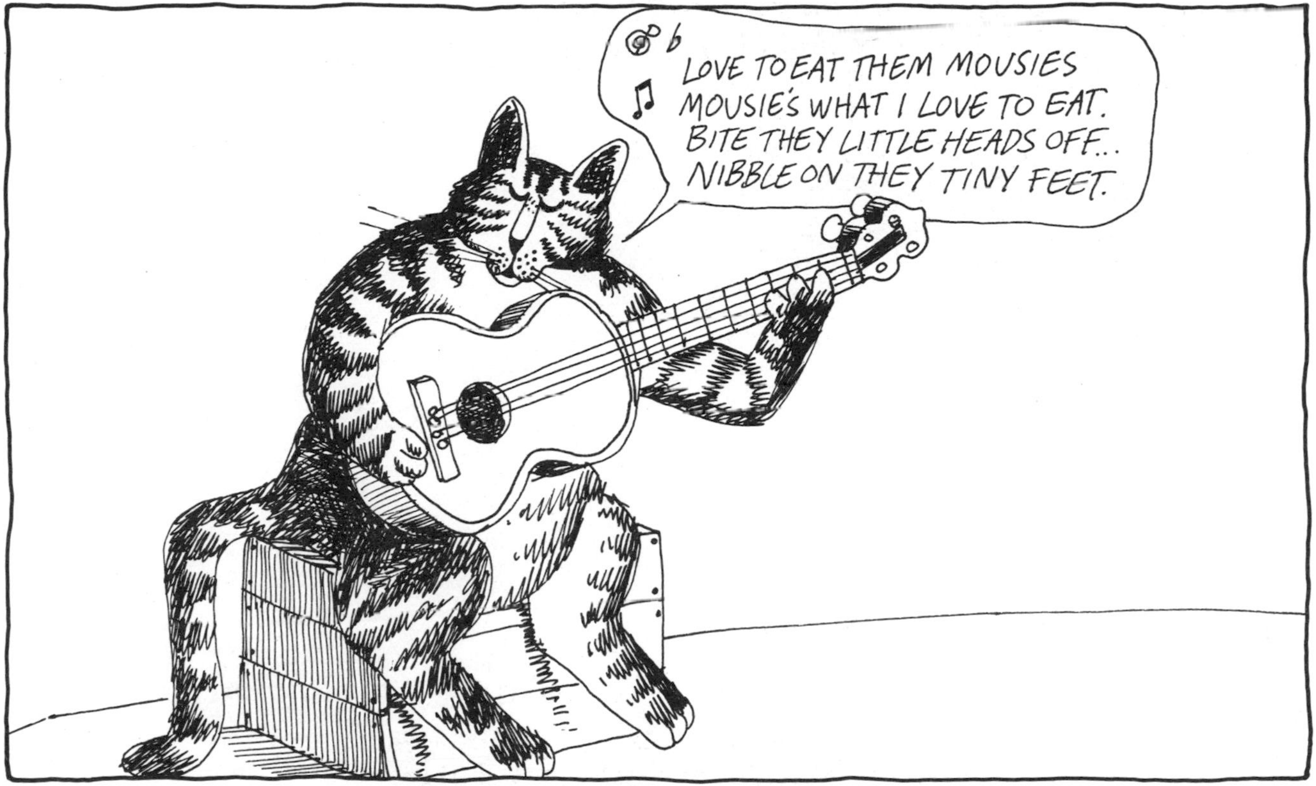
LOVE TO EAT THEM MOUSIES
MOUSIE'S WHAT I LOVE TO EAT.
BITE THEY LITTLE HEADS OFF...
NIBBLE ON THEY TINY FEET.

Sleight of Paw

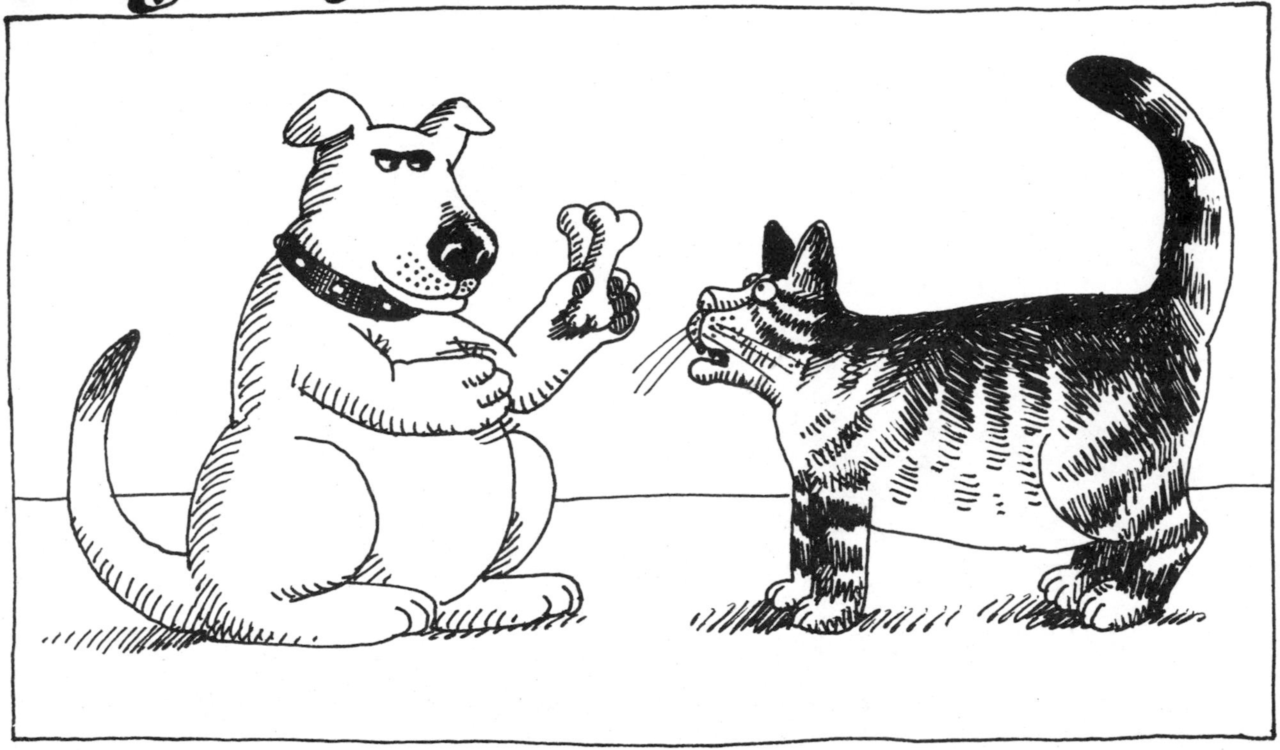

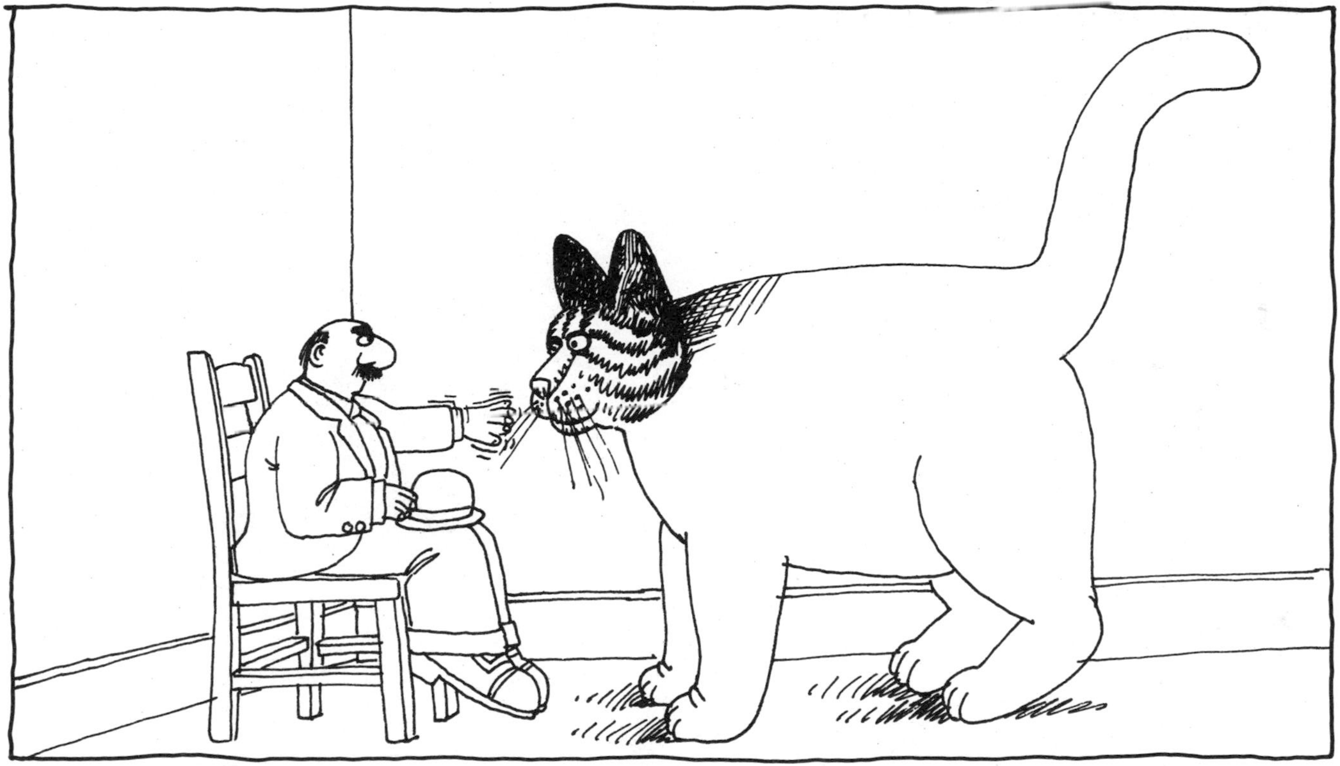

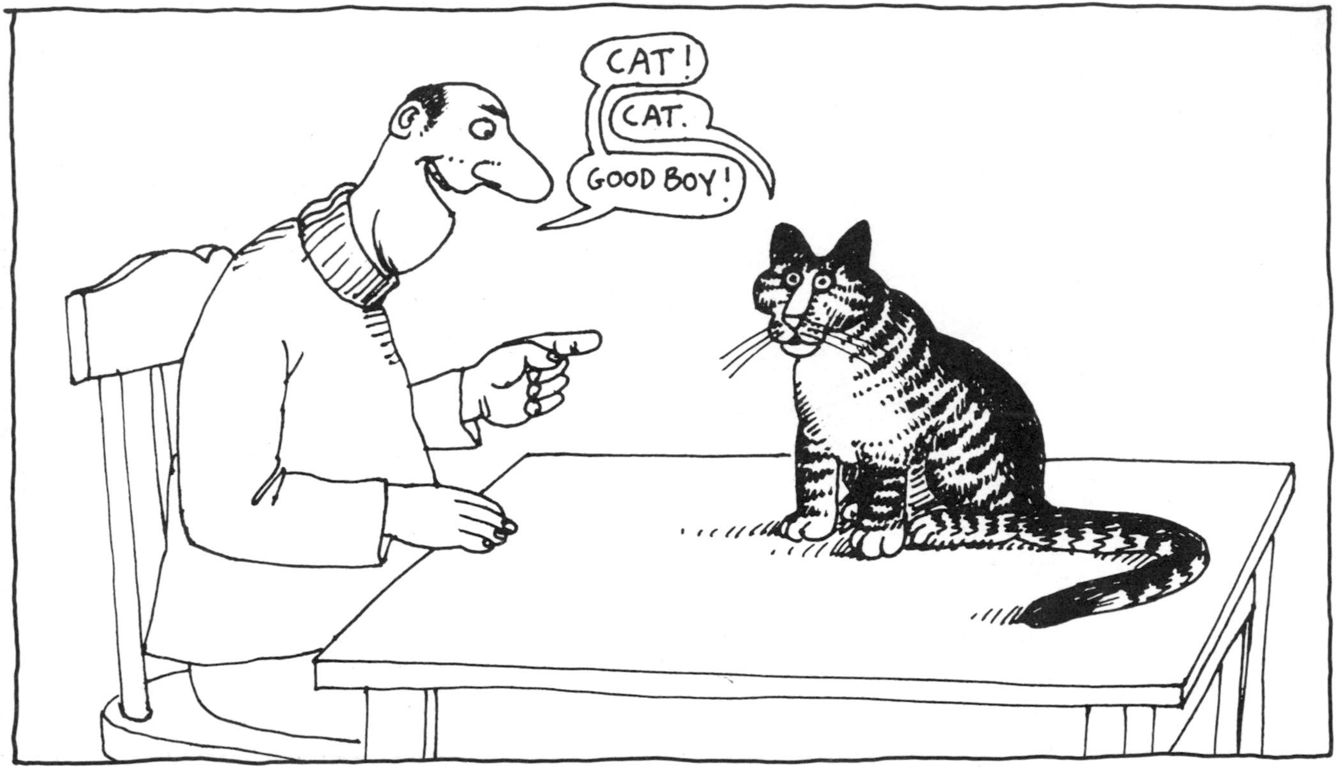
CAT!
CAT.
GOOD BOY!

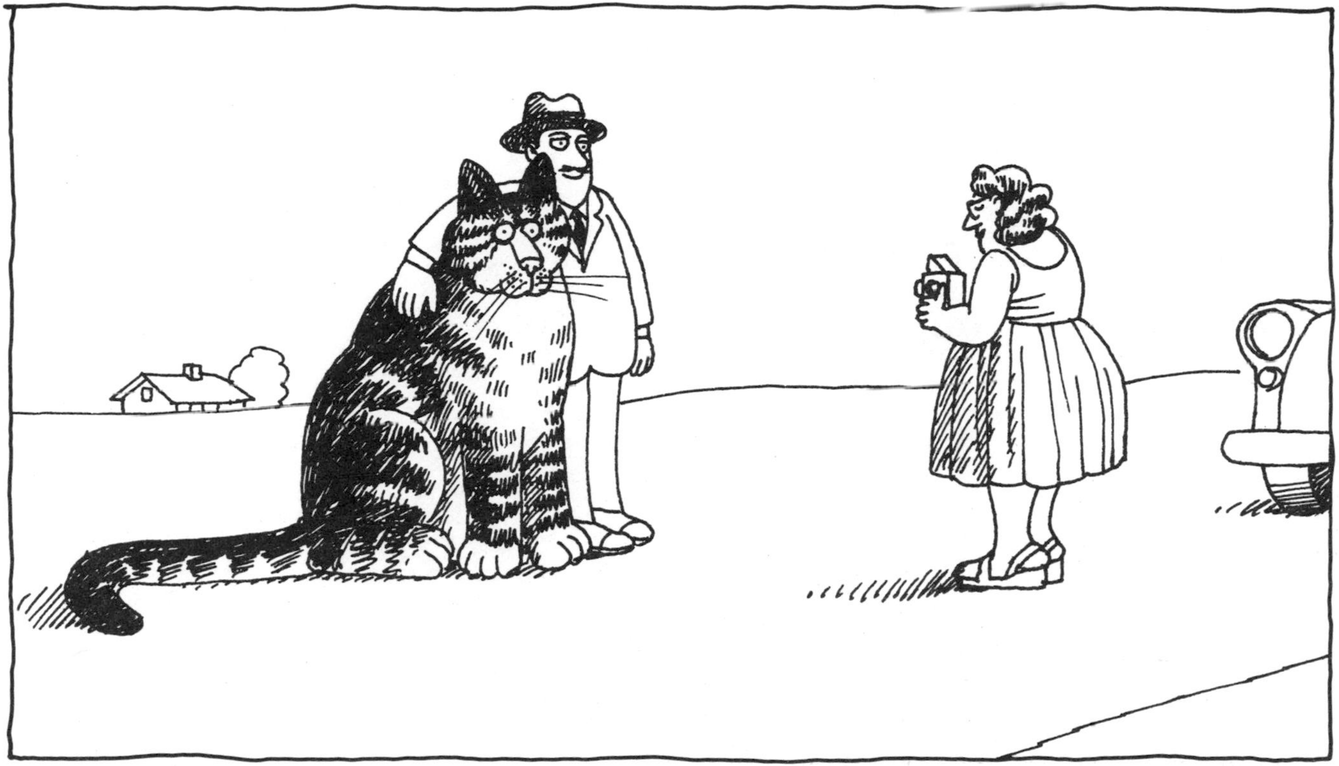

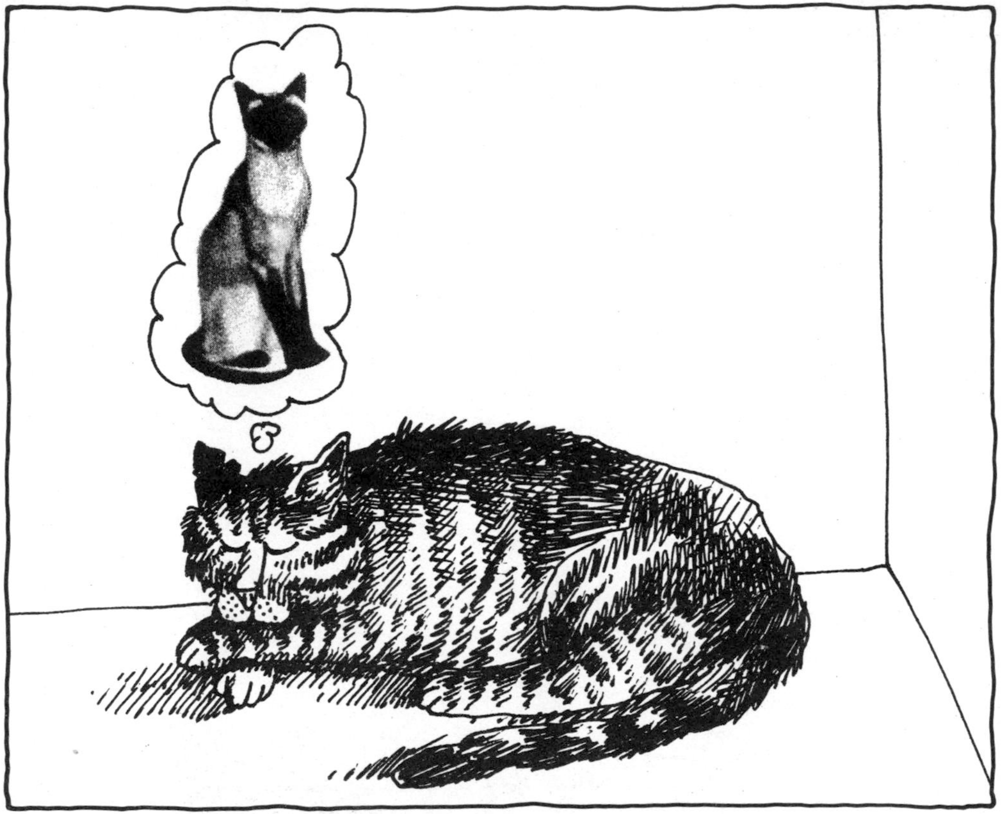

SUPERSTITIONS

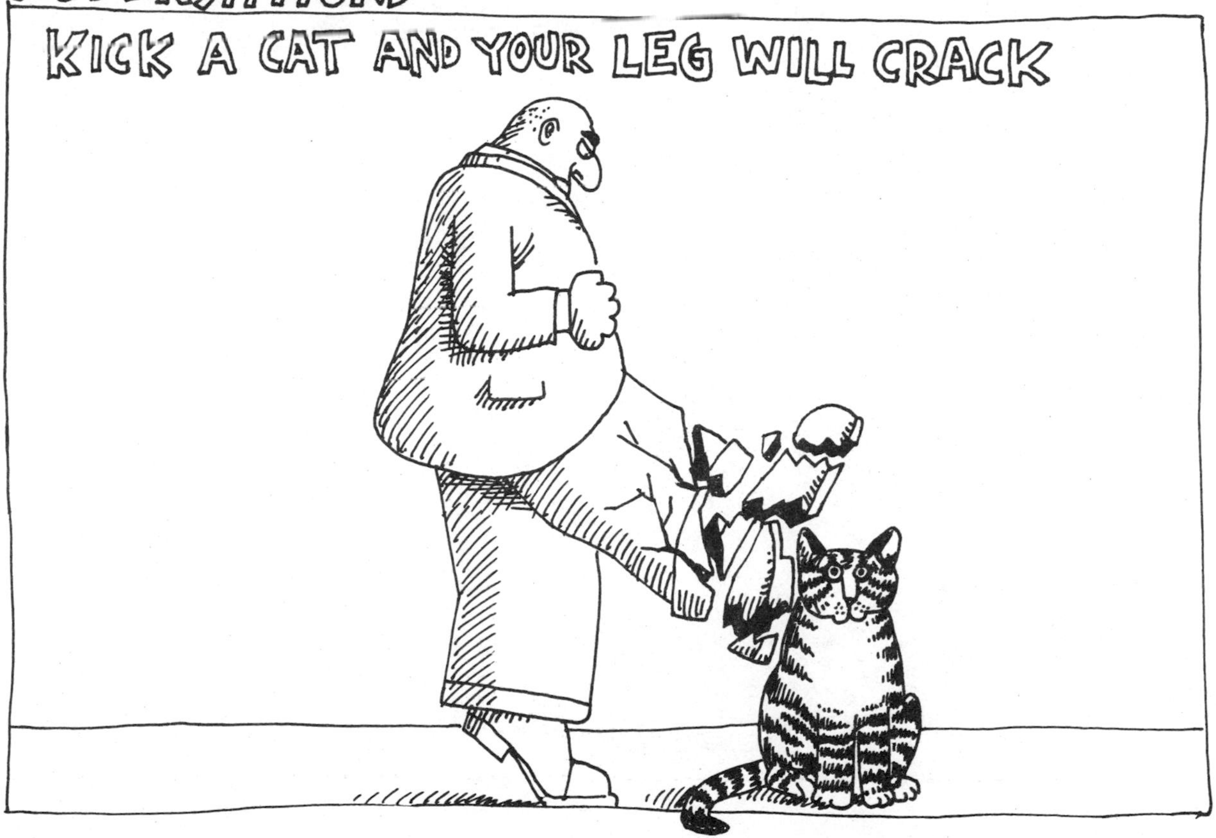
KICK A CAT AND YOUR LEG WILL CRACK

Cat and his mom

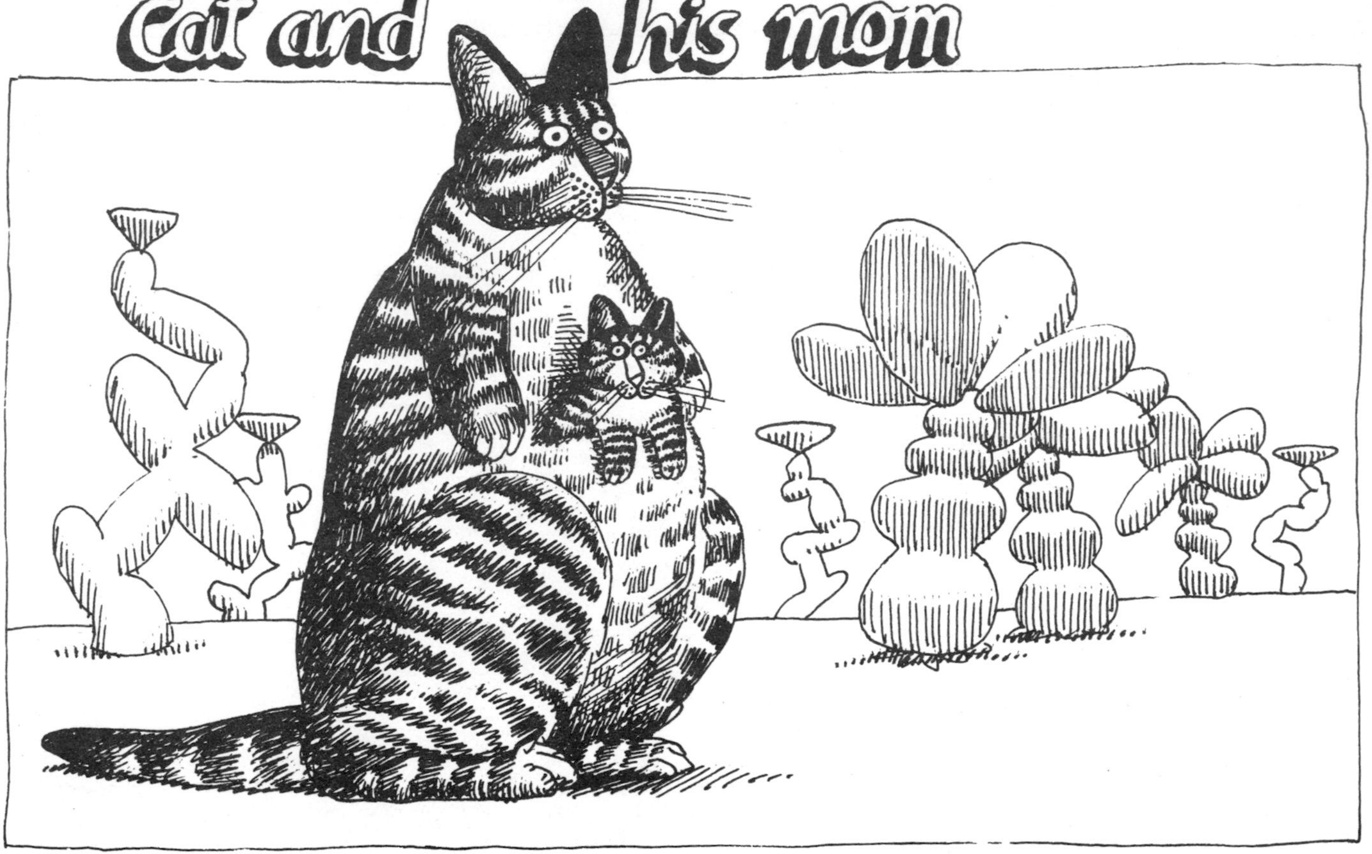

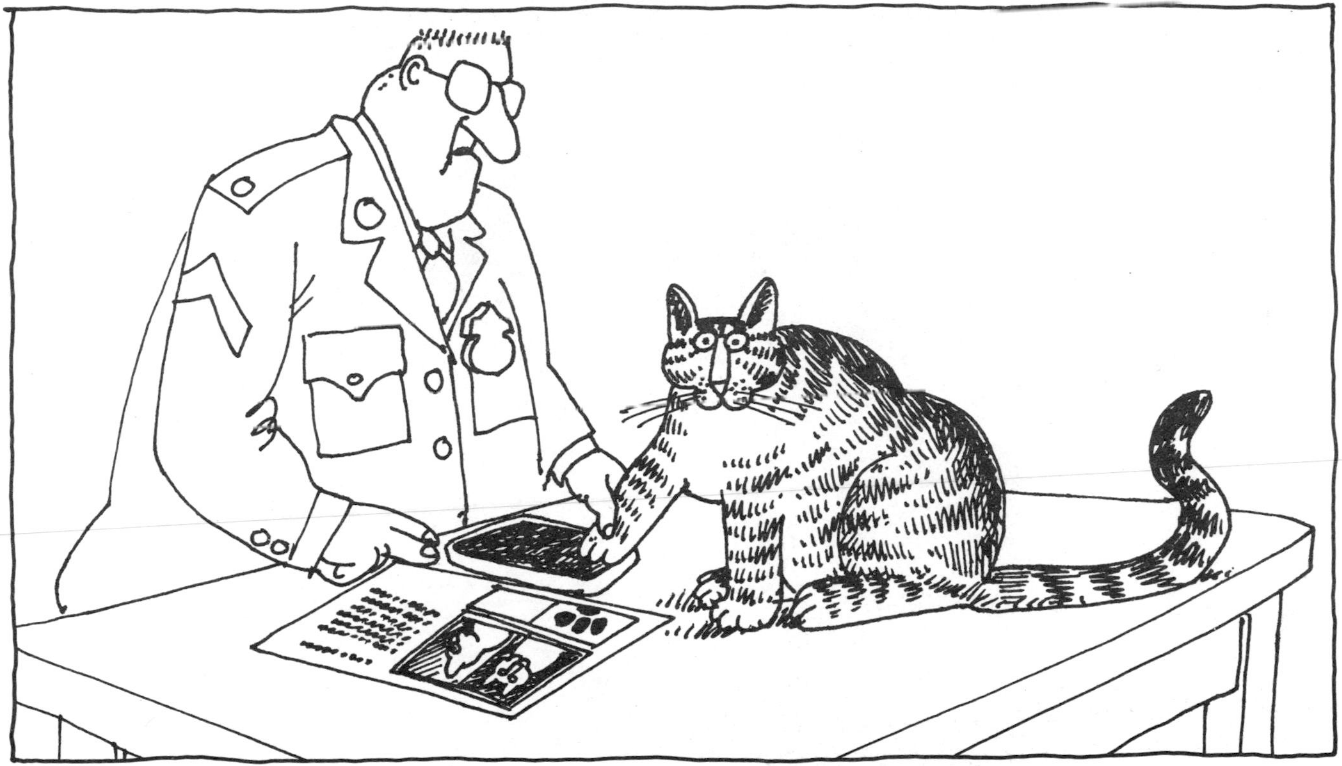

FAT FUZZY FELLOW

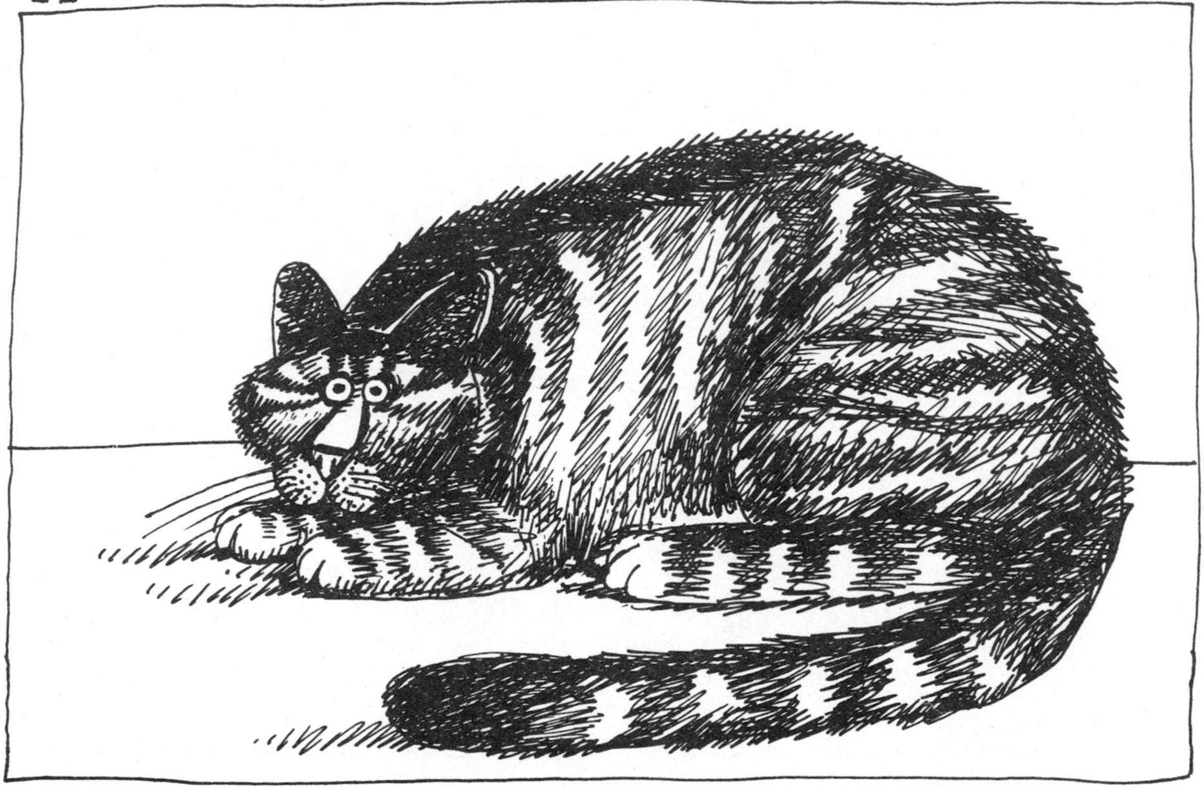

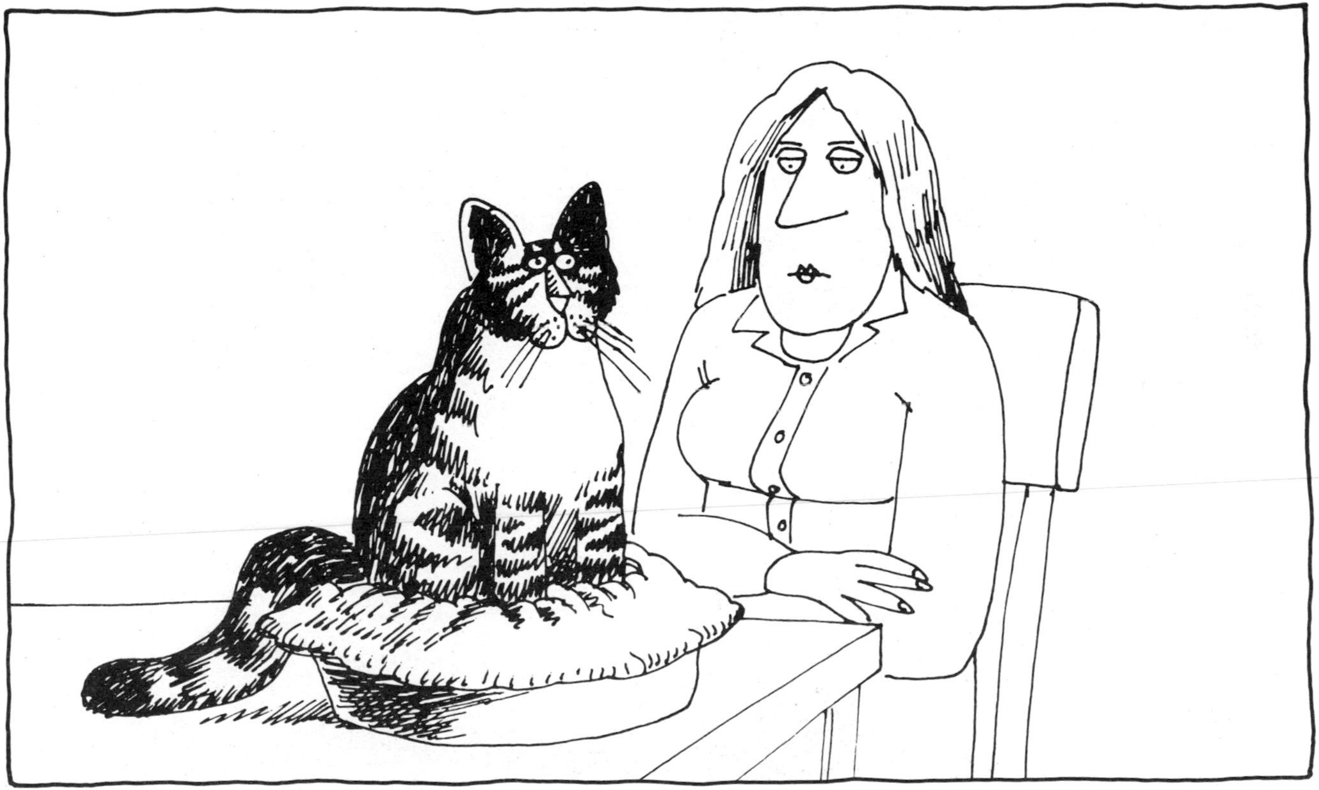

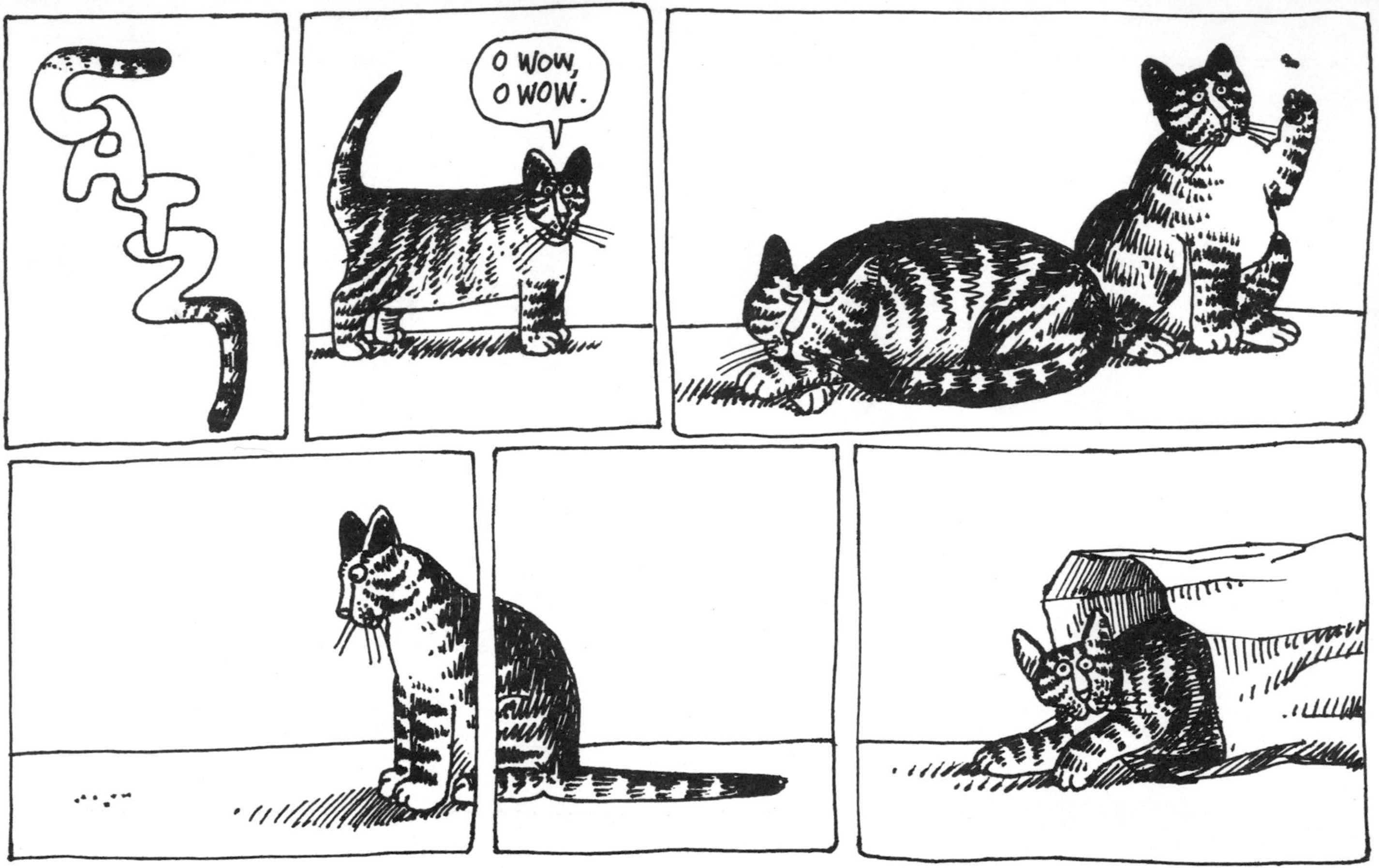
CATZ
O WOW,
O WOW.

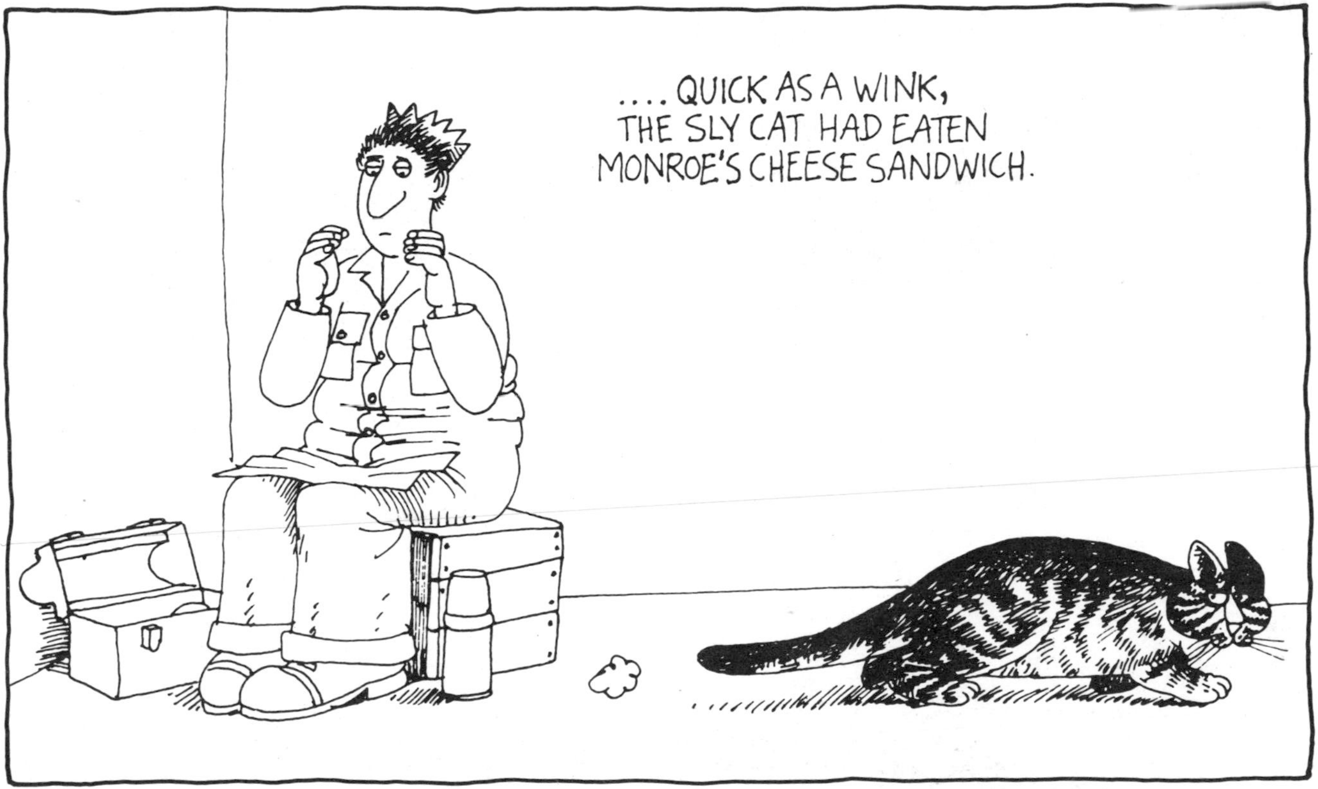
....QUICK AS A WINK,
THE SLY CAT HAD EATEN
MONROE'S CHEESE SANDWICH.

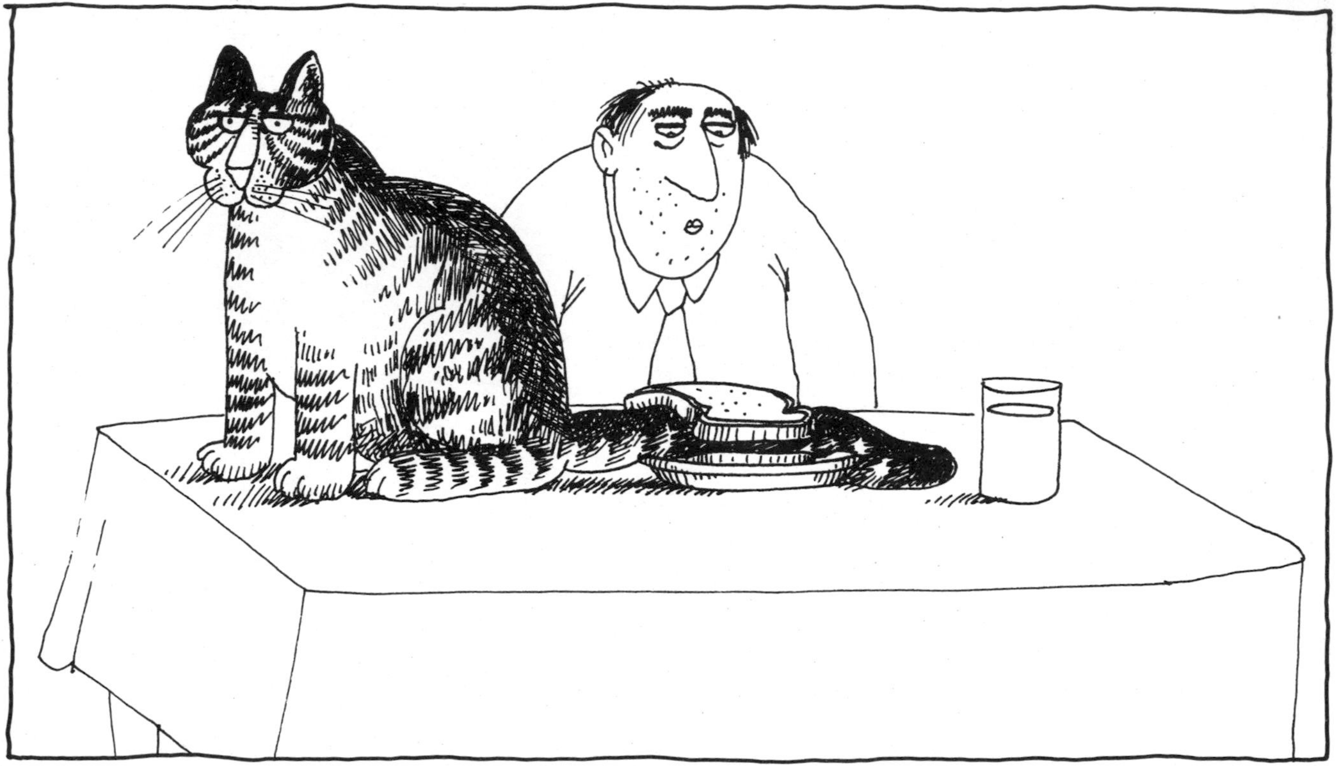

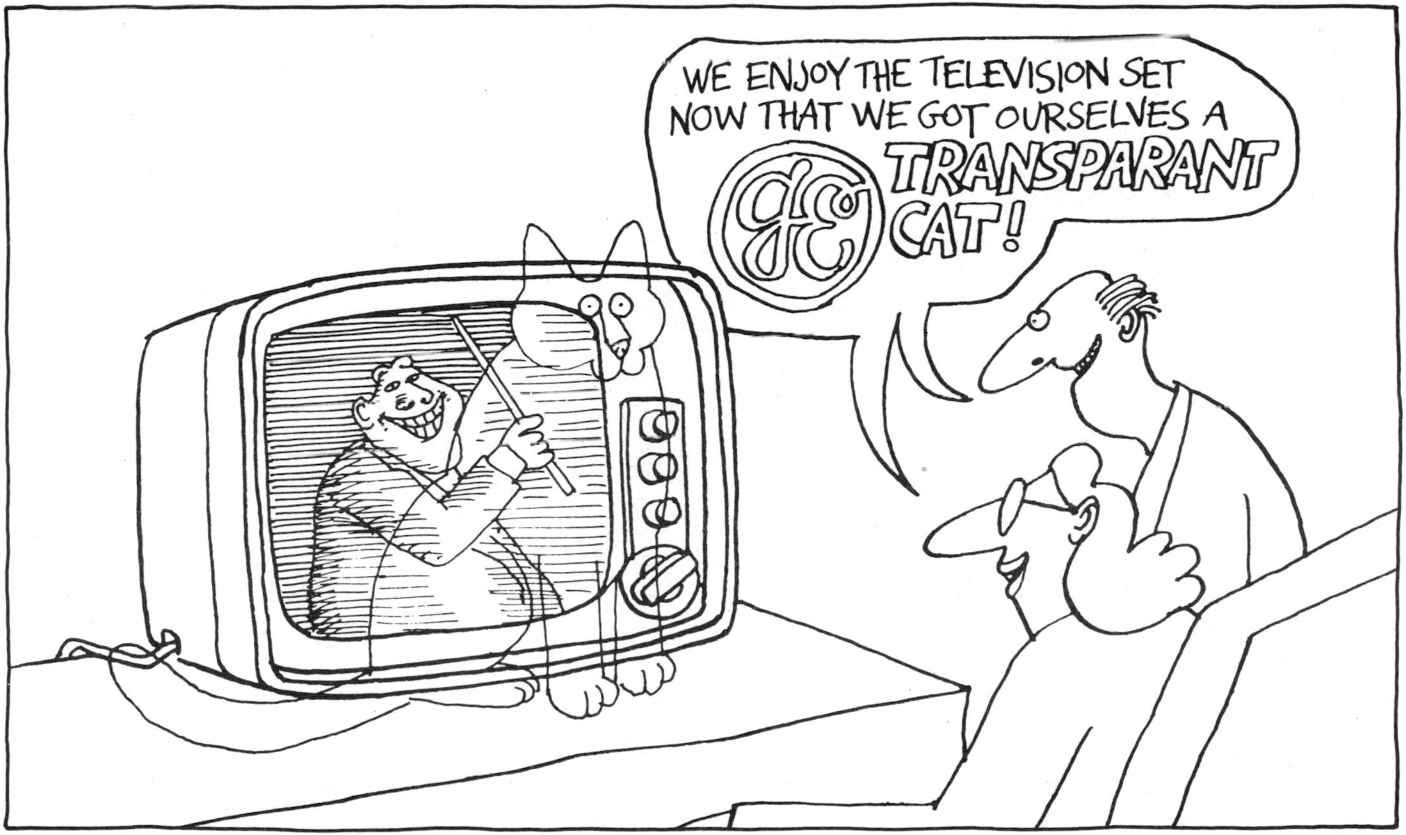
WE ENJOY THE TELEVISION SET NOW THAT WE GOT OURSELVES A TRANSPARANT CAT!

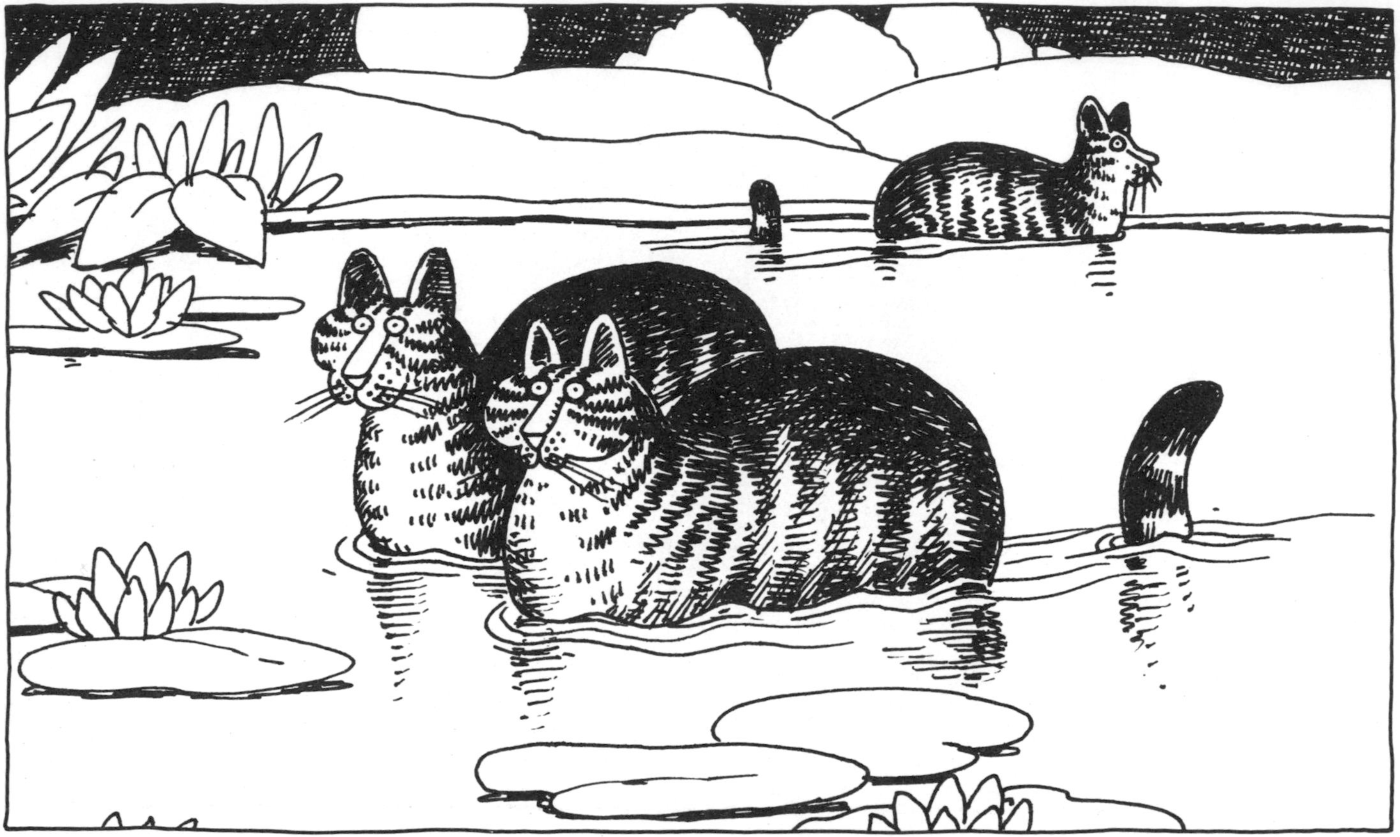

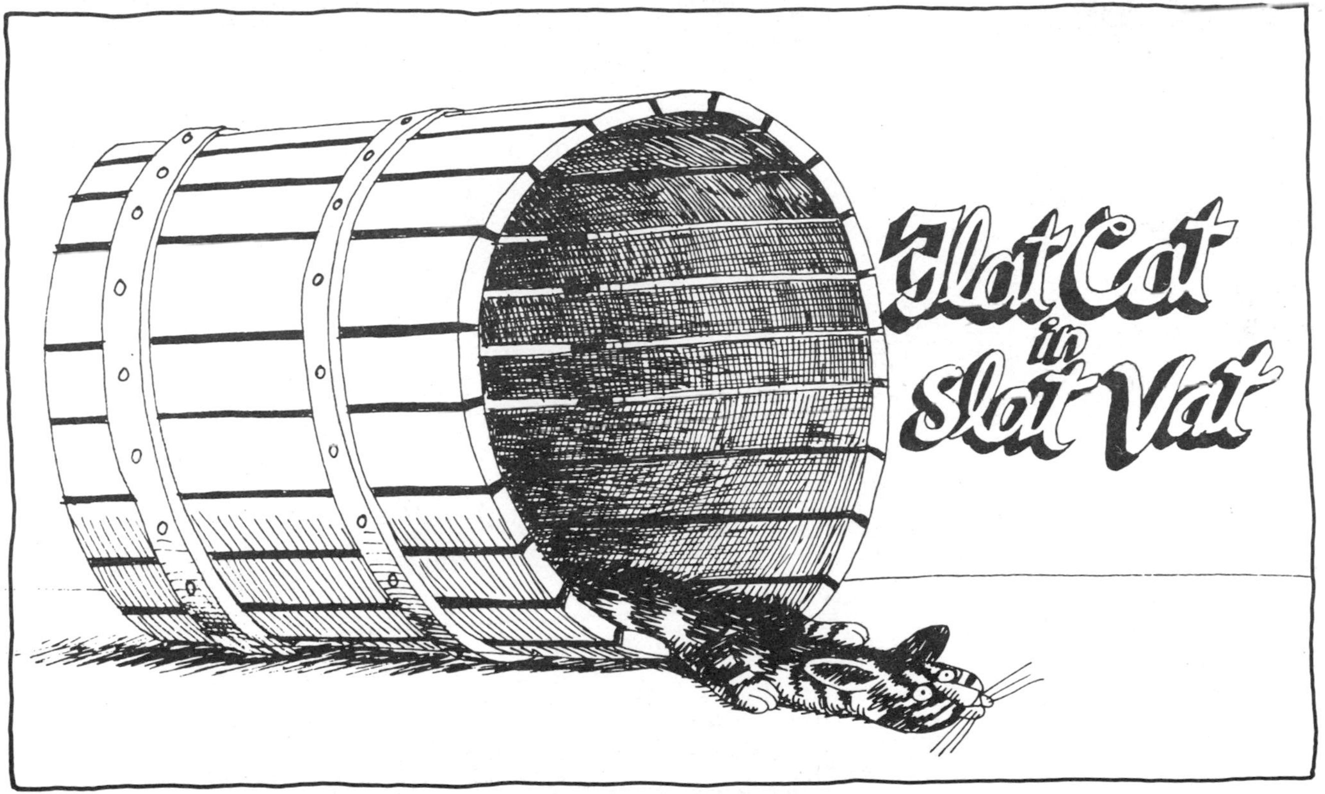
Flat Cat
in
Slot Vat

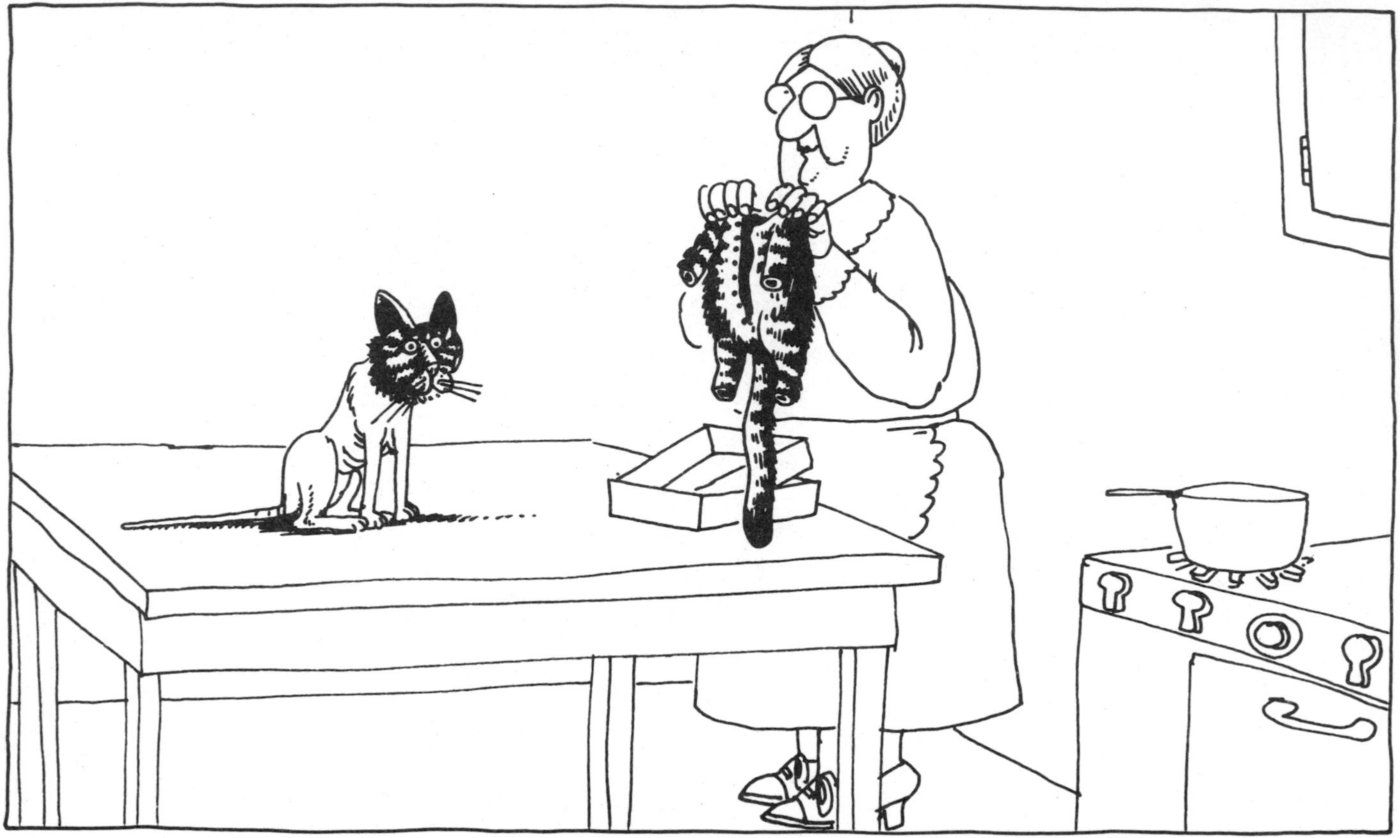

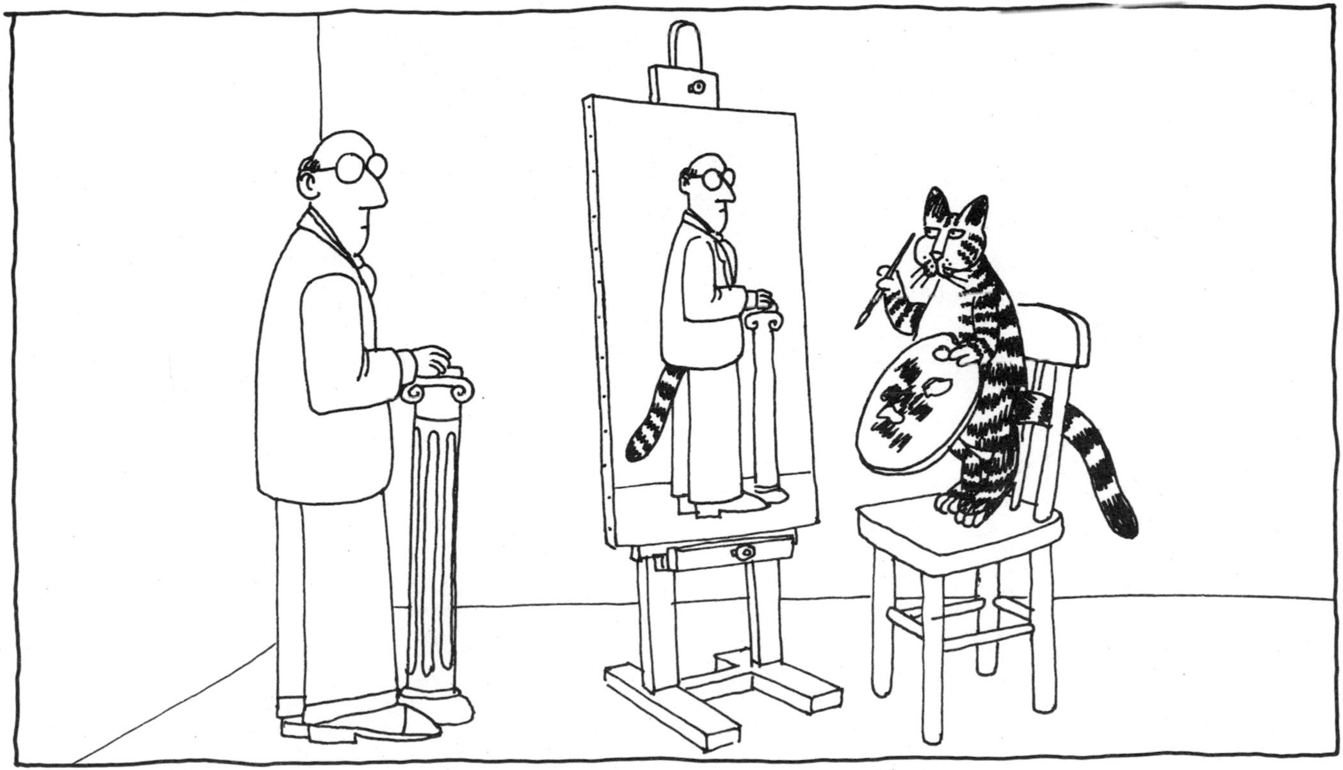

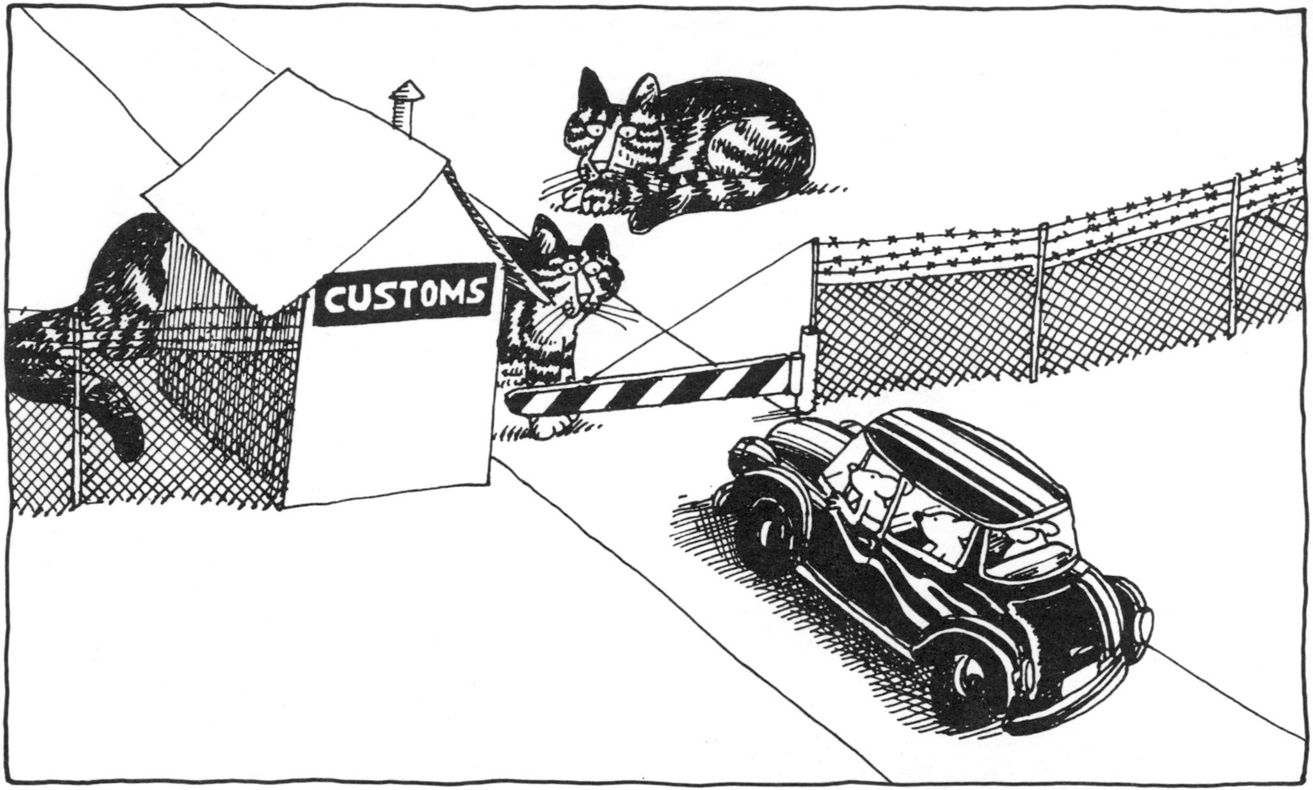
CUSTOMS

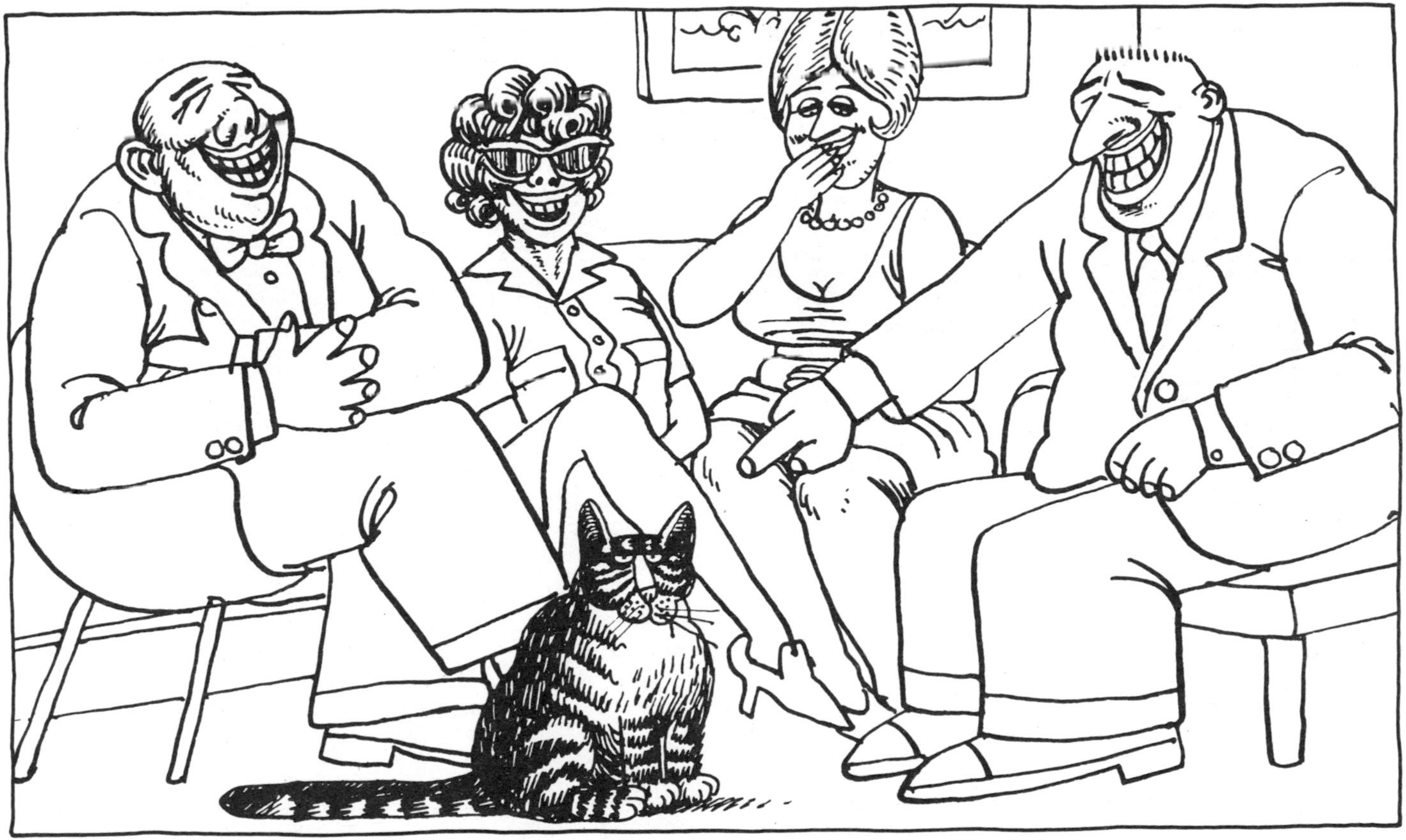

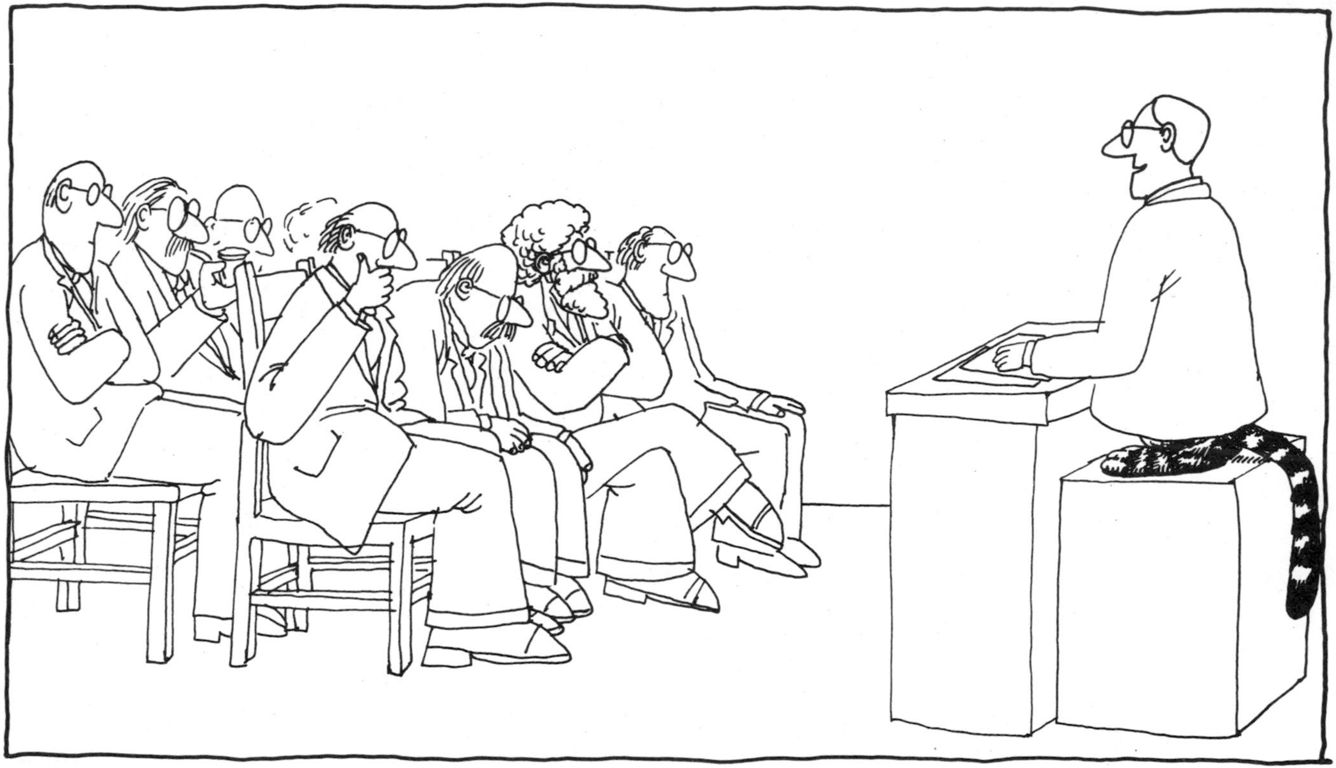

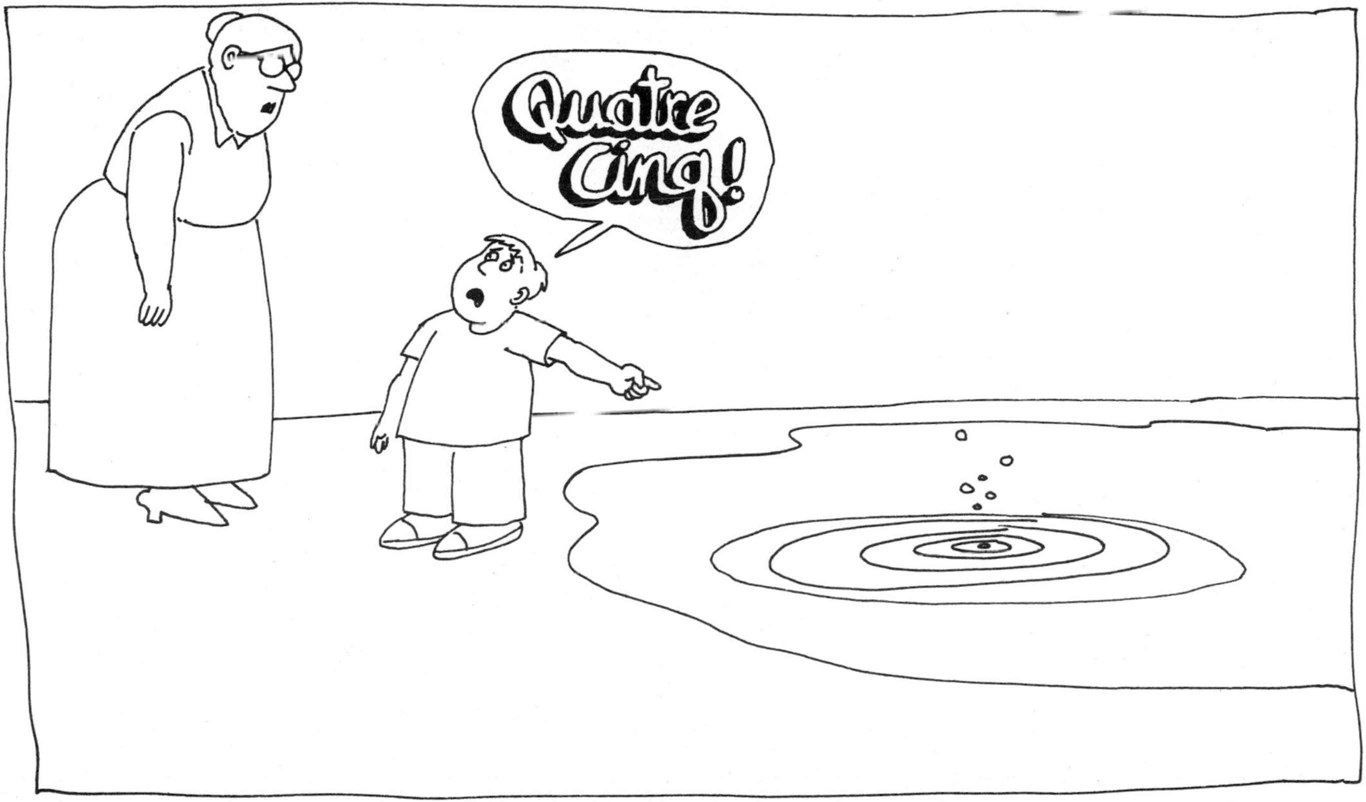
Quatre Cinq!

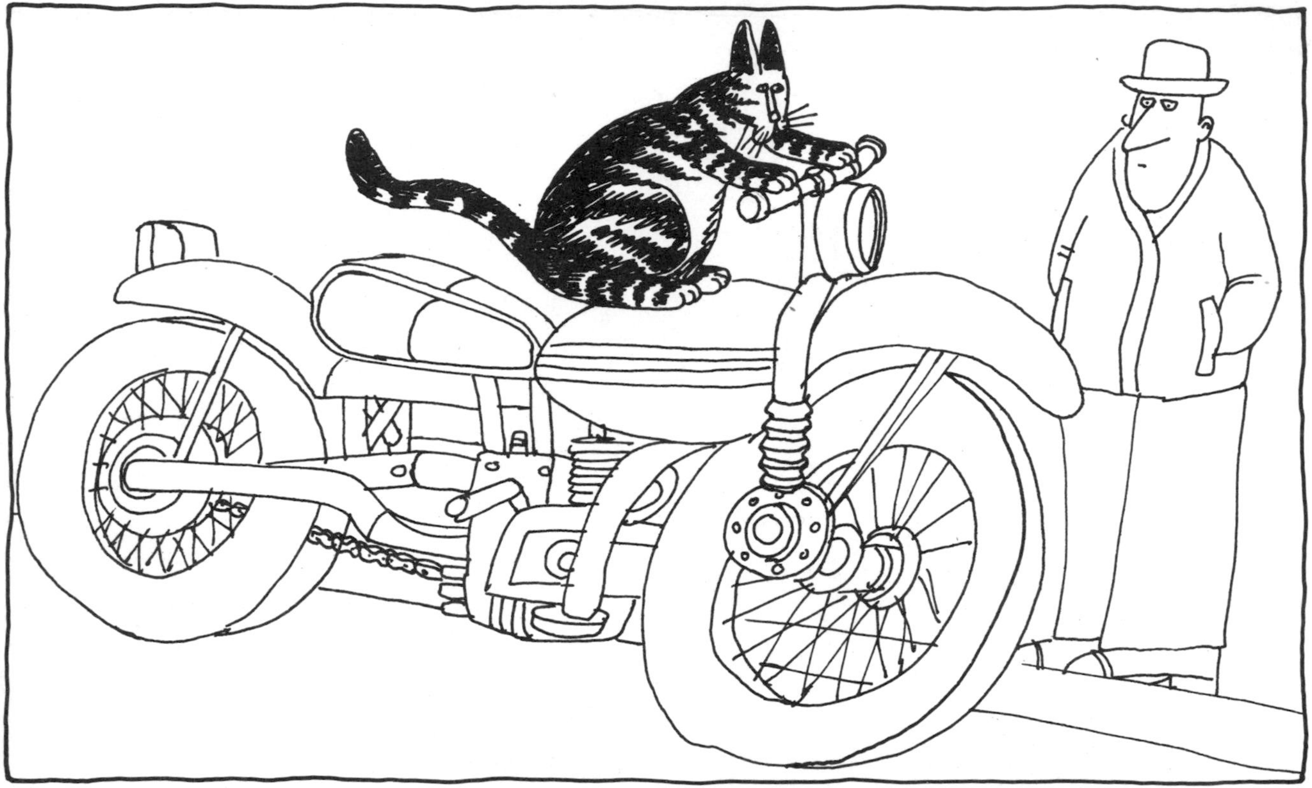

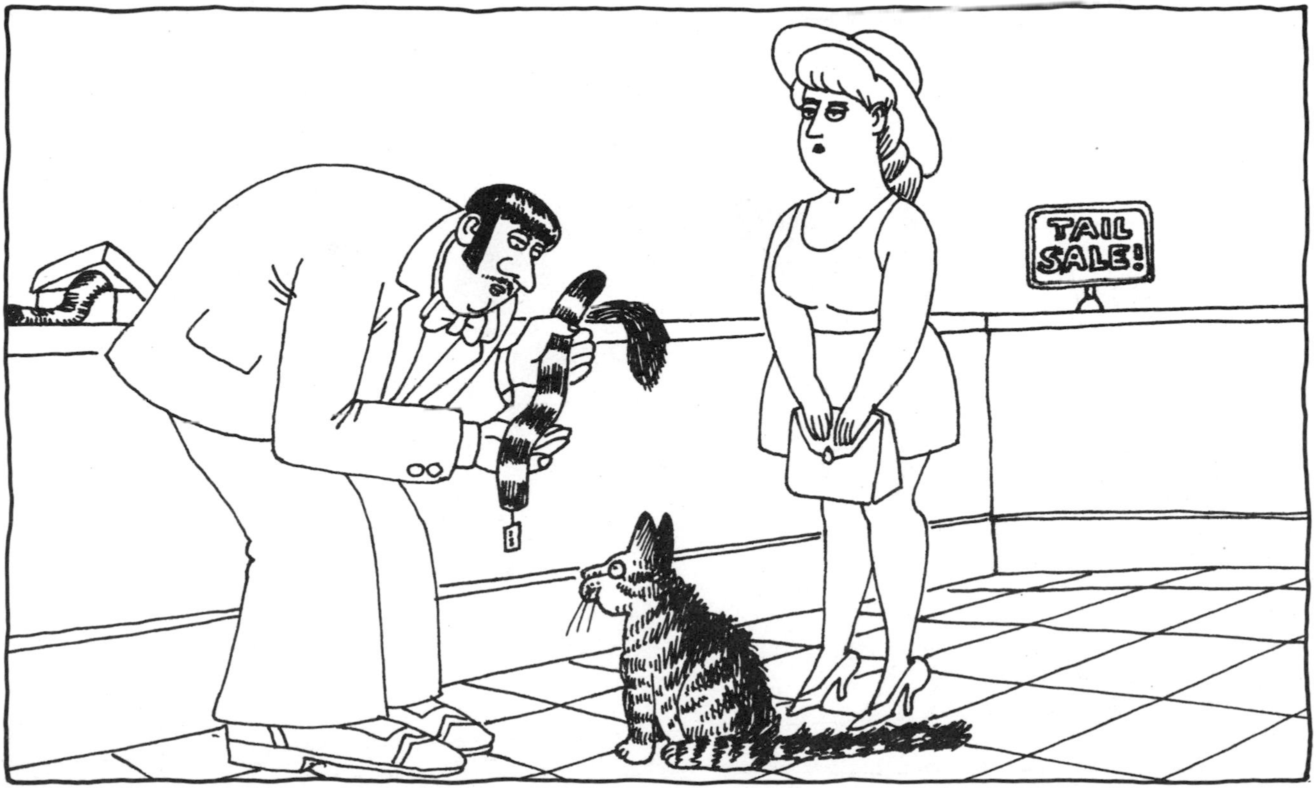
TAIL SALE!

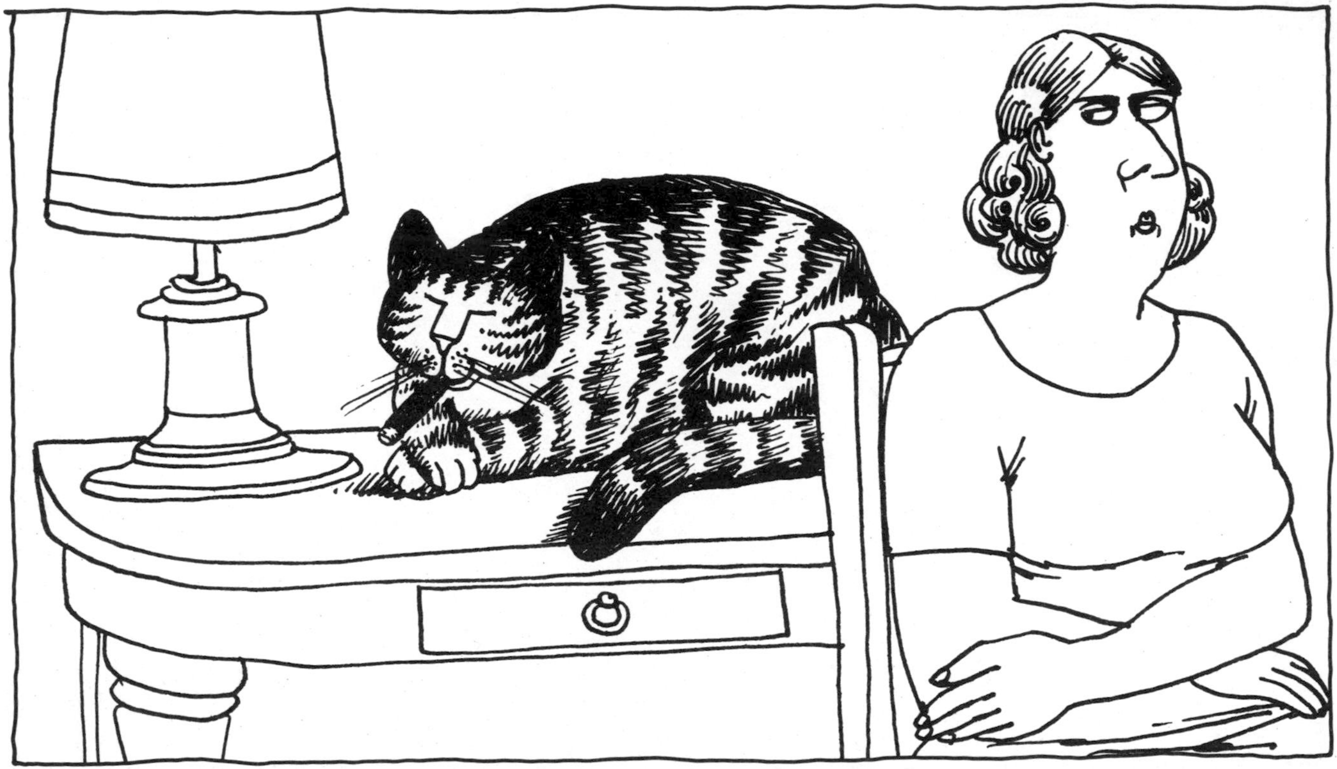

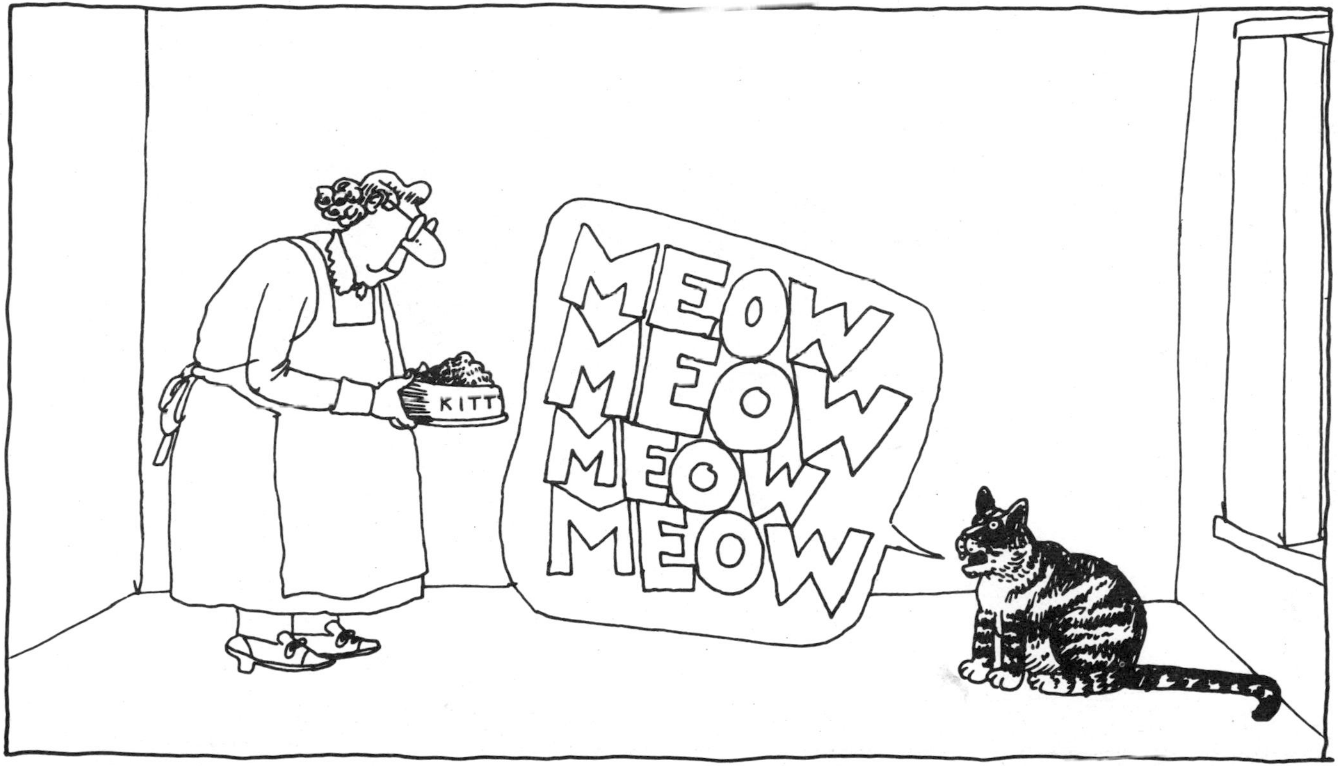
KITT
MEOW
MEOW
MEOW
MEOW

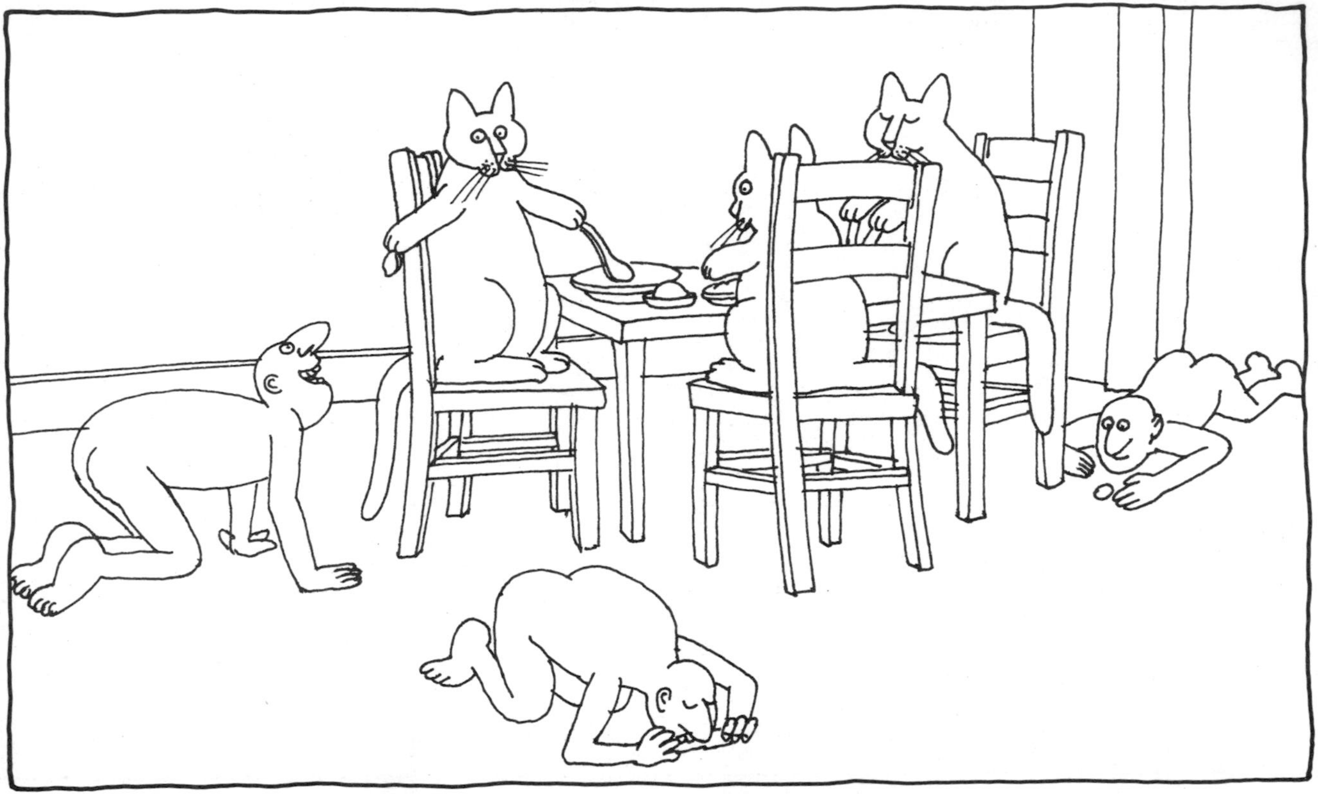

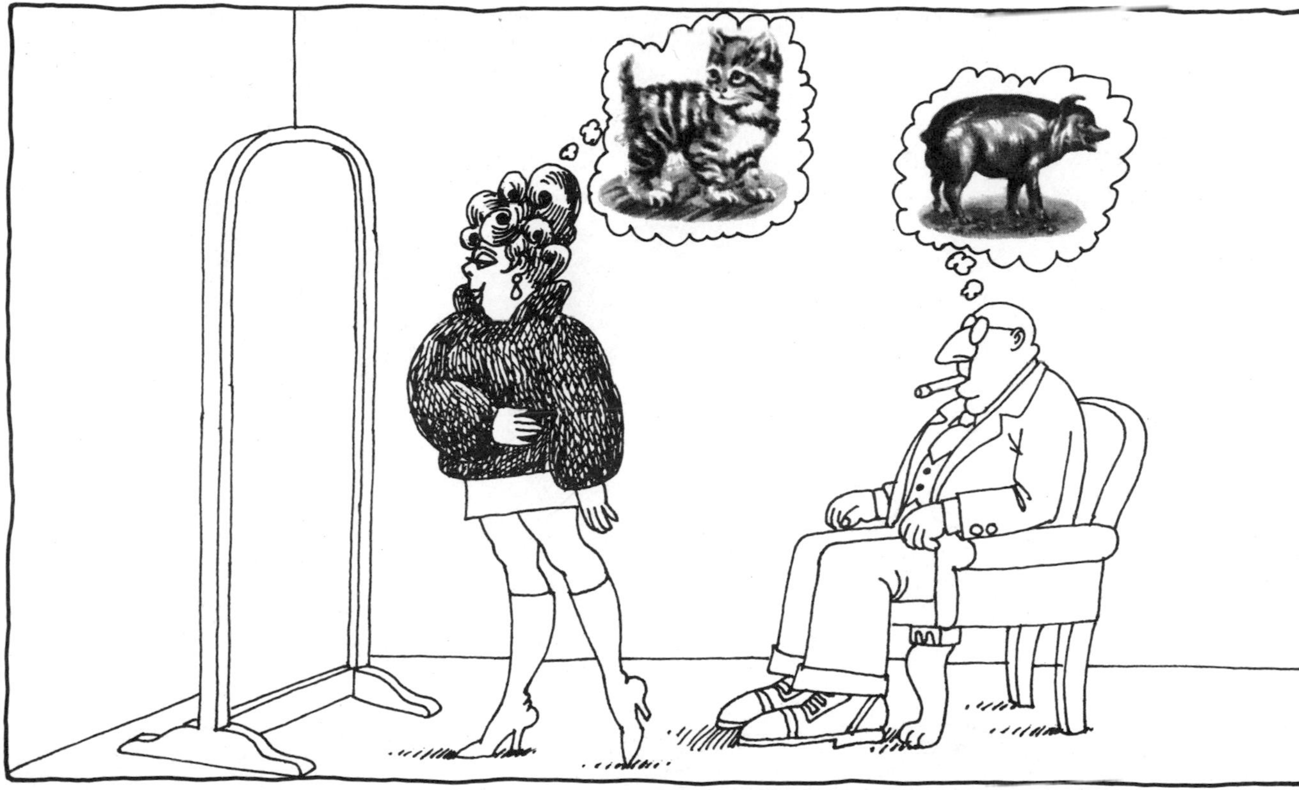

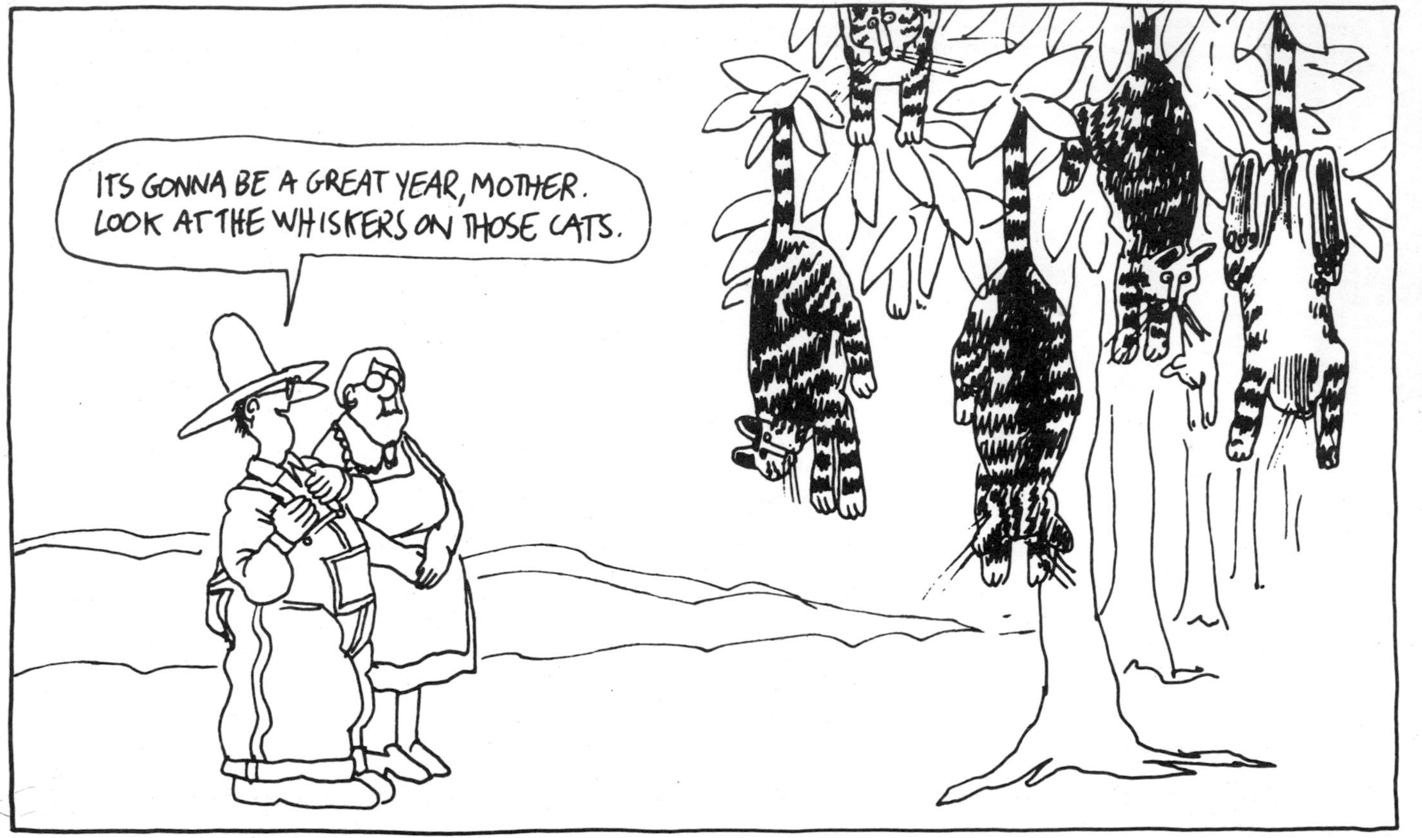
ITS GONNA BE A GREAT YEAR, MOTHER. LOOK AT THE WHISKERS ON THOSE CATS.

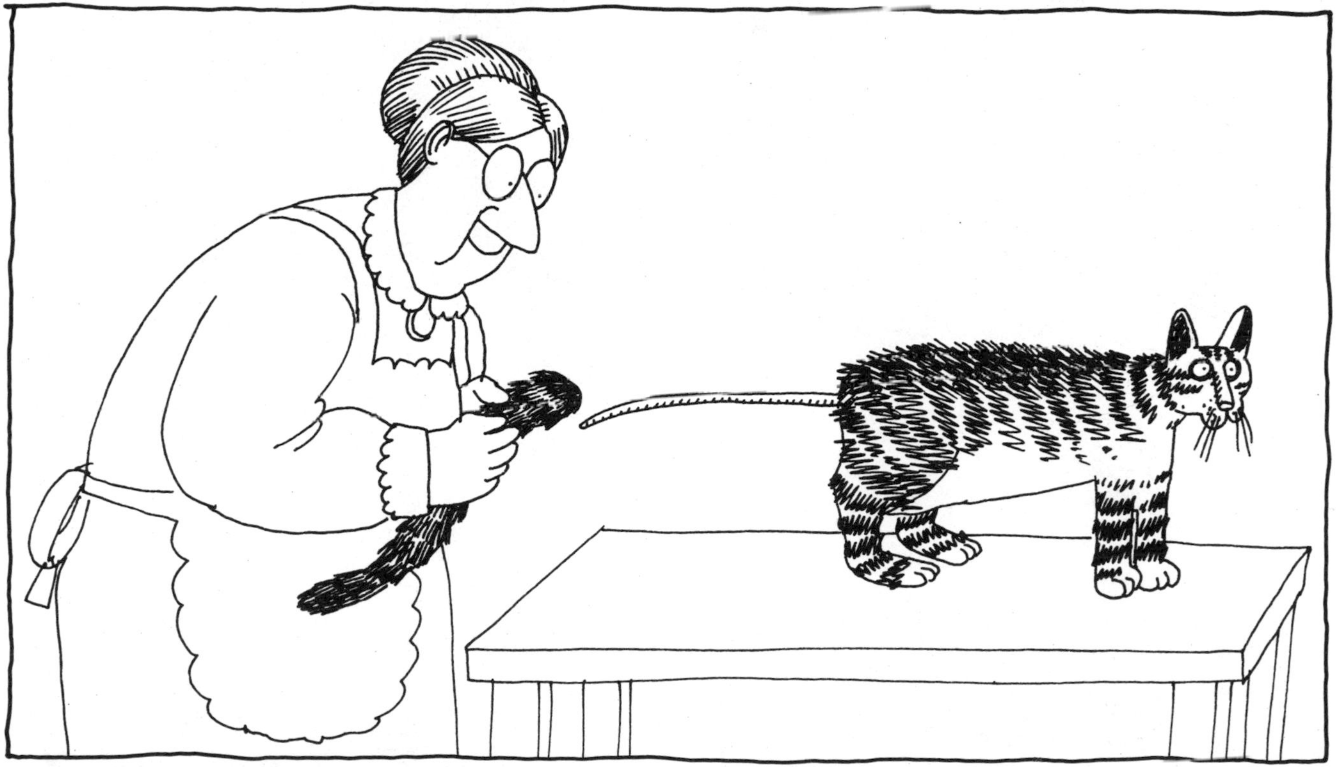

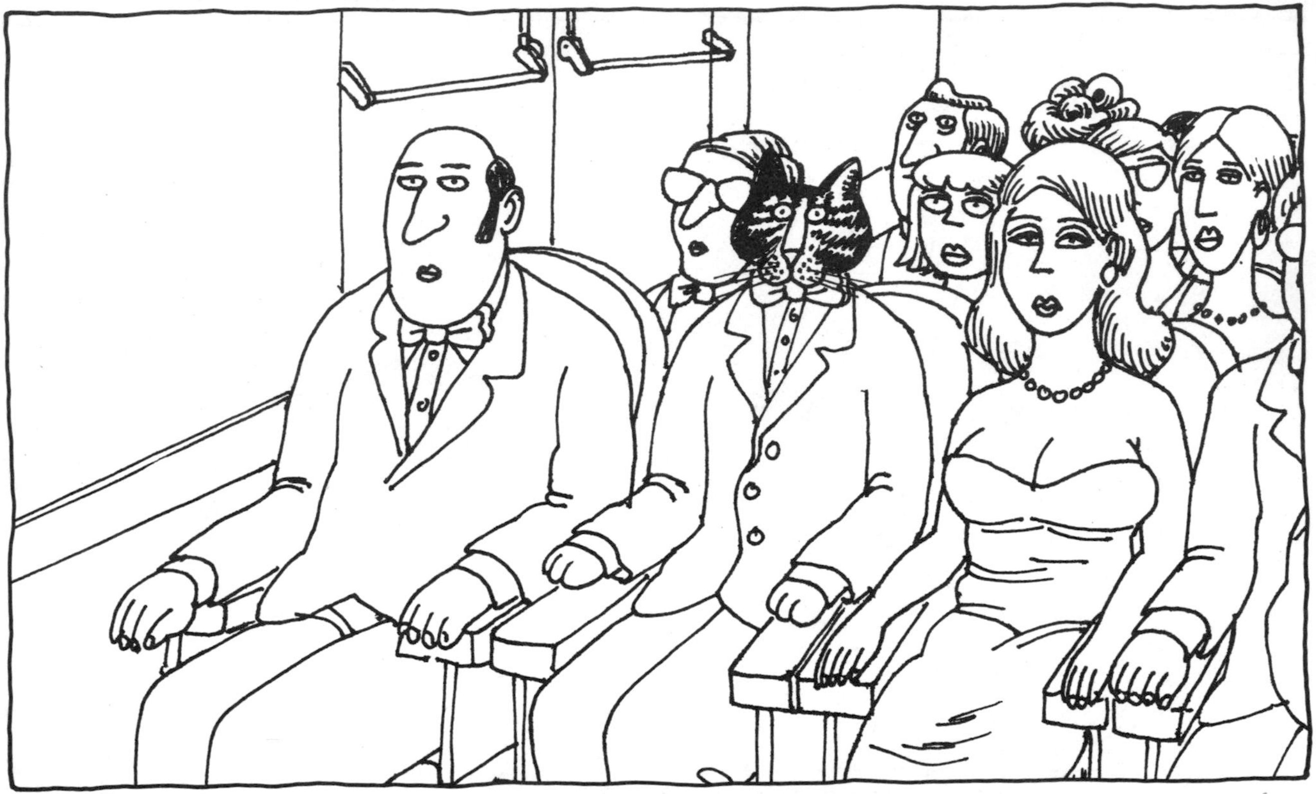

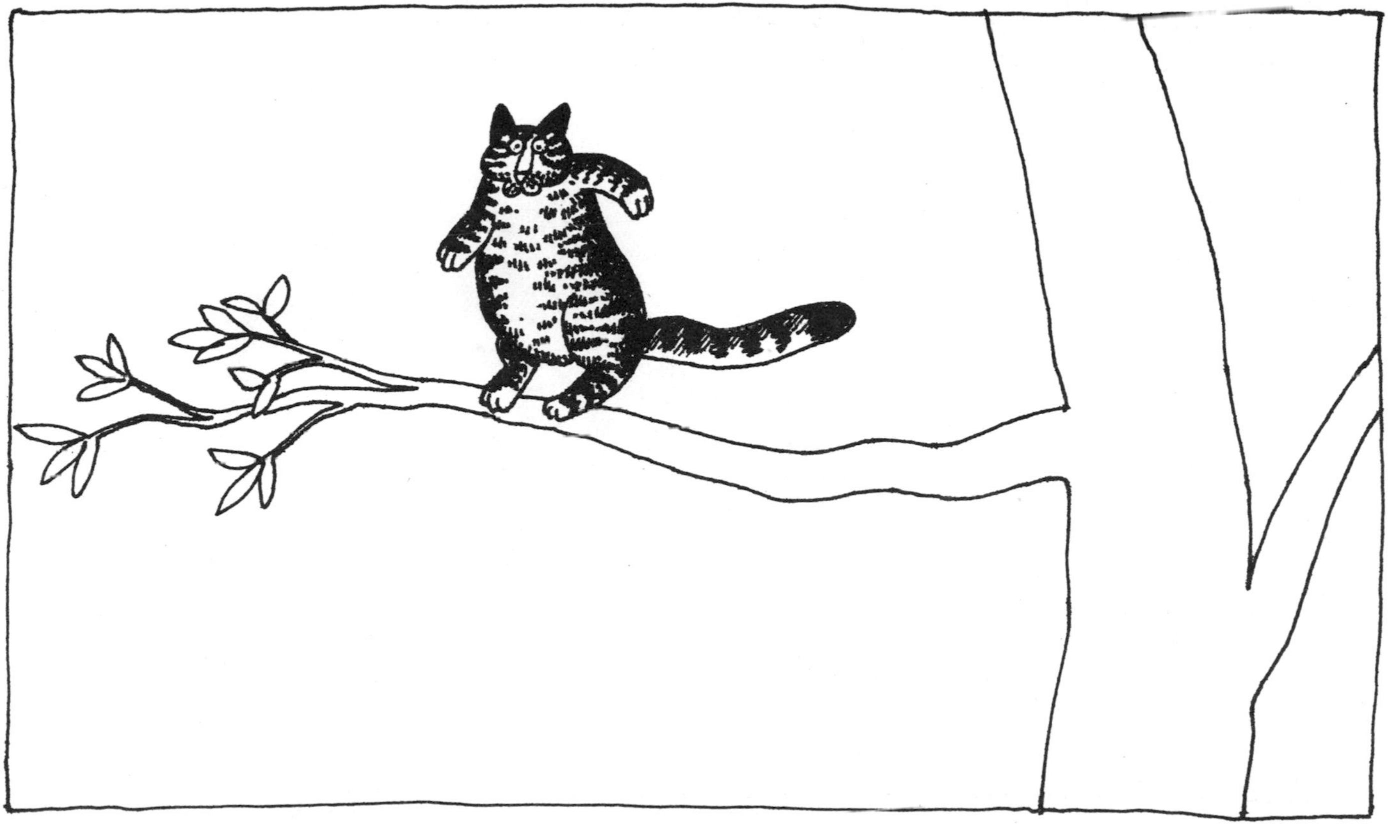

How they do it

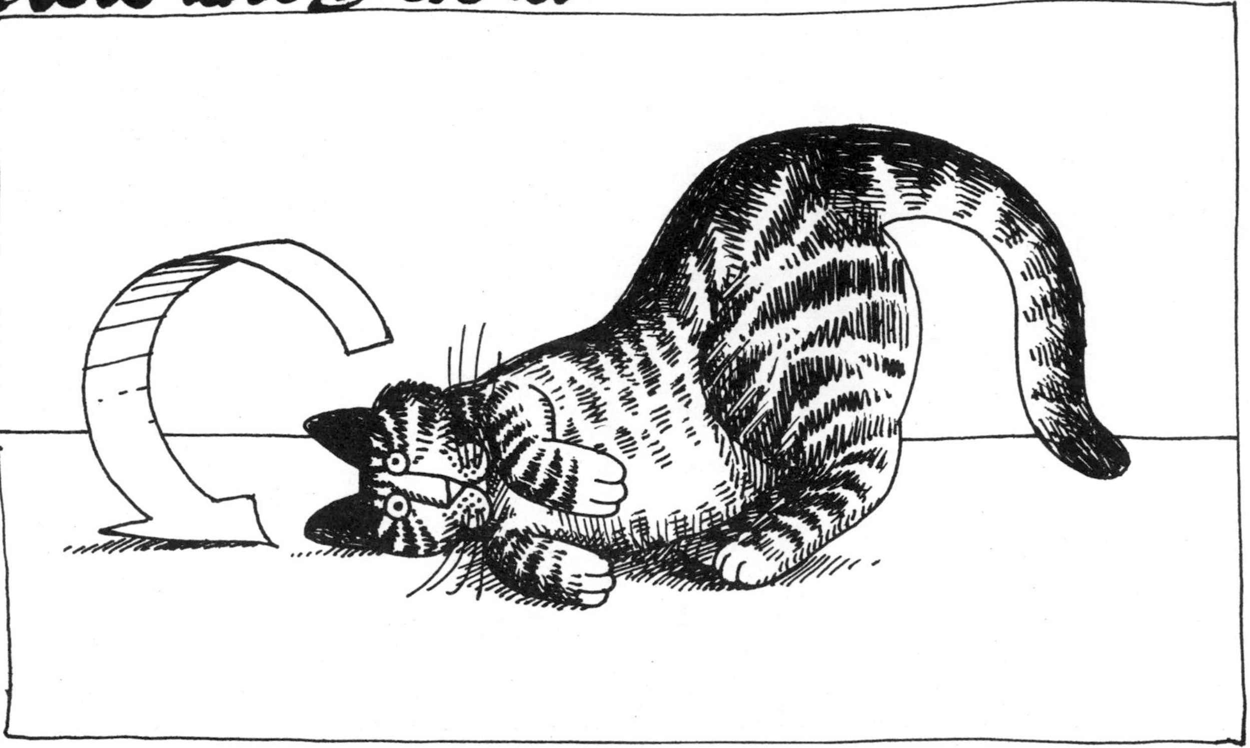

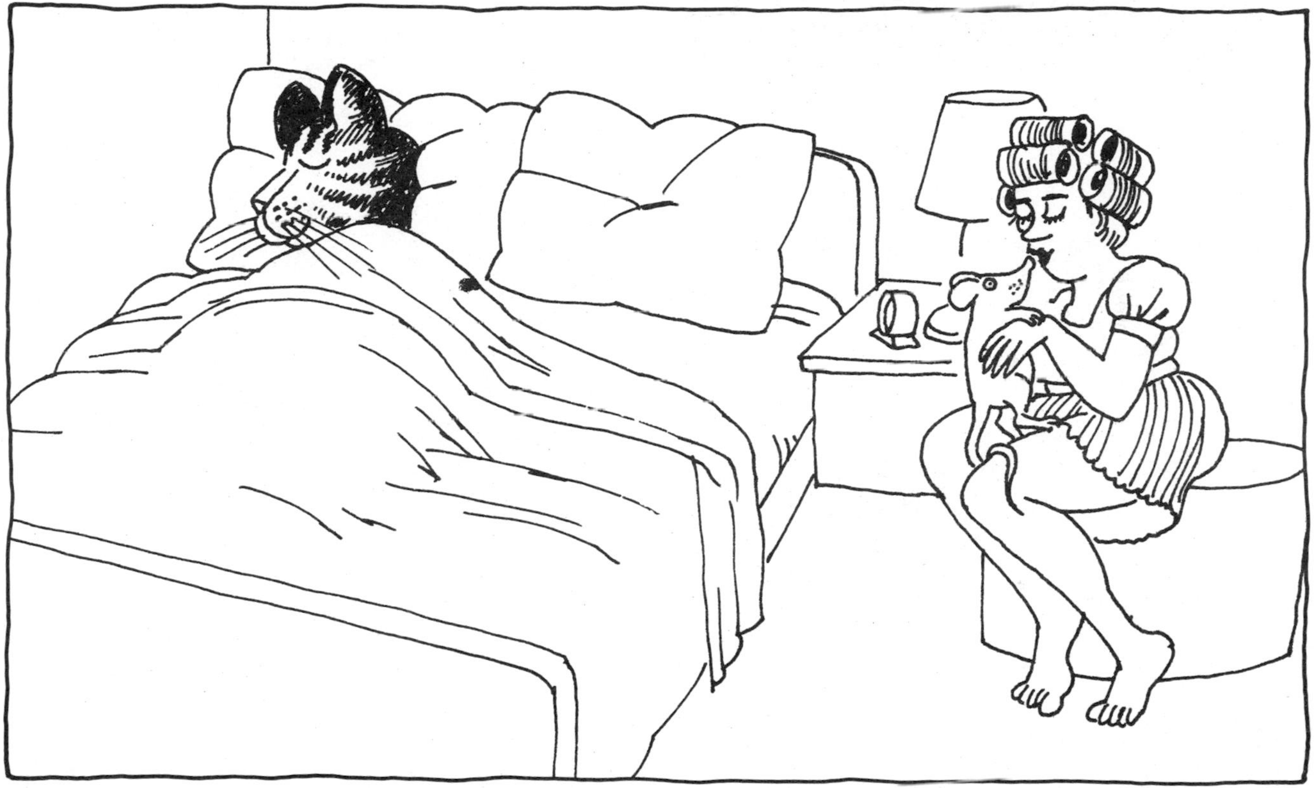

Nosechair Cat

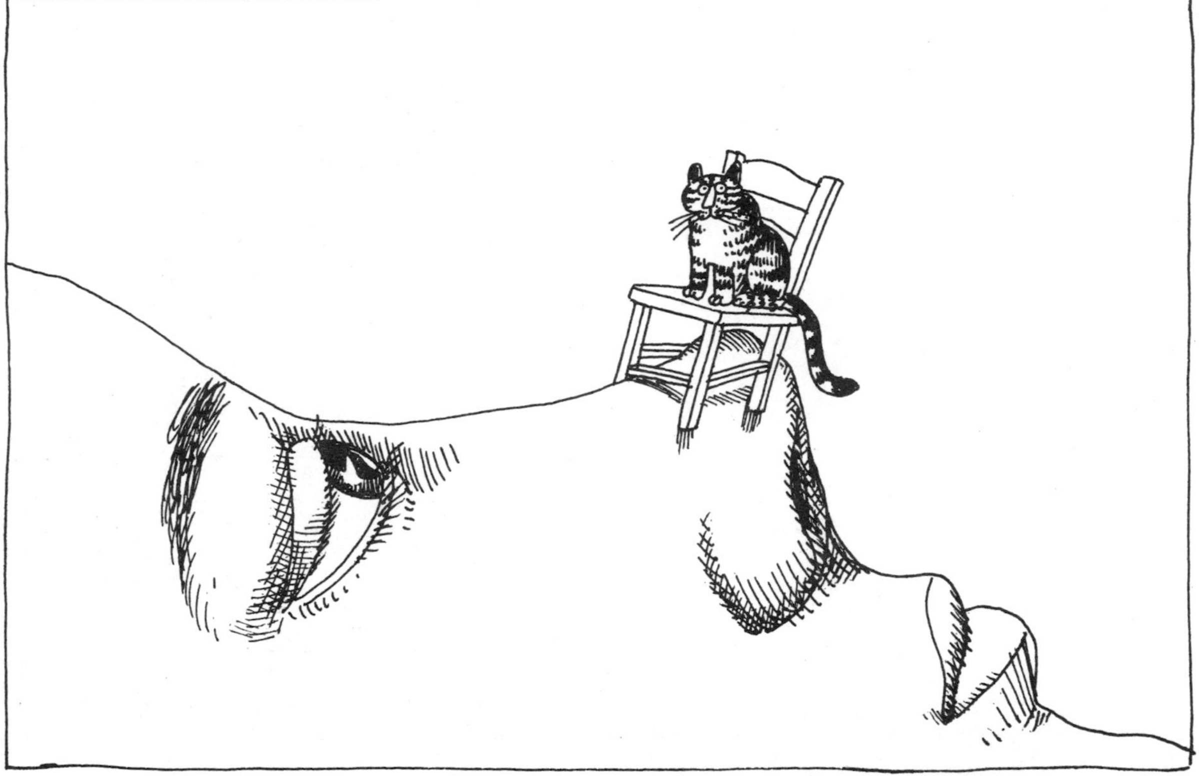

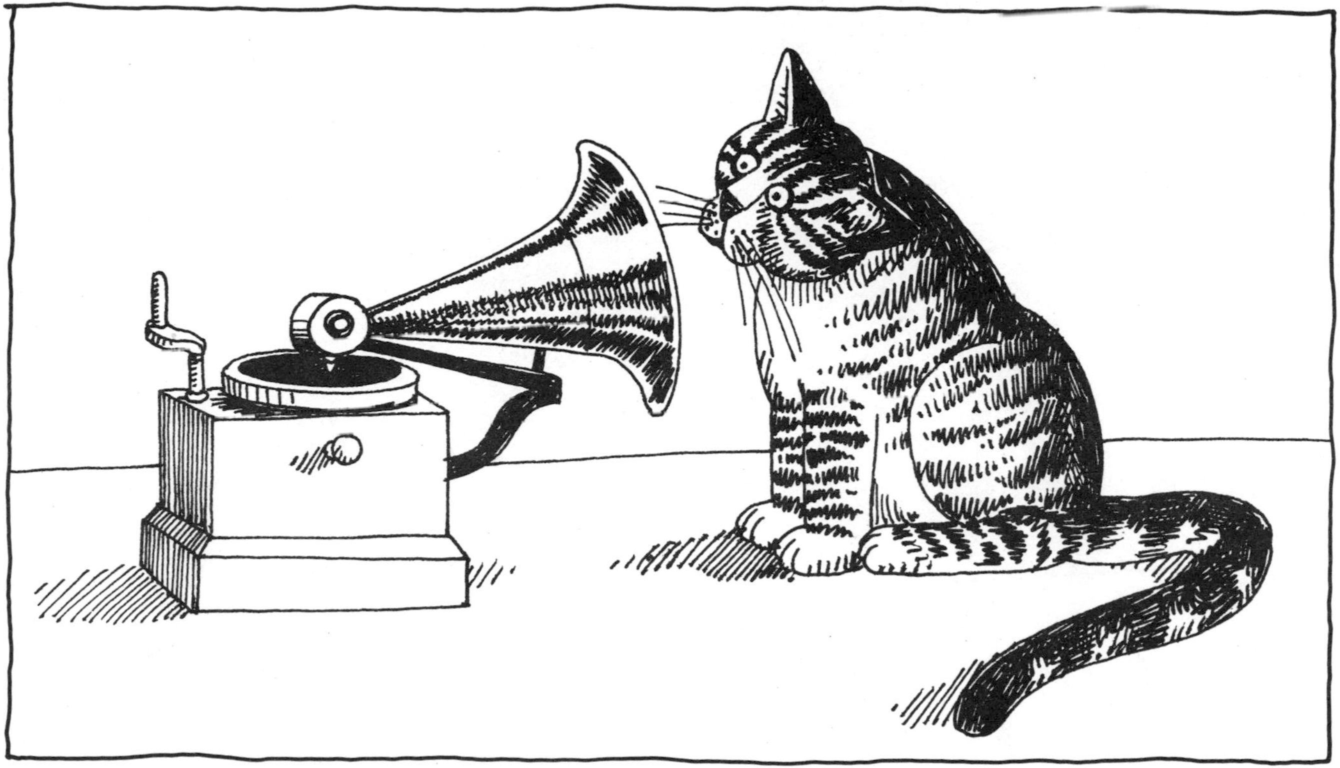

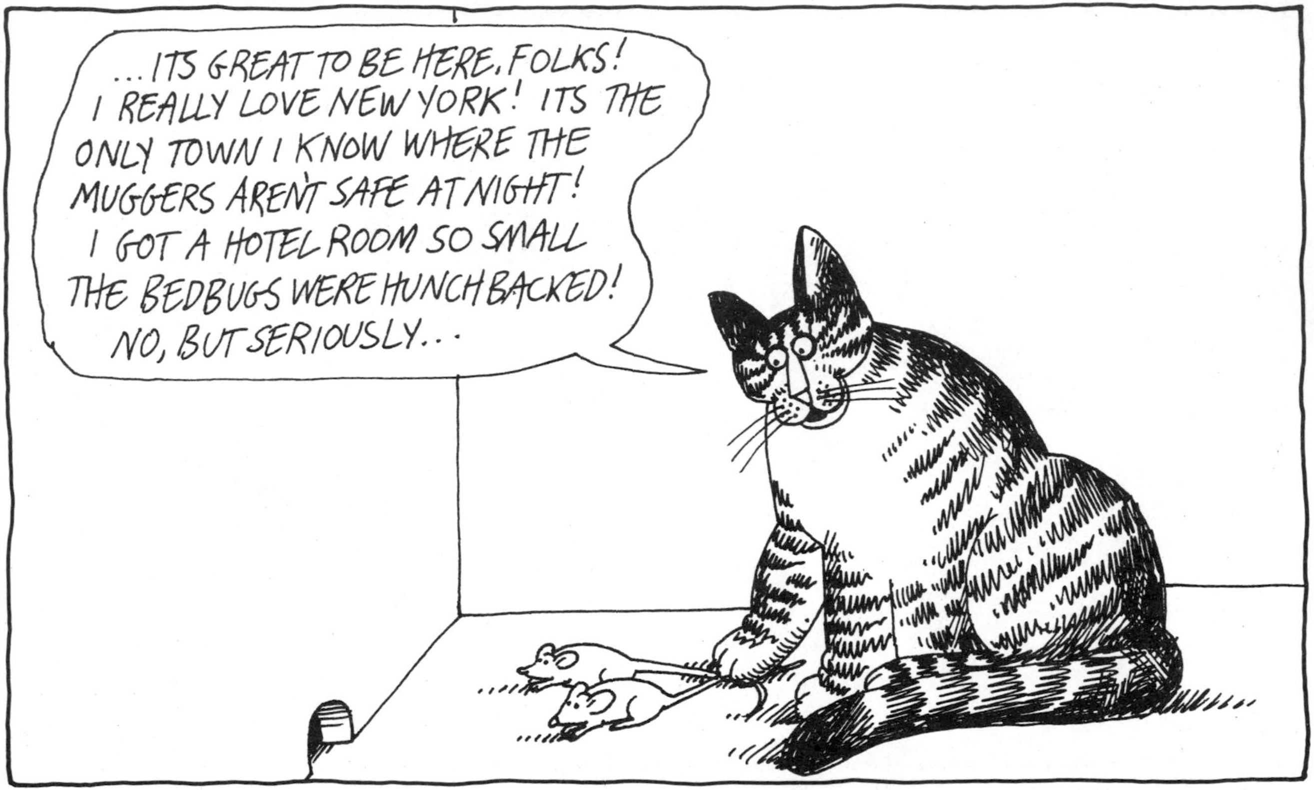
...ITS GREAT TO BE HERE, FOLKS! I REALLY LOVE NEW YORK! ITS THE ONLY TOWN I KNOW WHERE THE MUGGERS AREN'T SAFE AT NIGHT! I GOT A HOTEL ROOM SO SMALL THE BEDBUGS WERE HUNCHBACKED! NO, BUT SERIOUSLY...

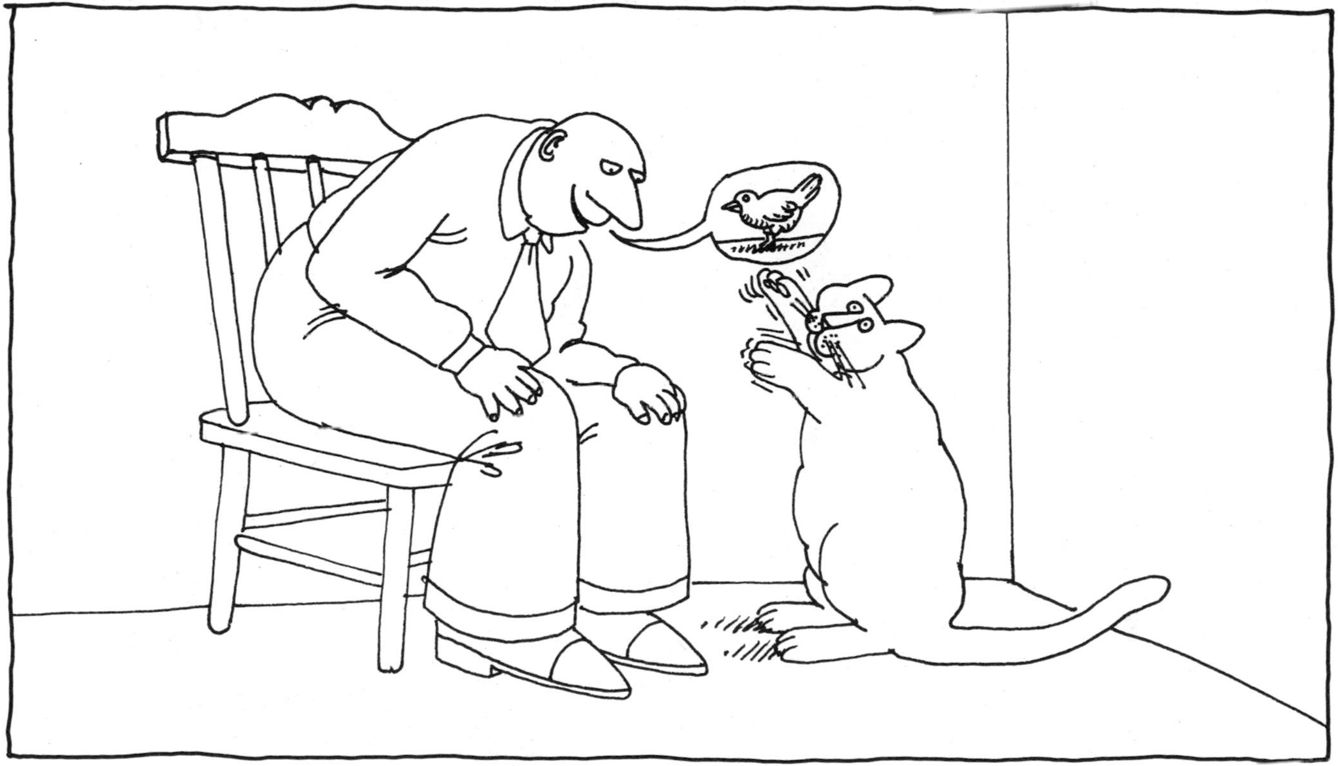

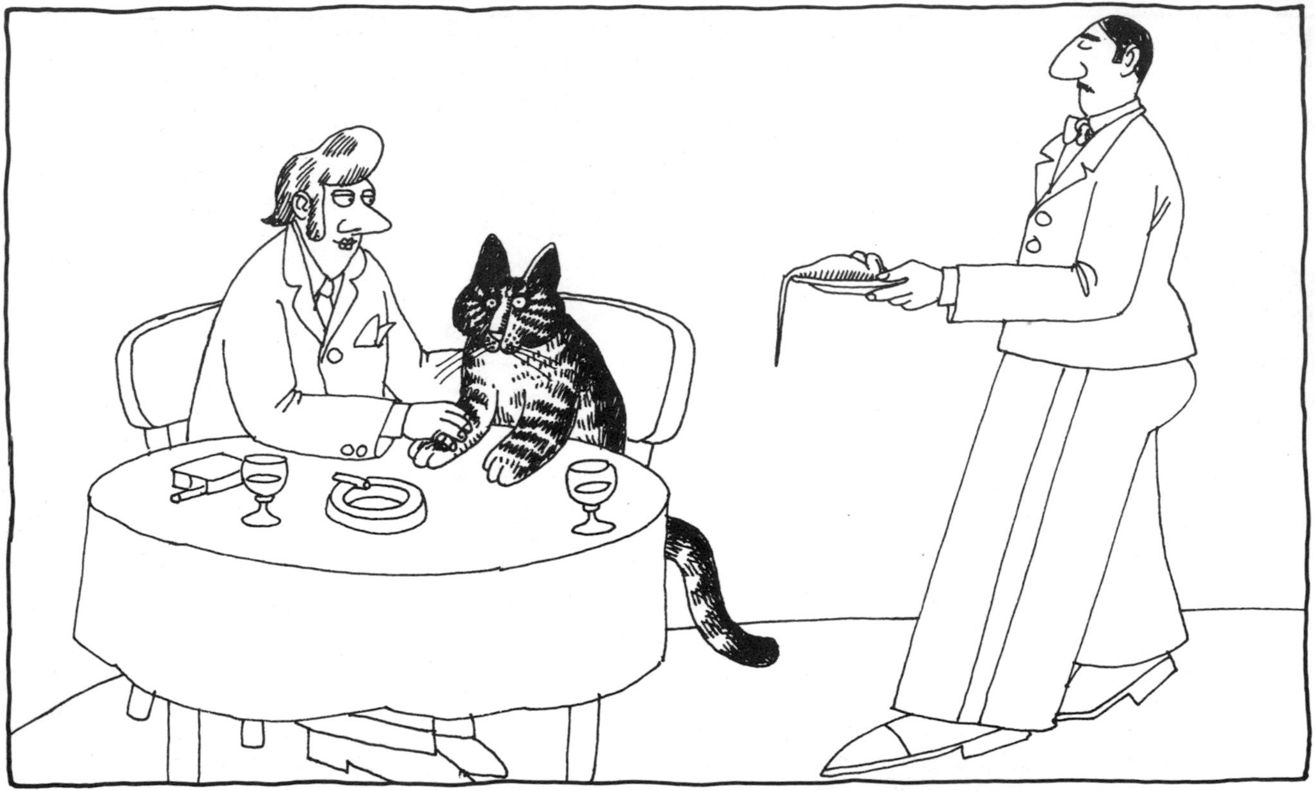

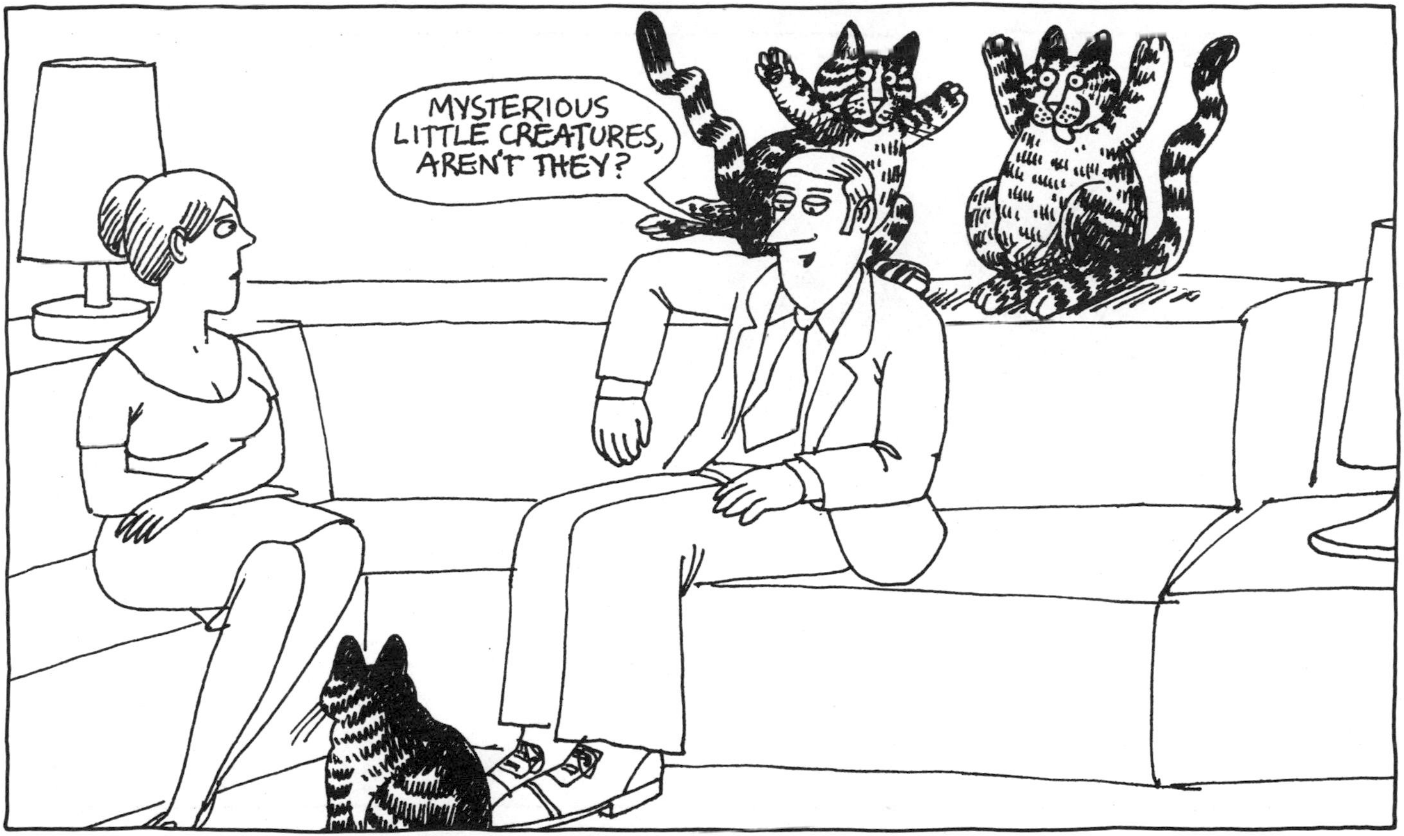
MYSTERIOUS LITTLE CREATURES, AREN'T THEY?

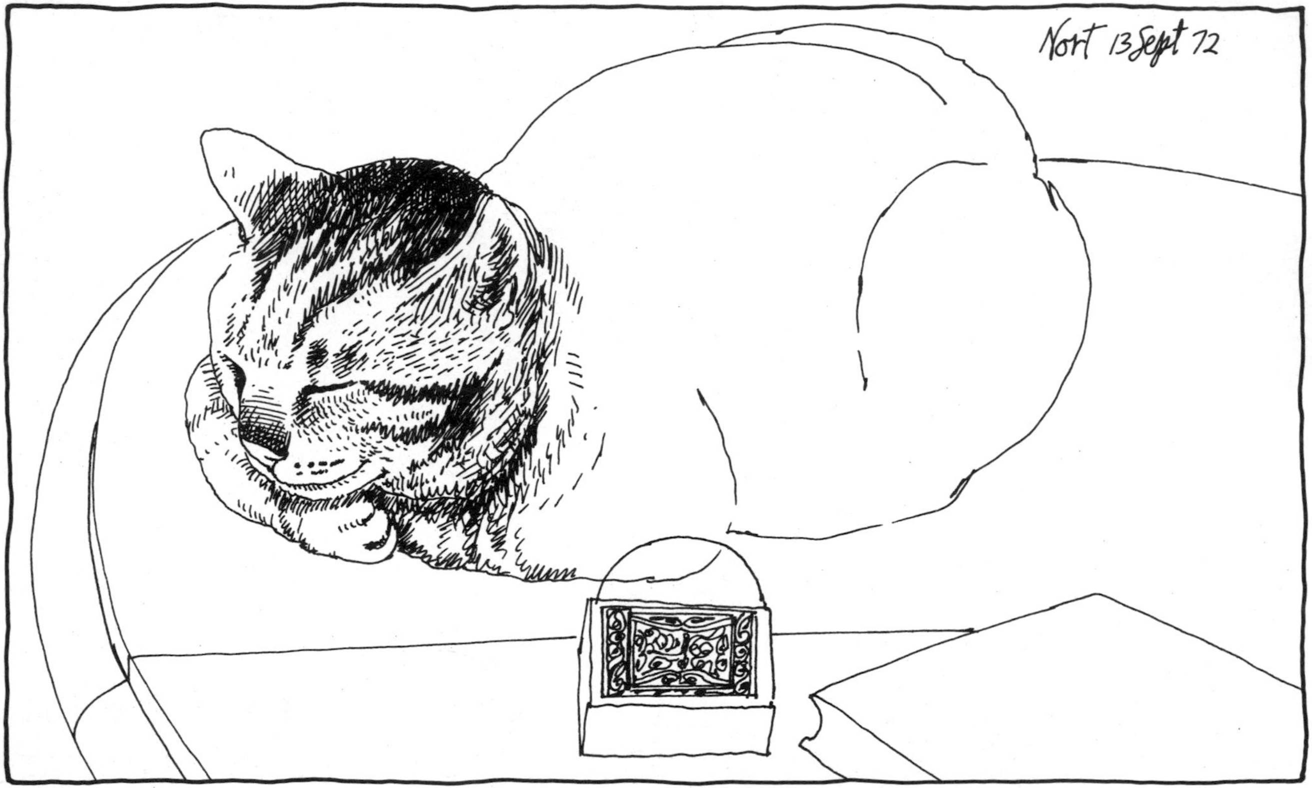
Nort 13 Sept 72

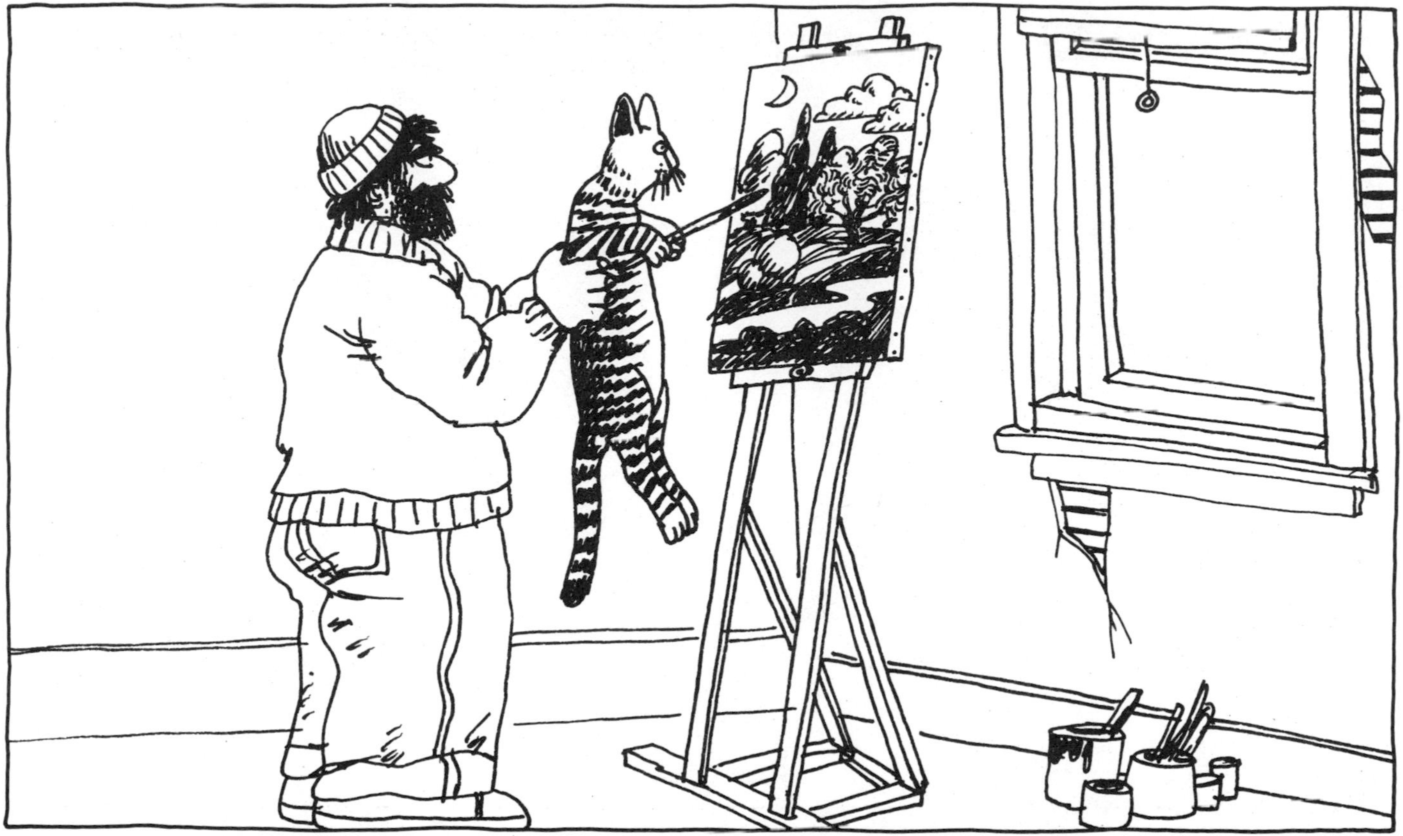

HOW TO TELL A CAT FROM A MEAT LOAF

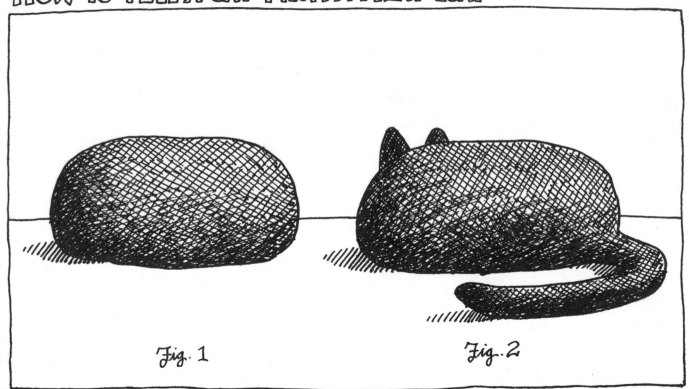

Fig. 1

Fig. 2

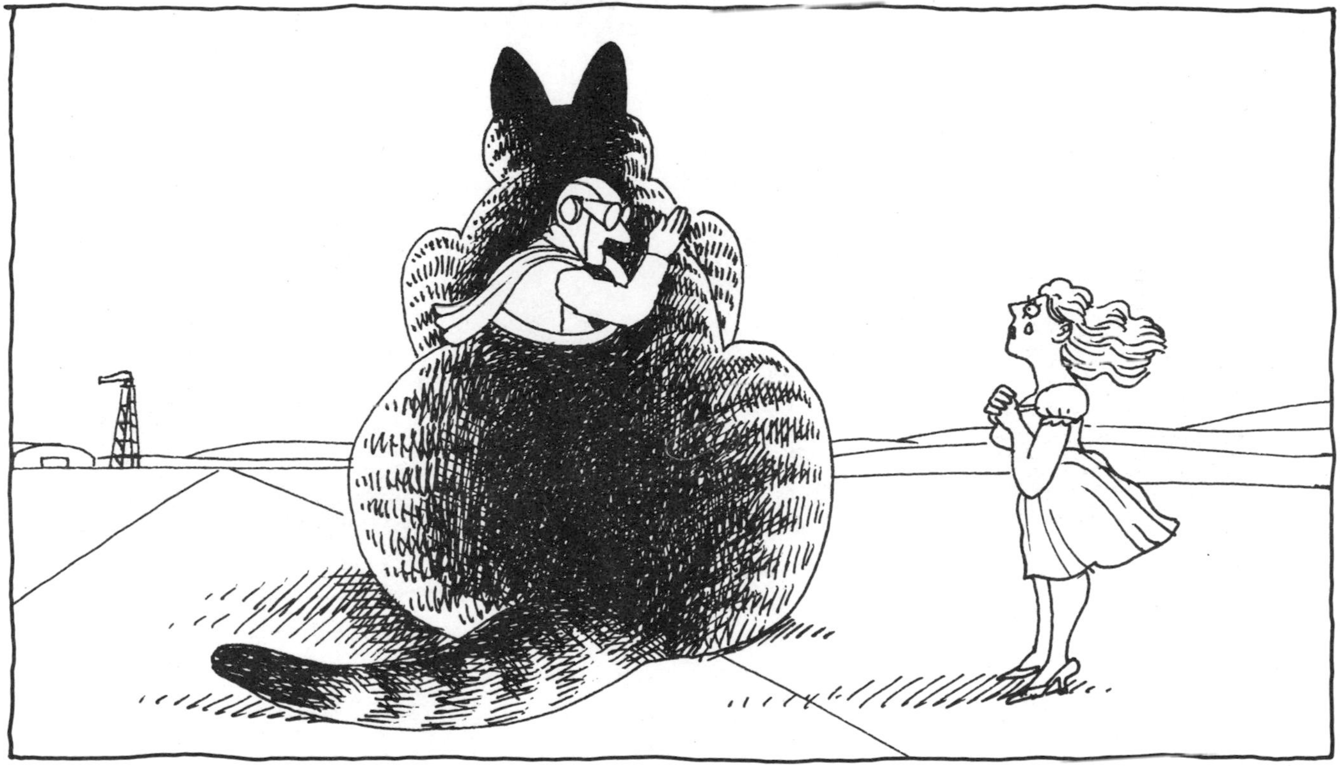

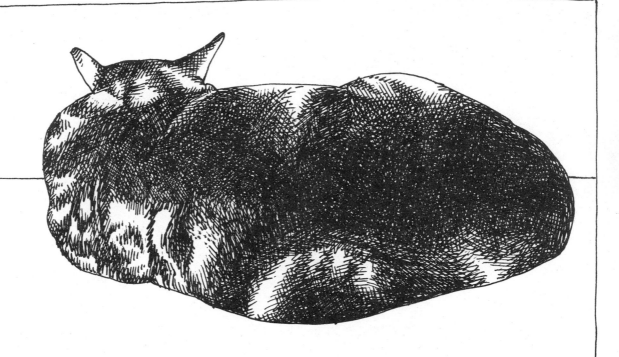

Nort NOV 72

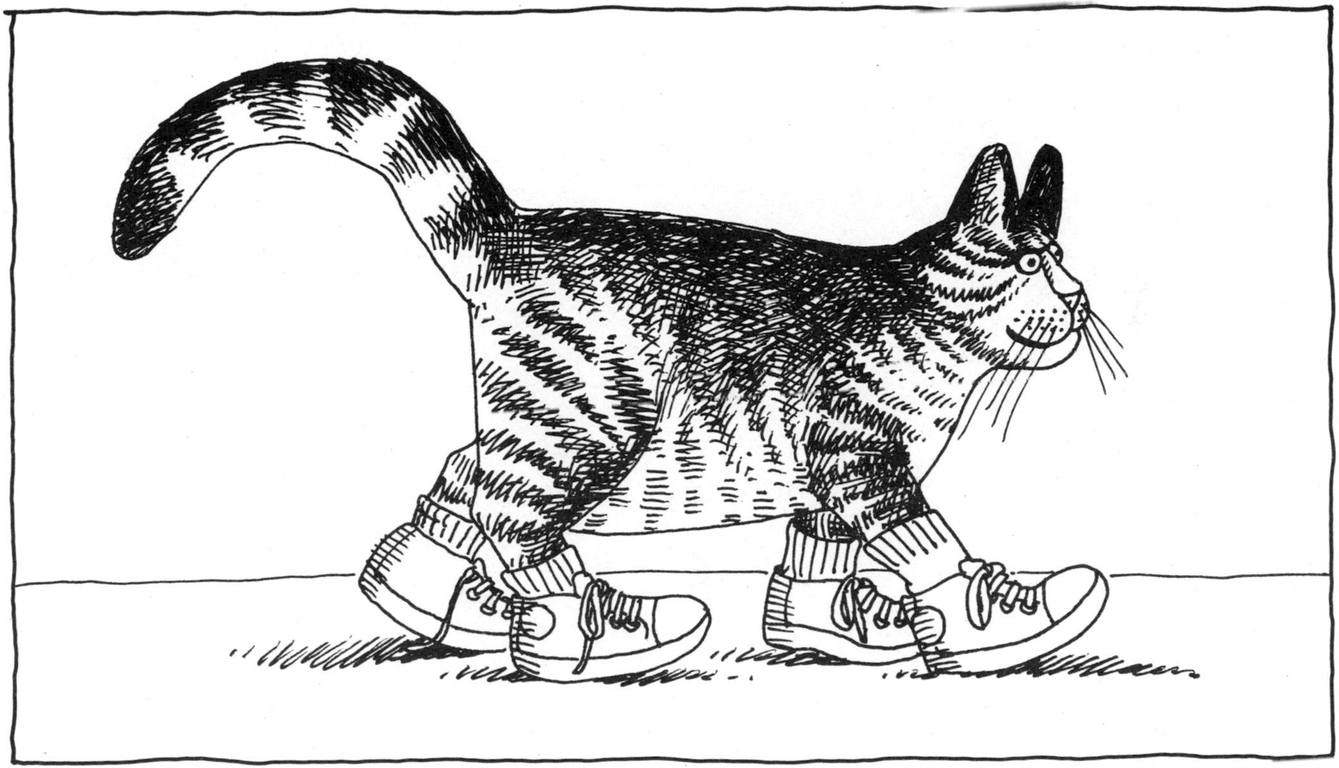

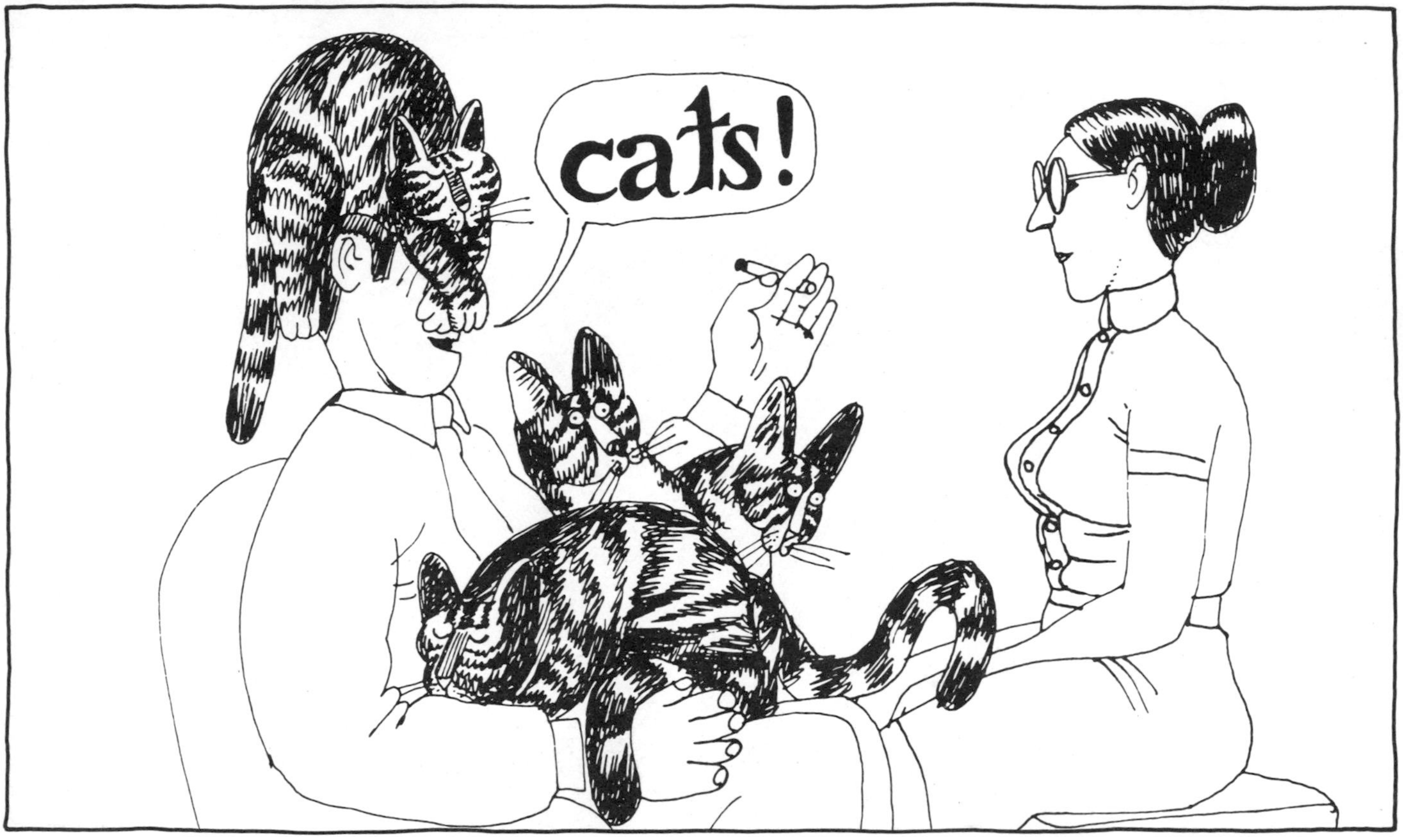
cats!

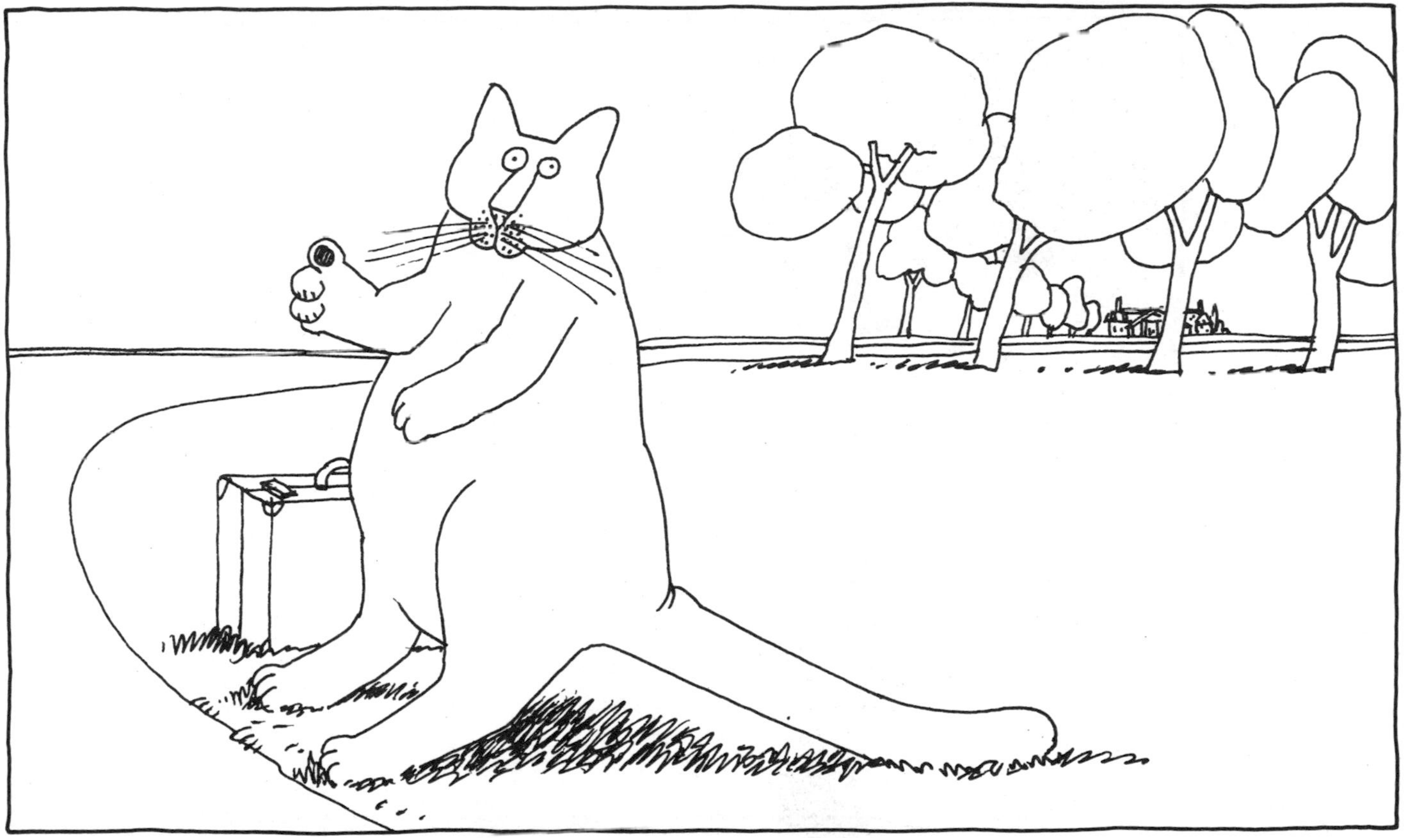

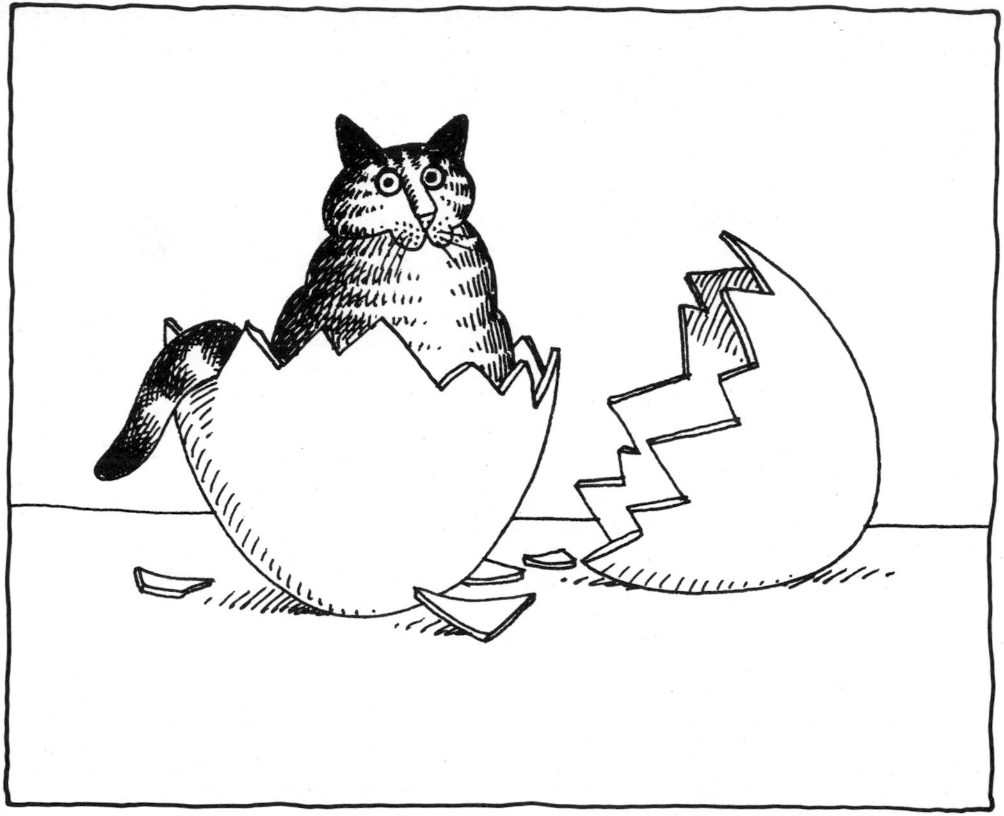

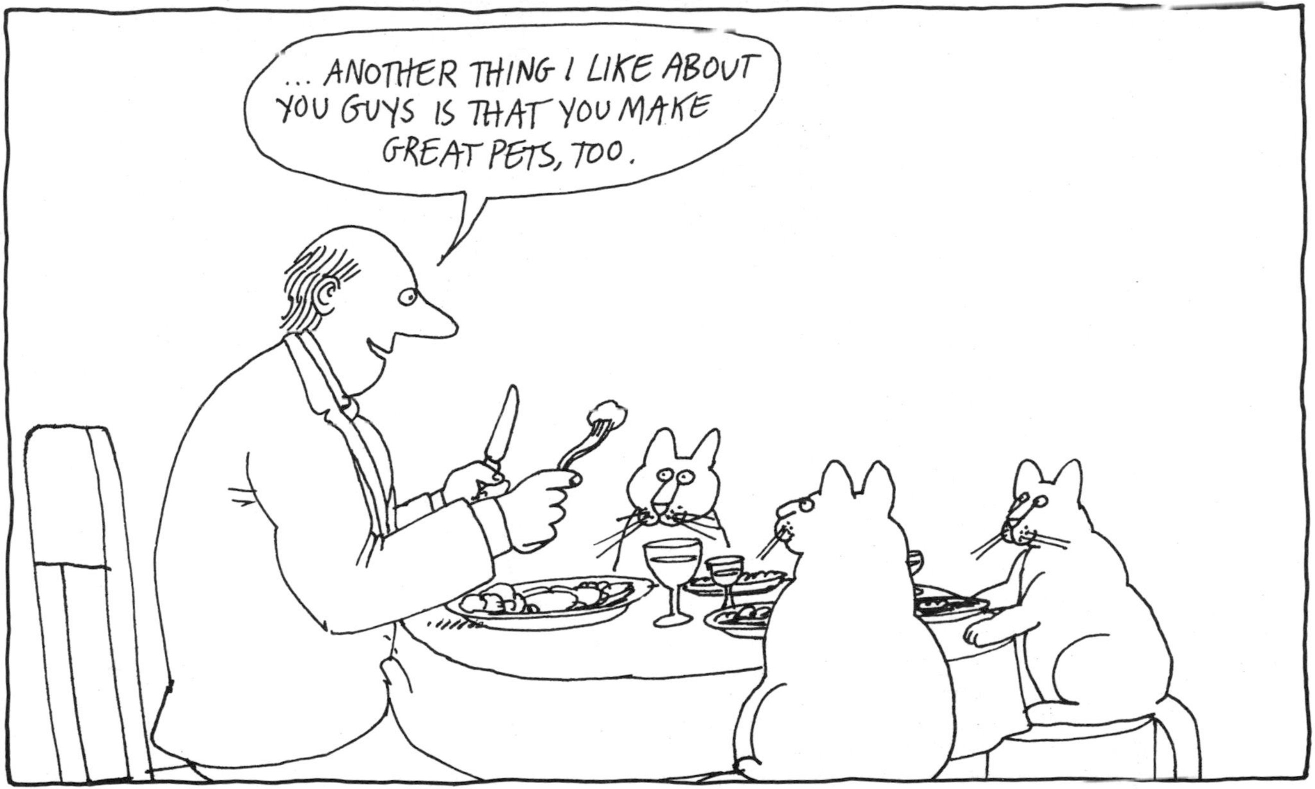
... ANOTHER THING I LIKE ABOUT YOU GUYS IS THAT YOU MAKE GREAT PETS, TOO.

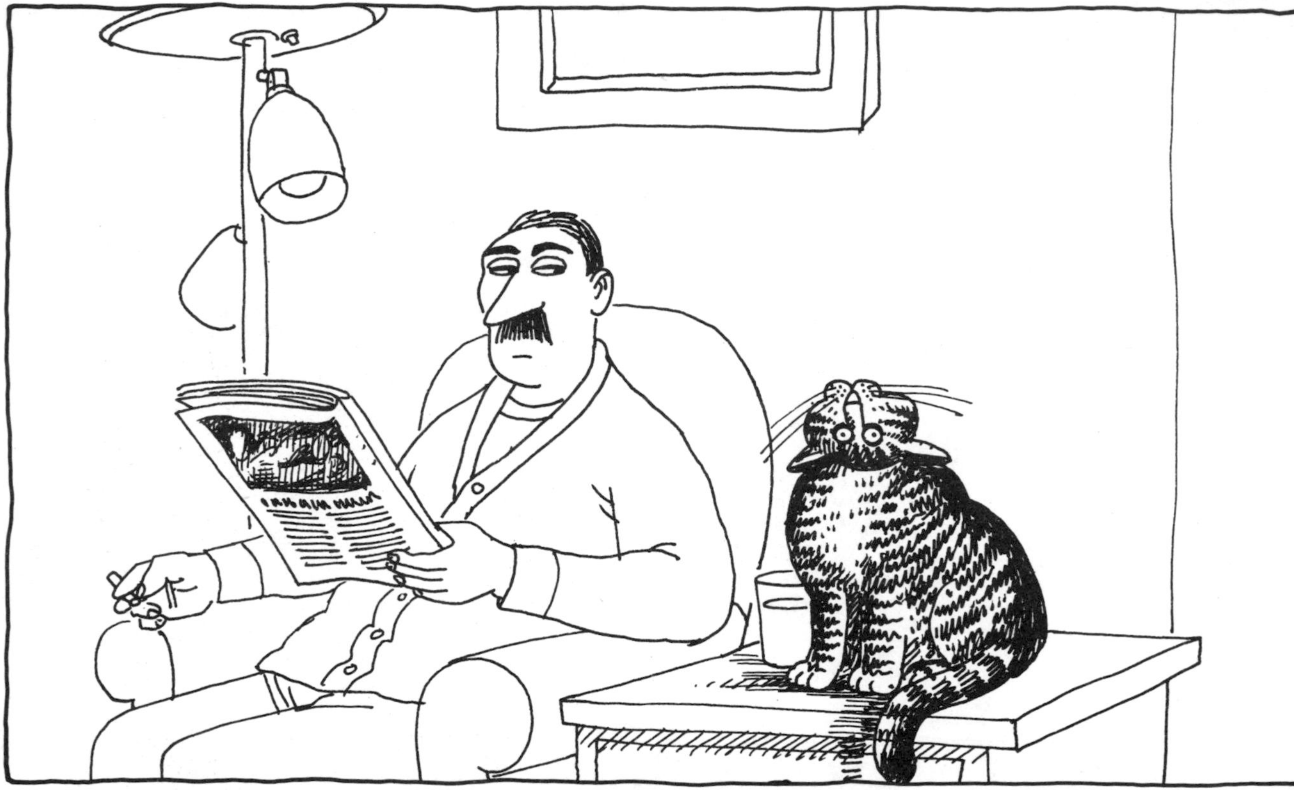

Cats

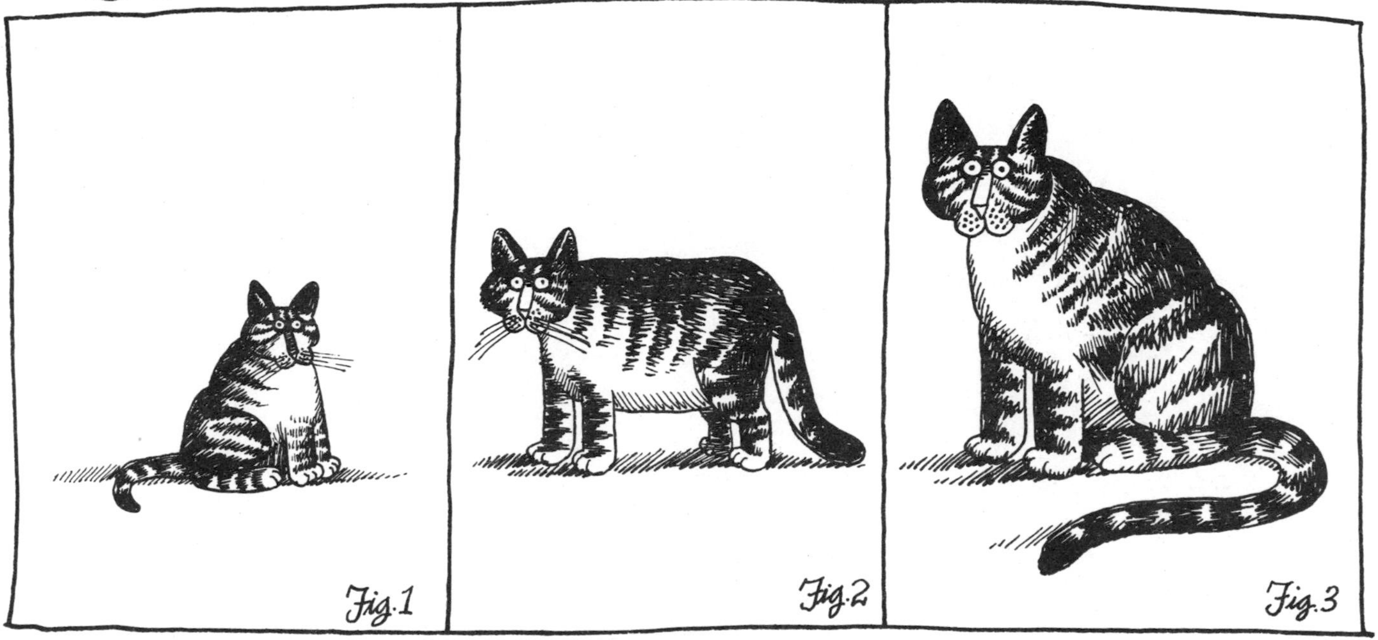
Fig.1
Fig.2
Fig.3

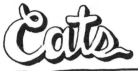

SMALL MEDIUM LARGE

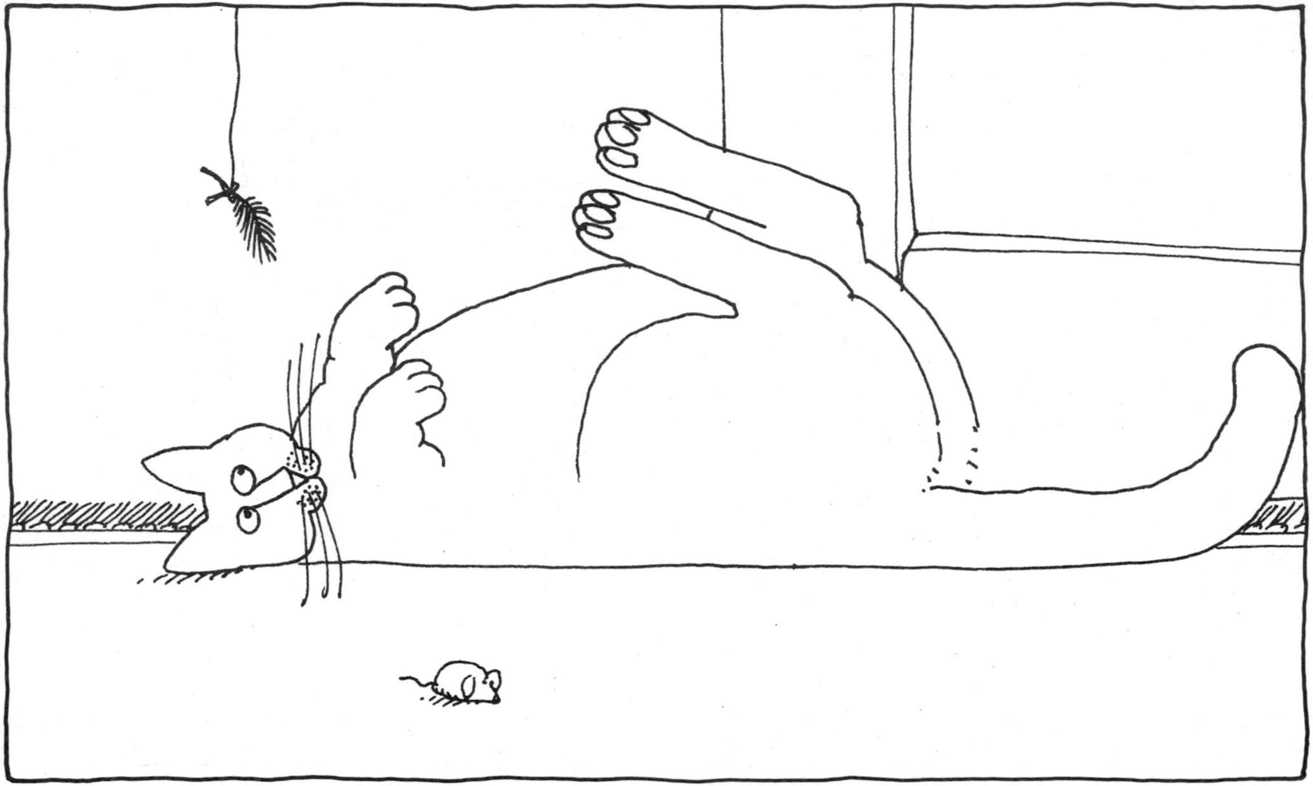

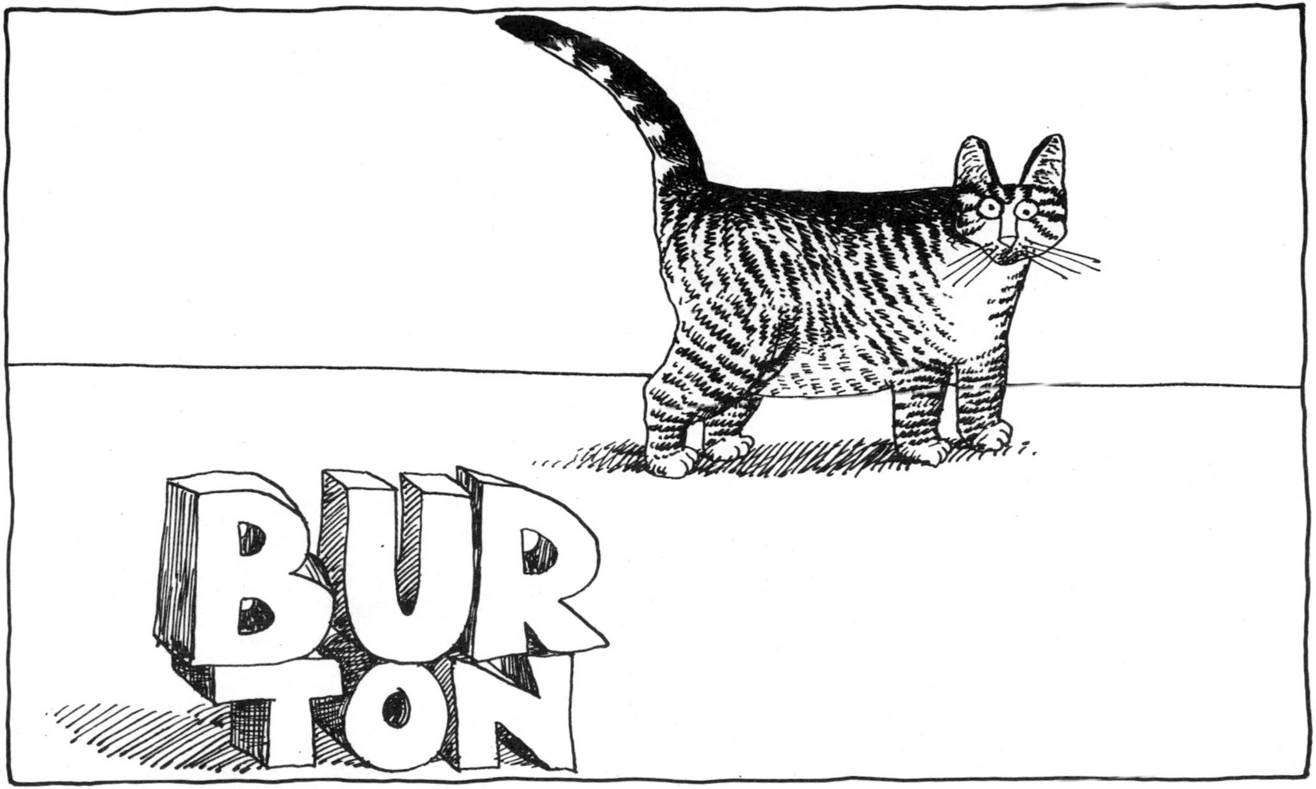
BURTON

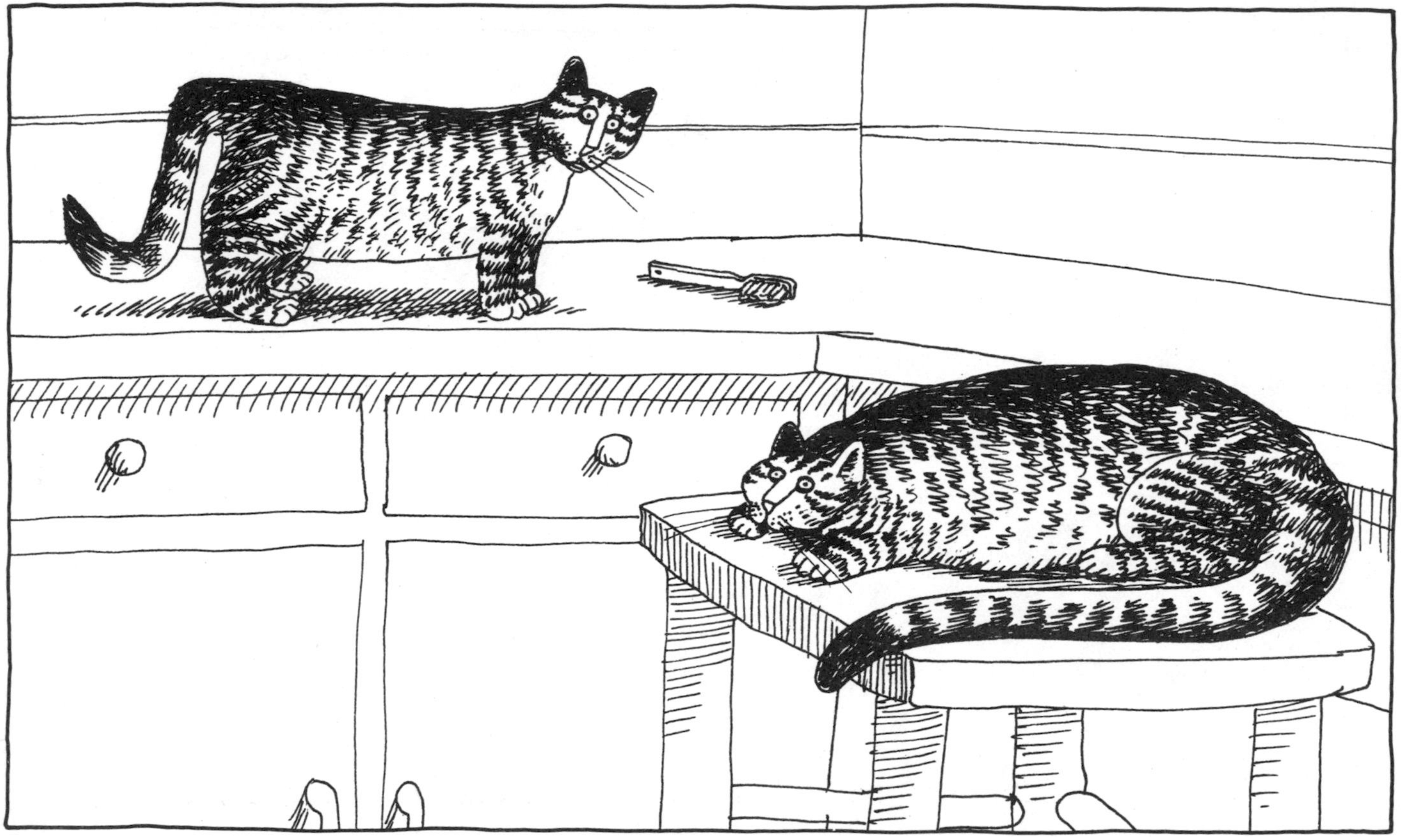

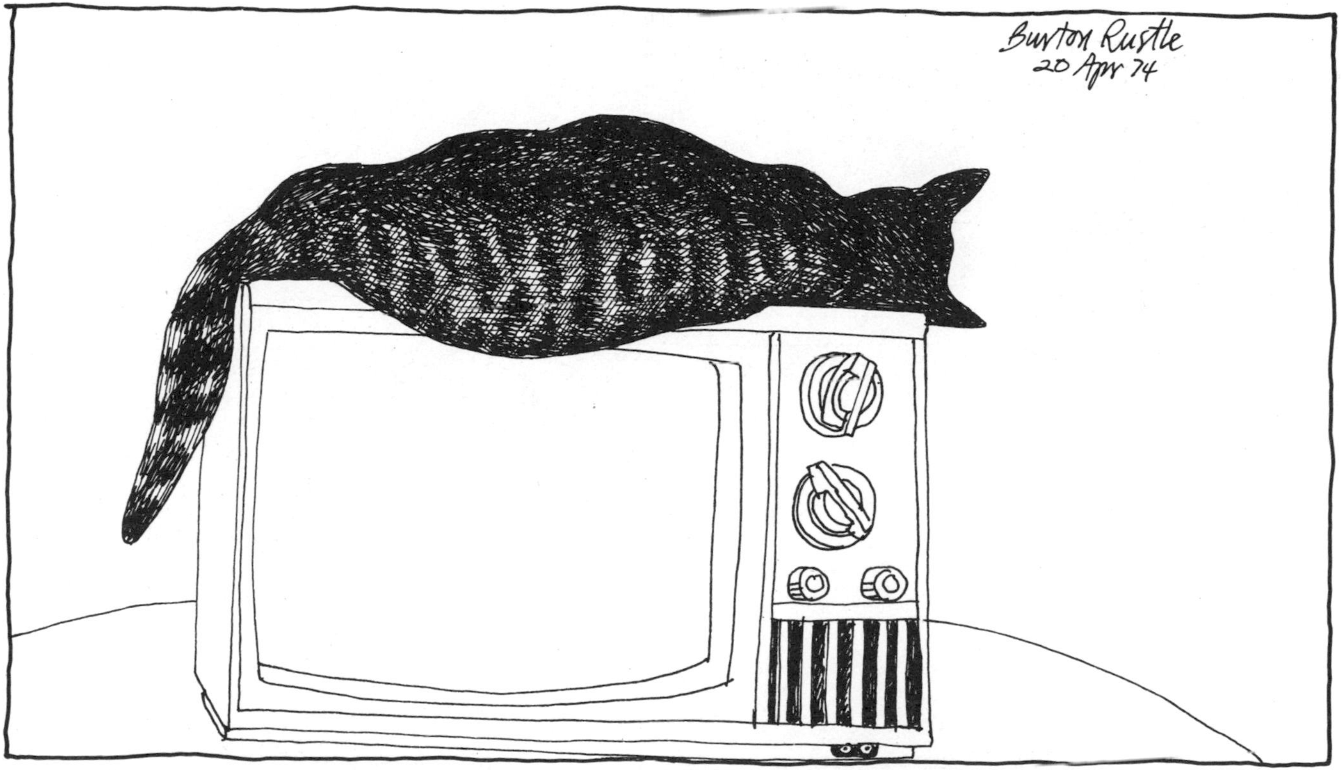
Burton Rustle
20 Apr 74

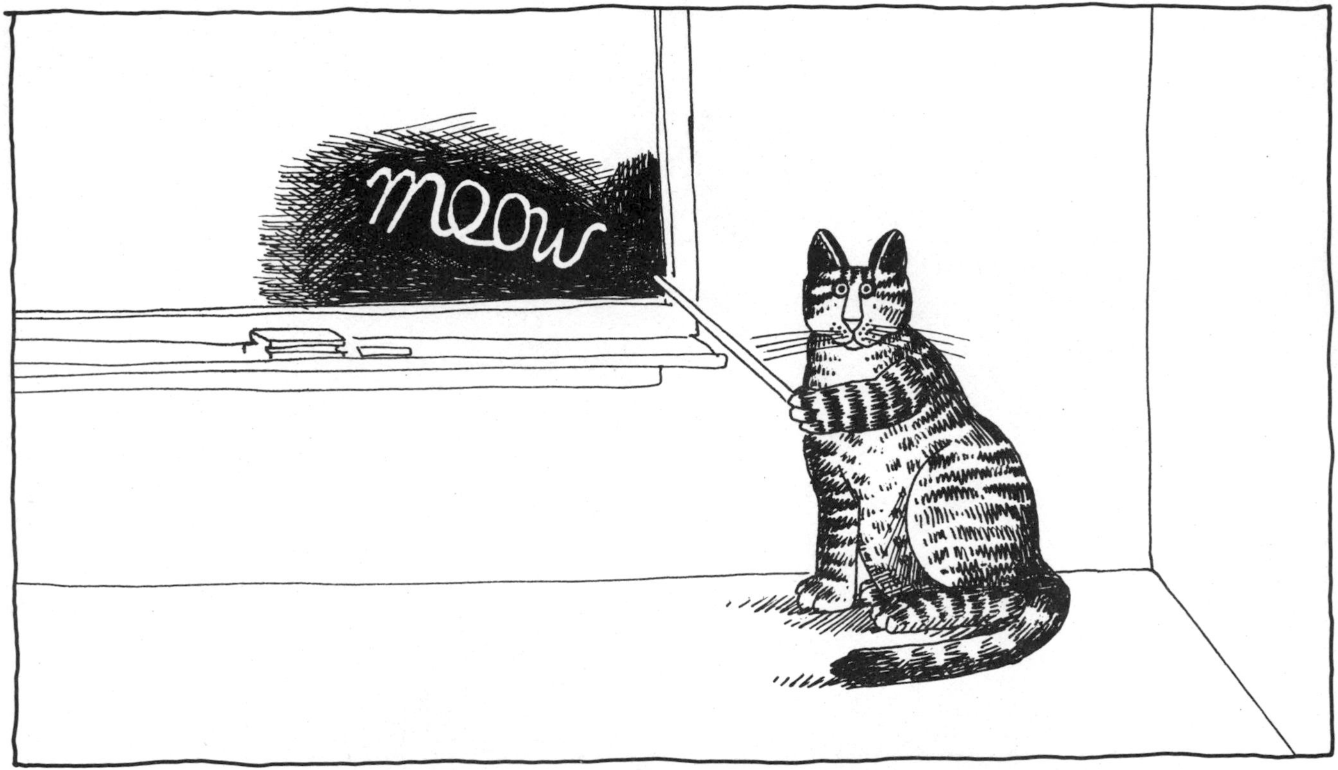
meow

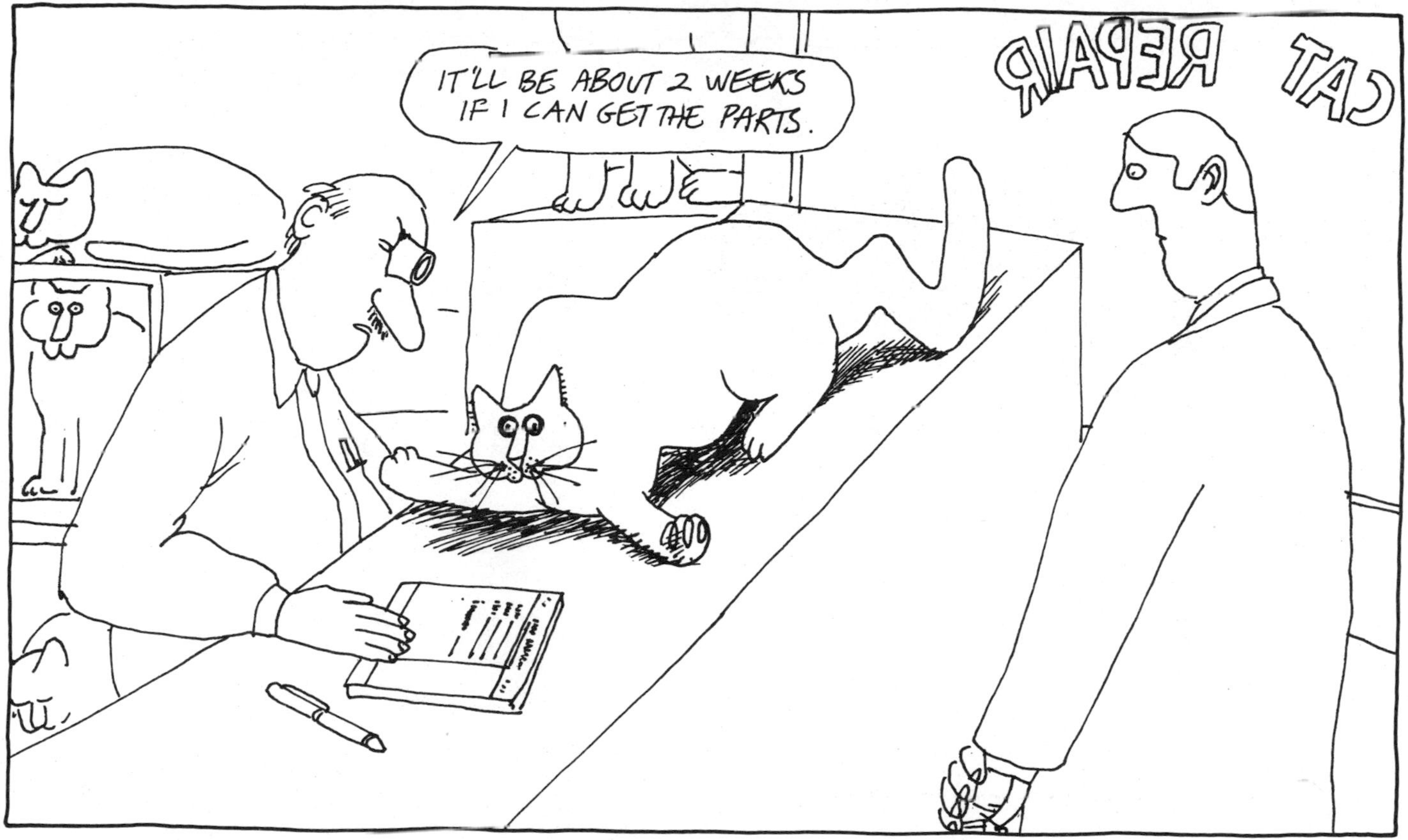
IT'LL BE ABOUT 2 WEEKS IF I CAN GET THE PARTS.
CAT REPAIR

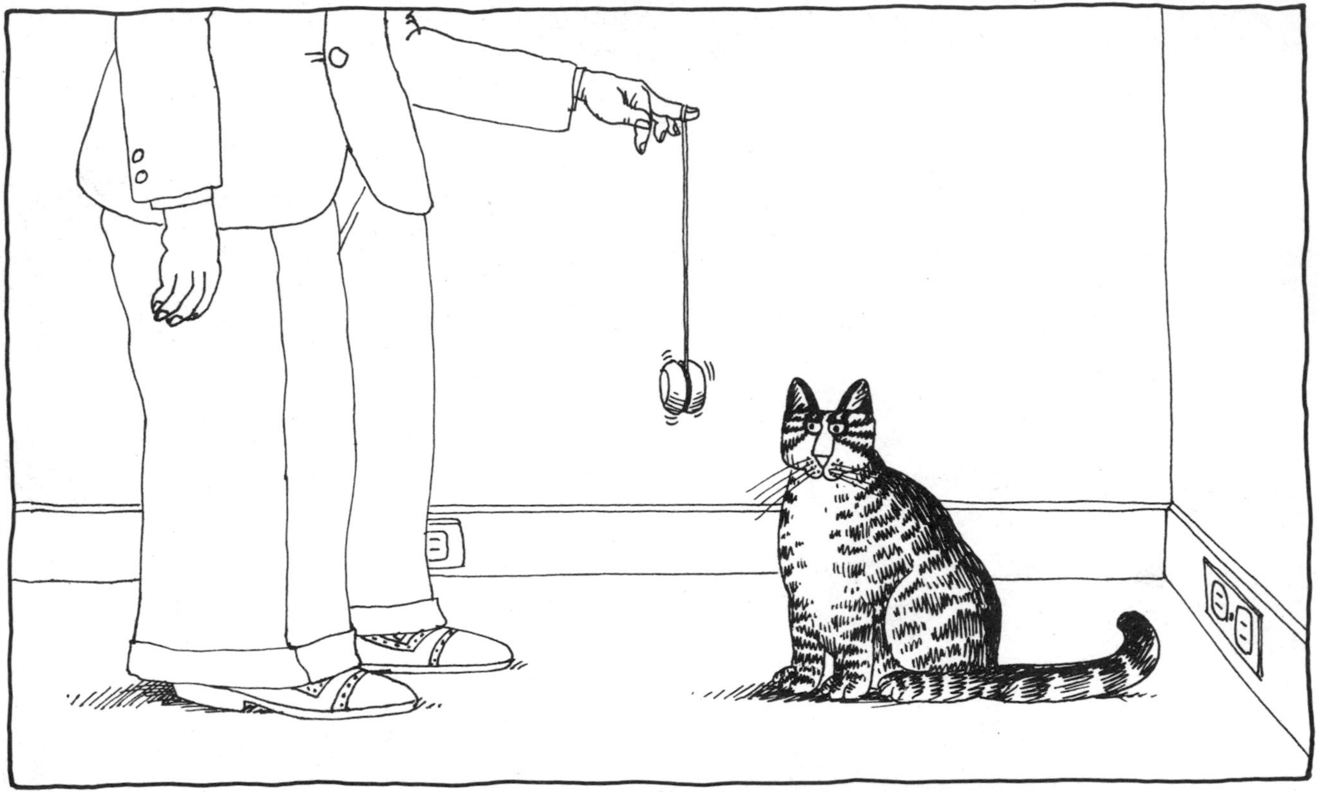

Nit & Burt at the Same Time

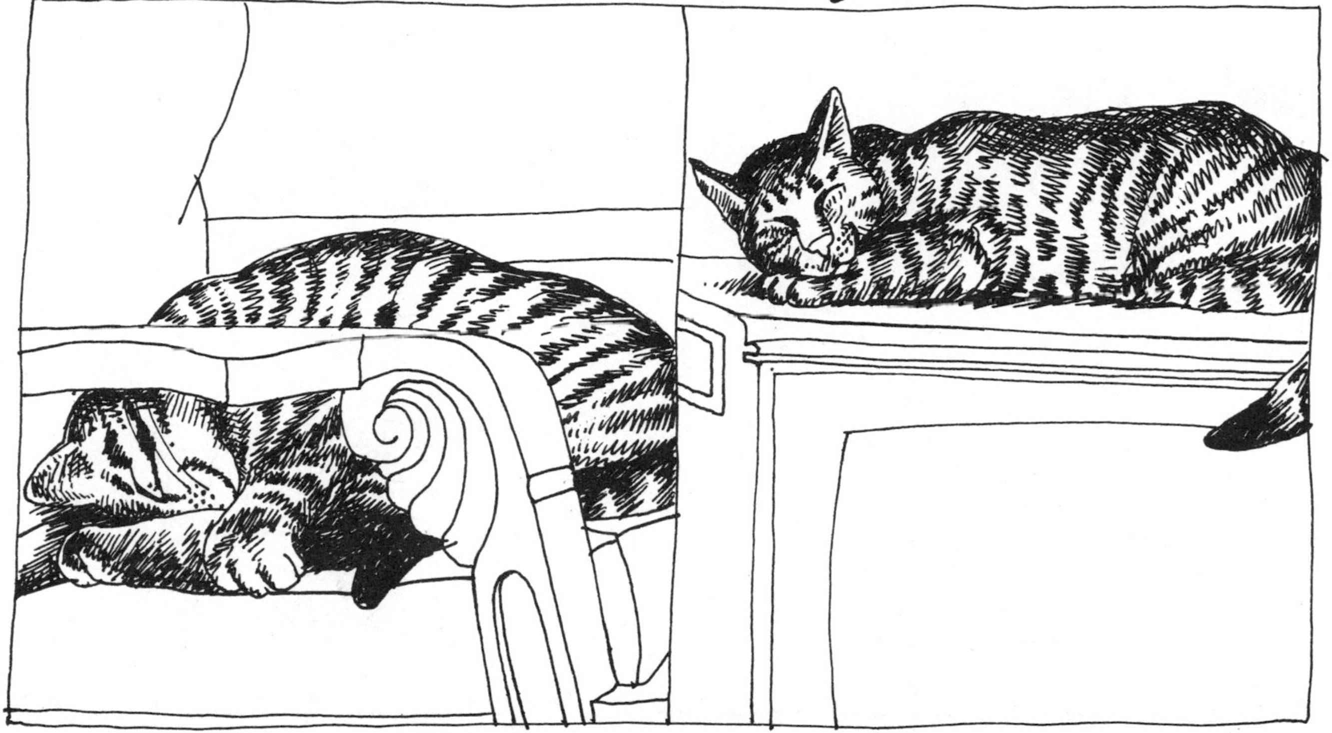

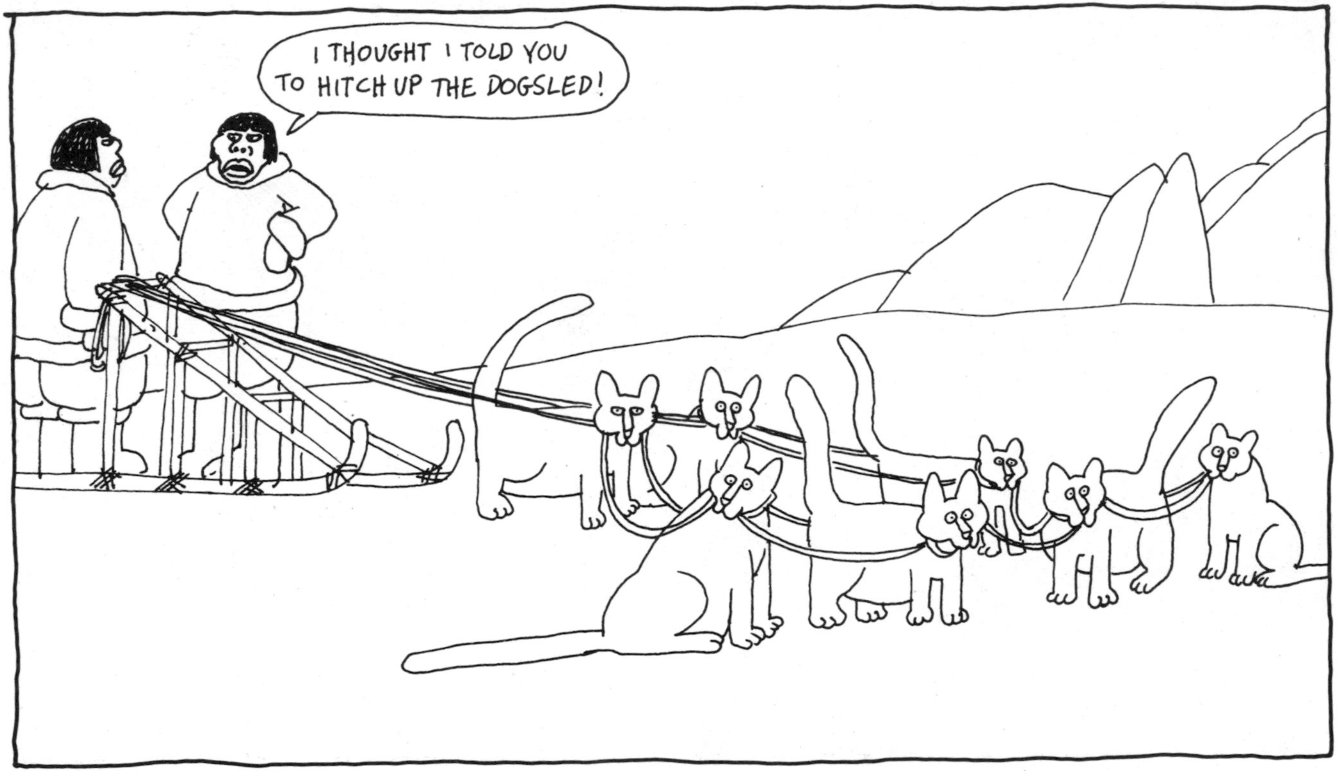
I THOUGHT I TOLD YOU TO HITCH UP THE DOGSLED!

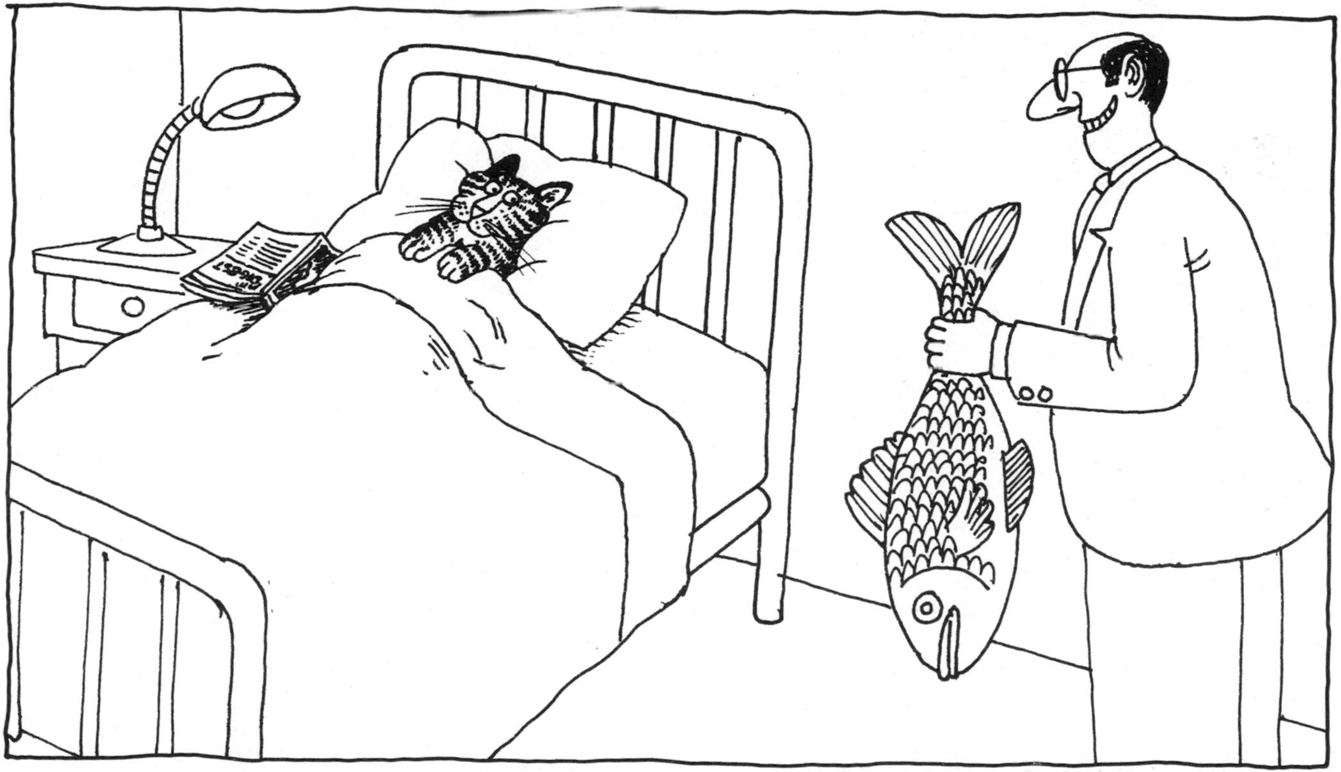
DIGEST

Kneecat

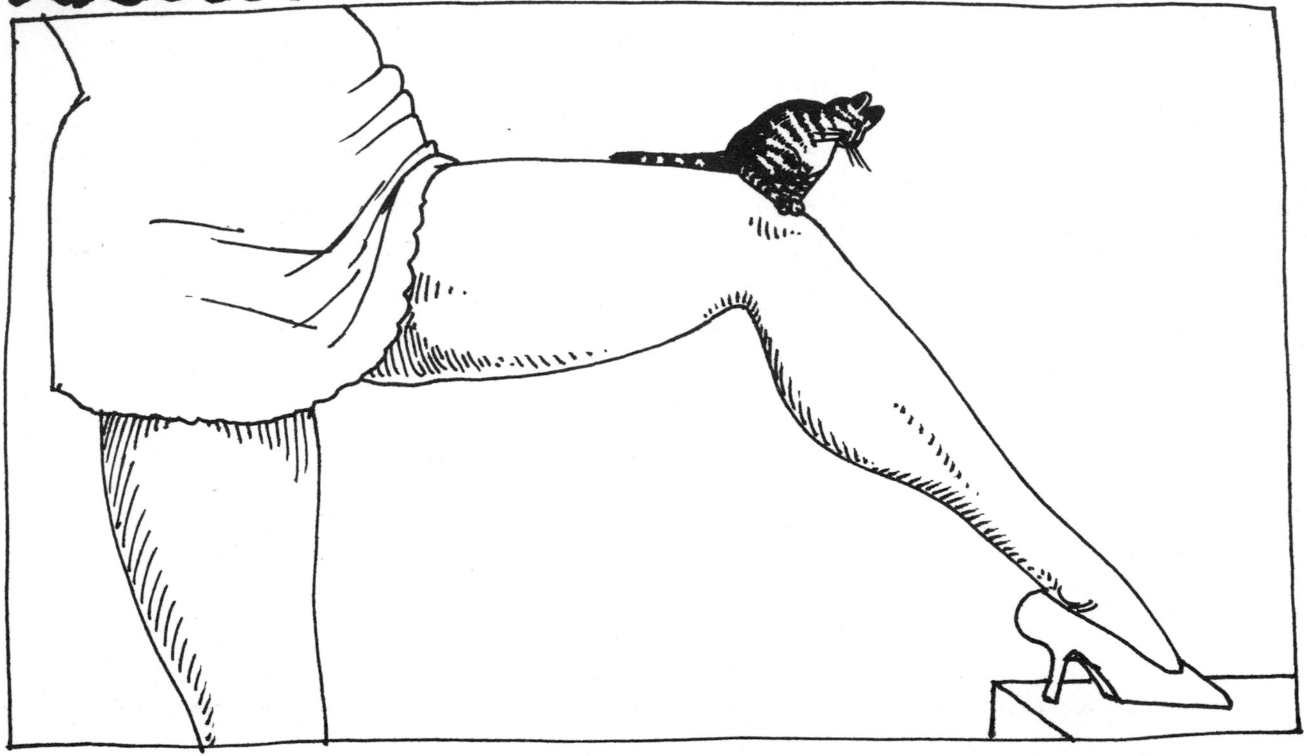

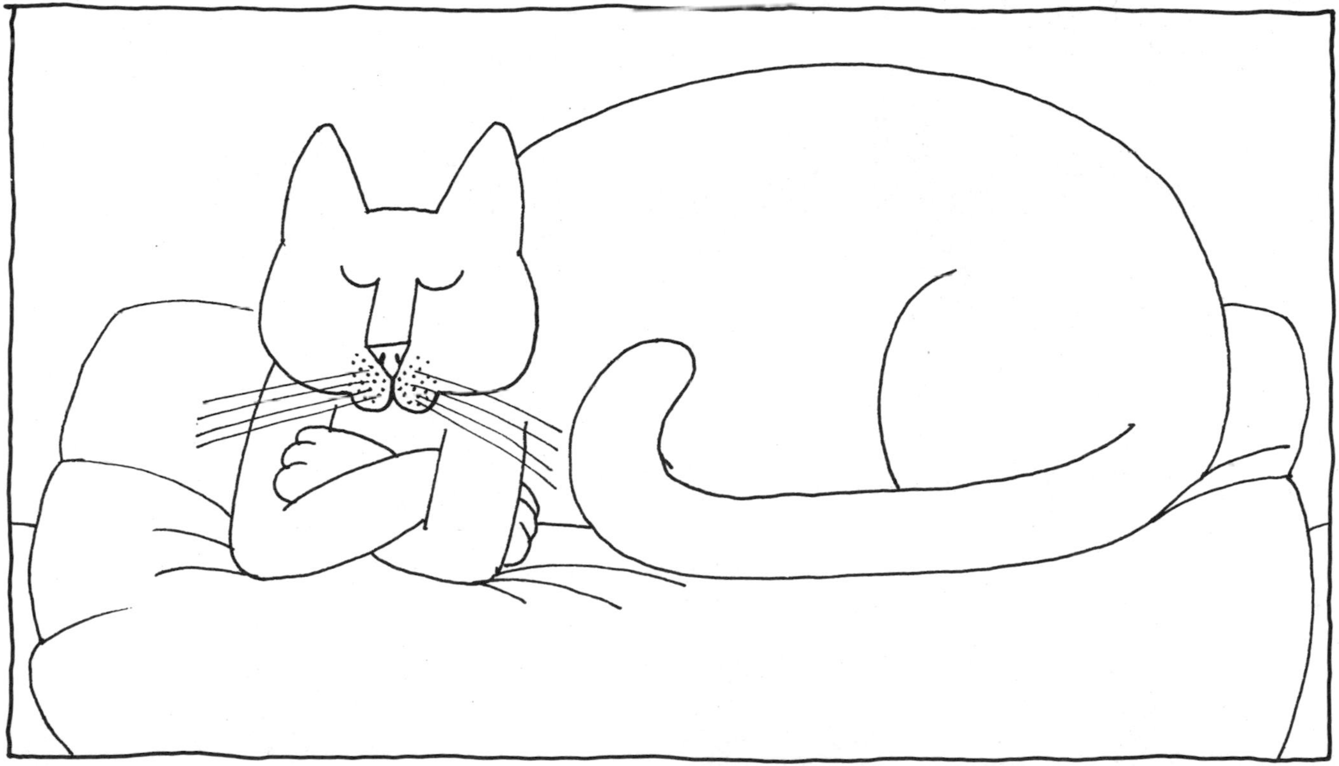

FAT NITTY

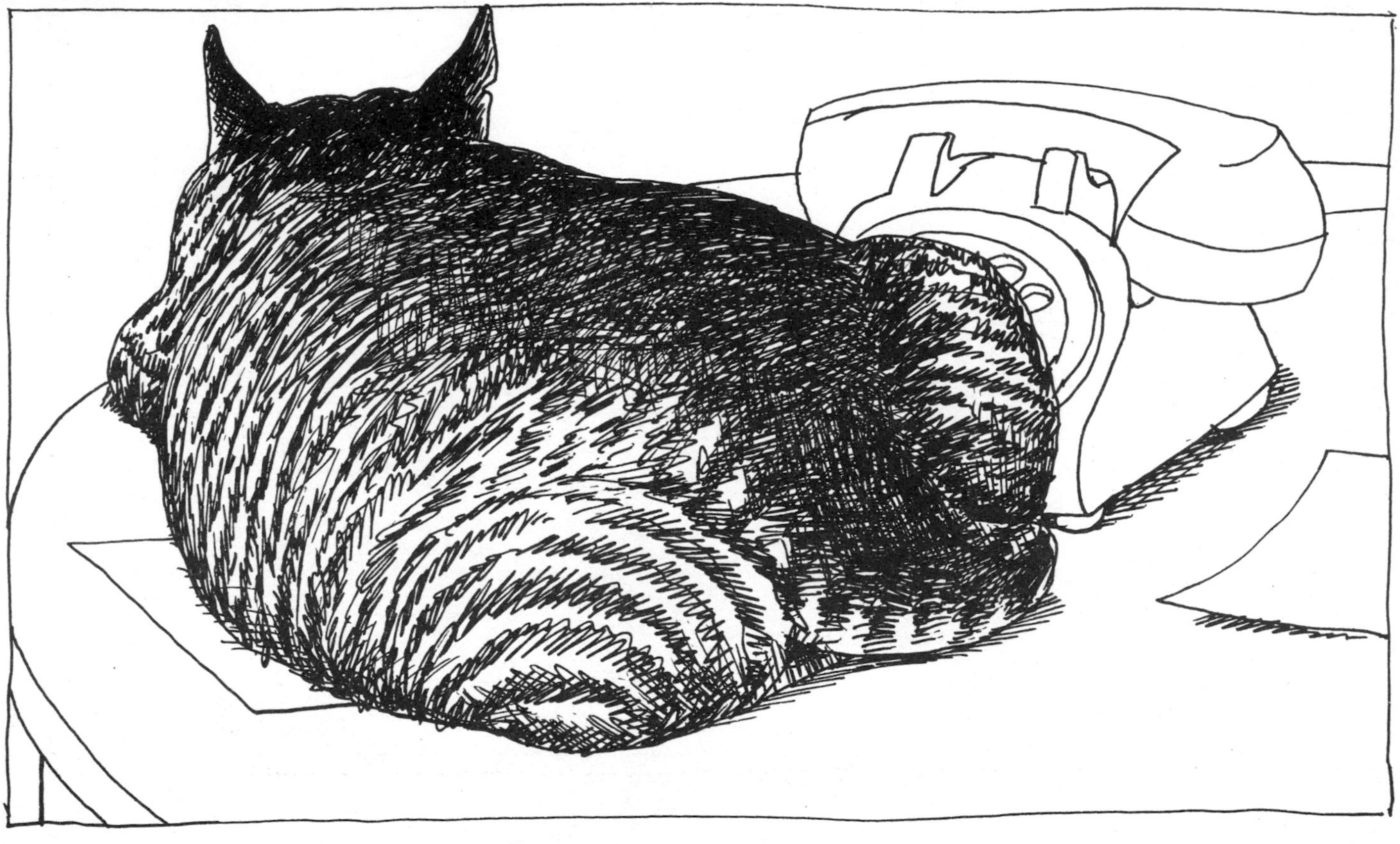

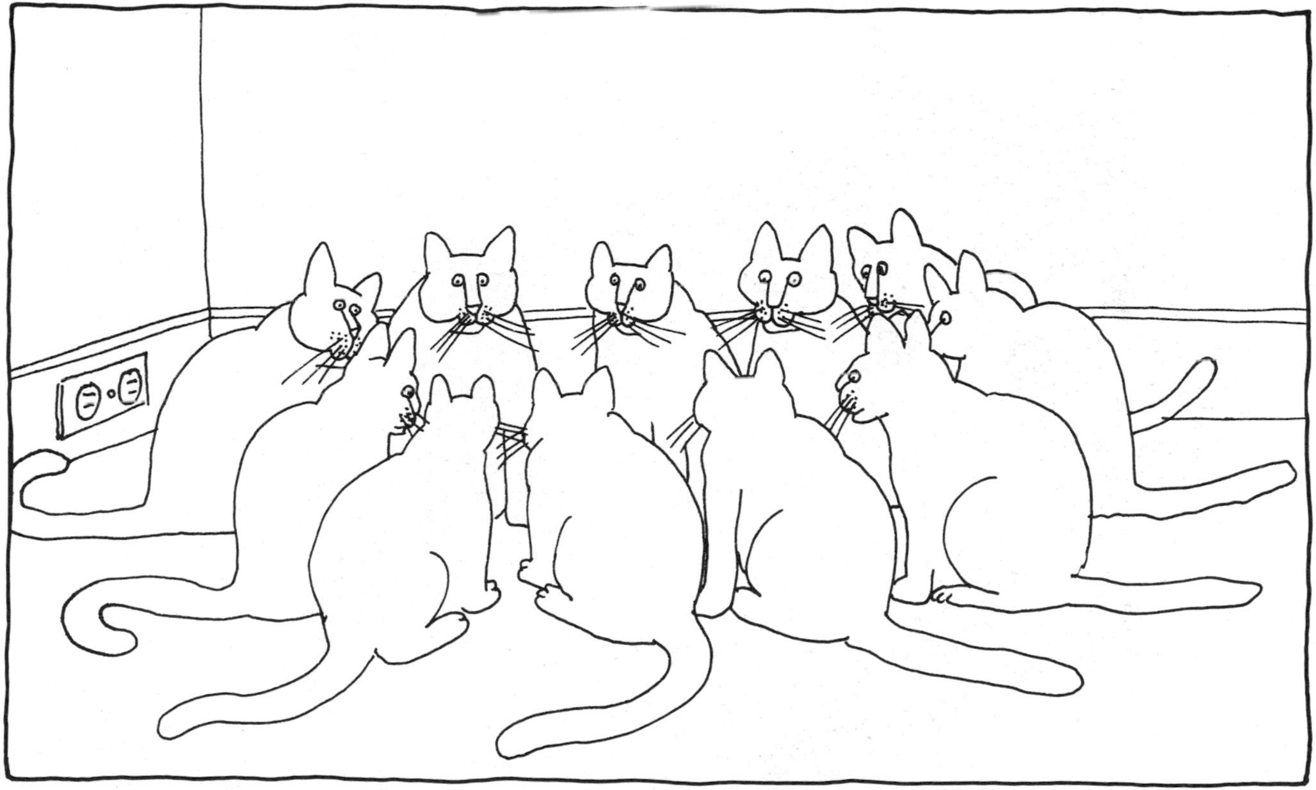

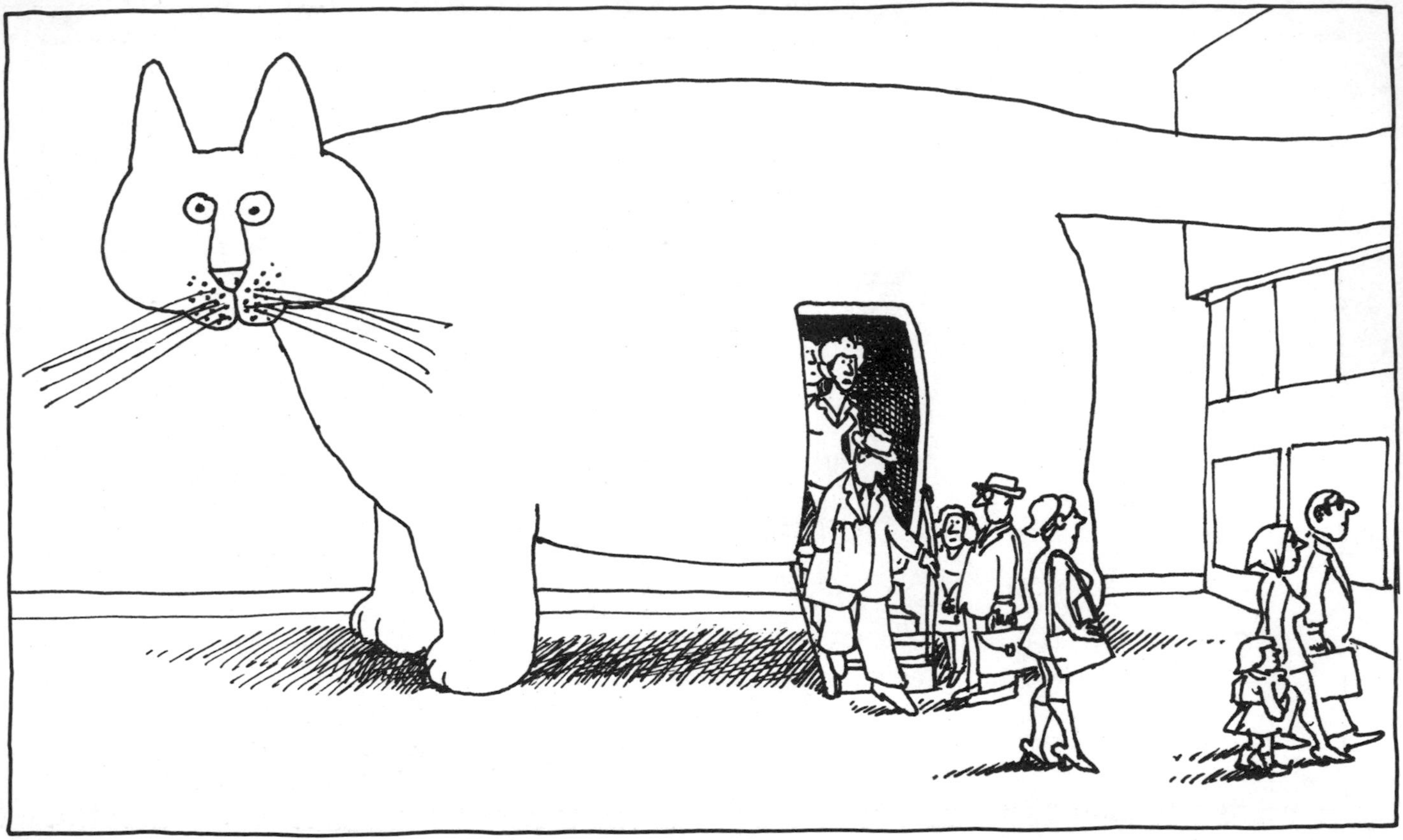

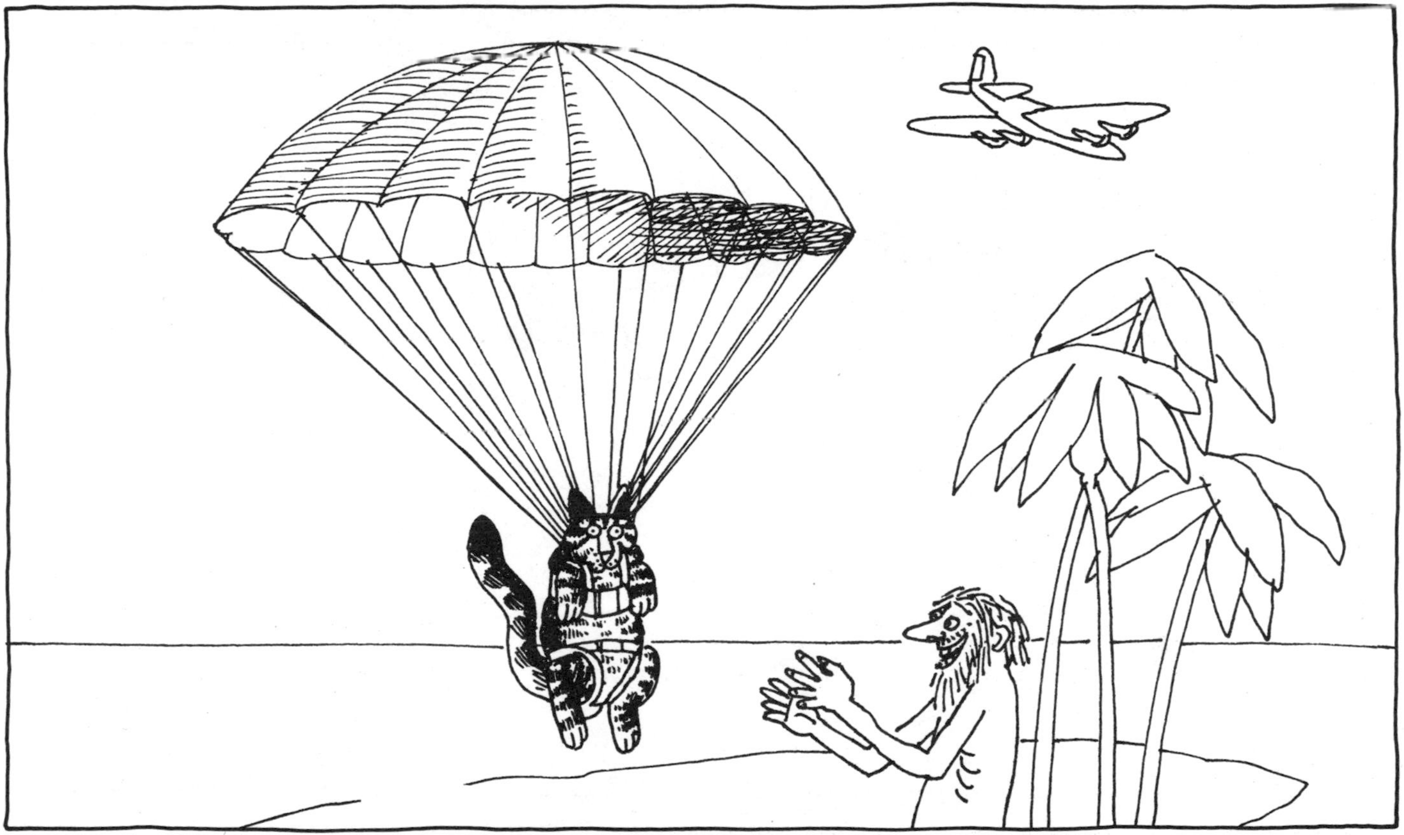

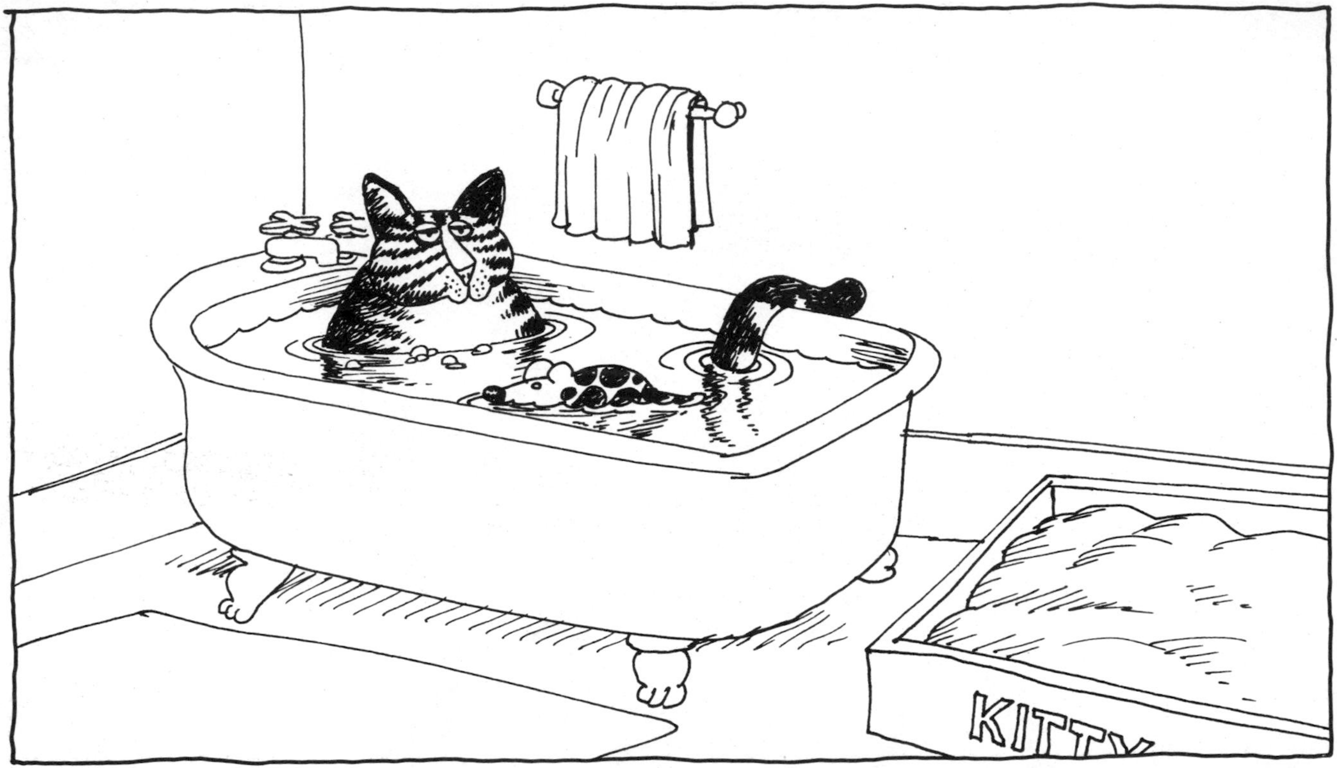

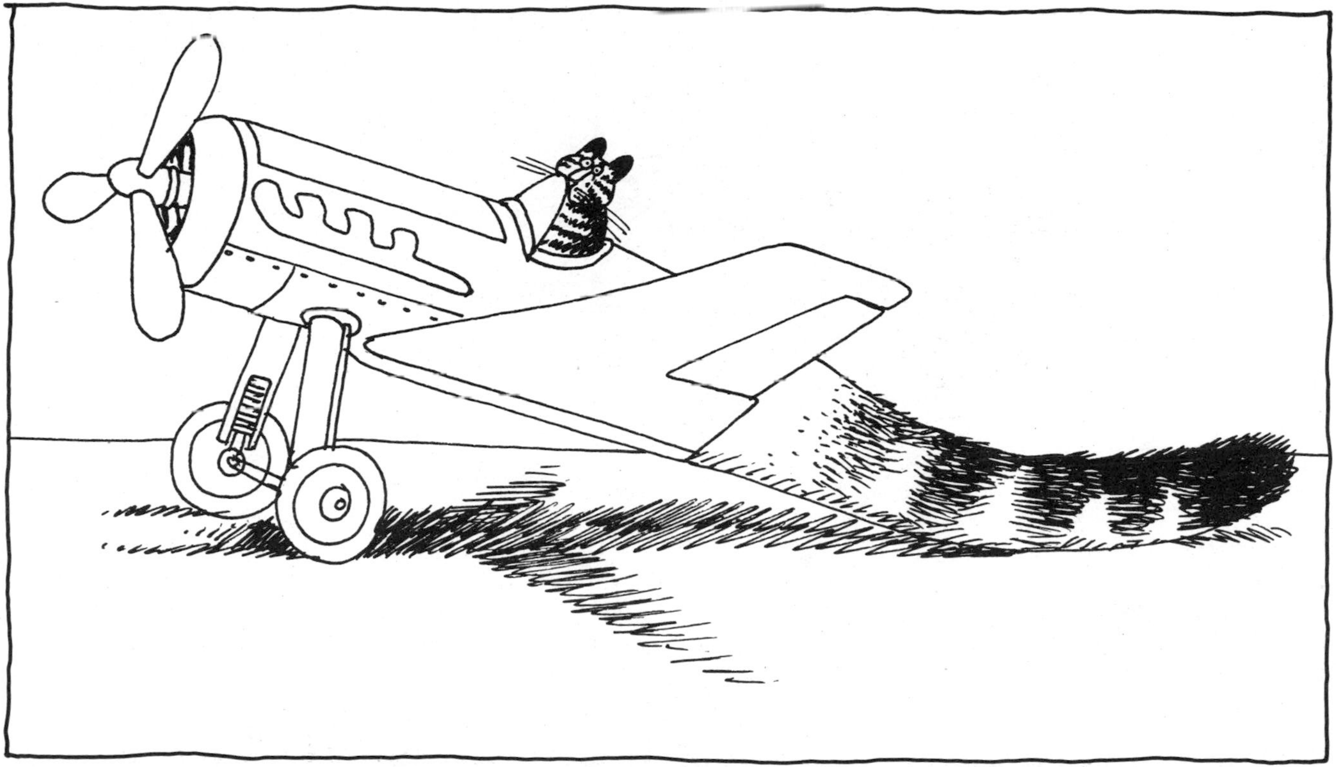

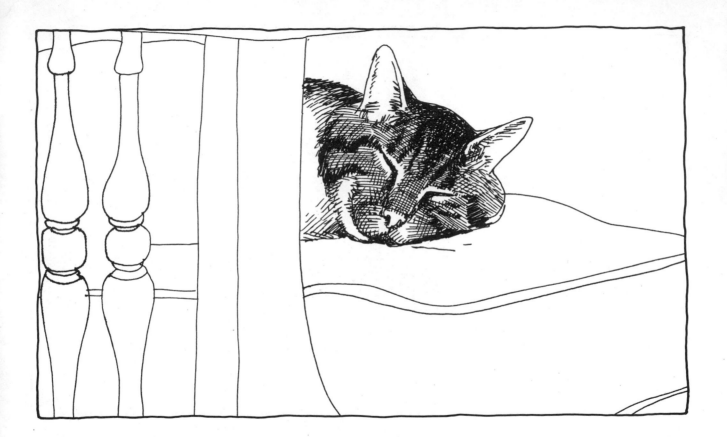

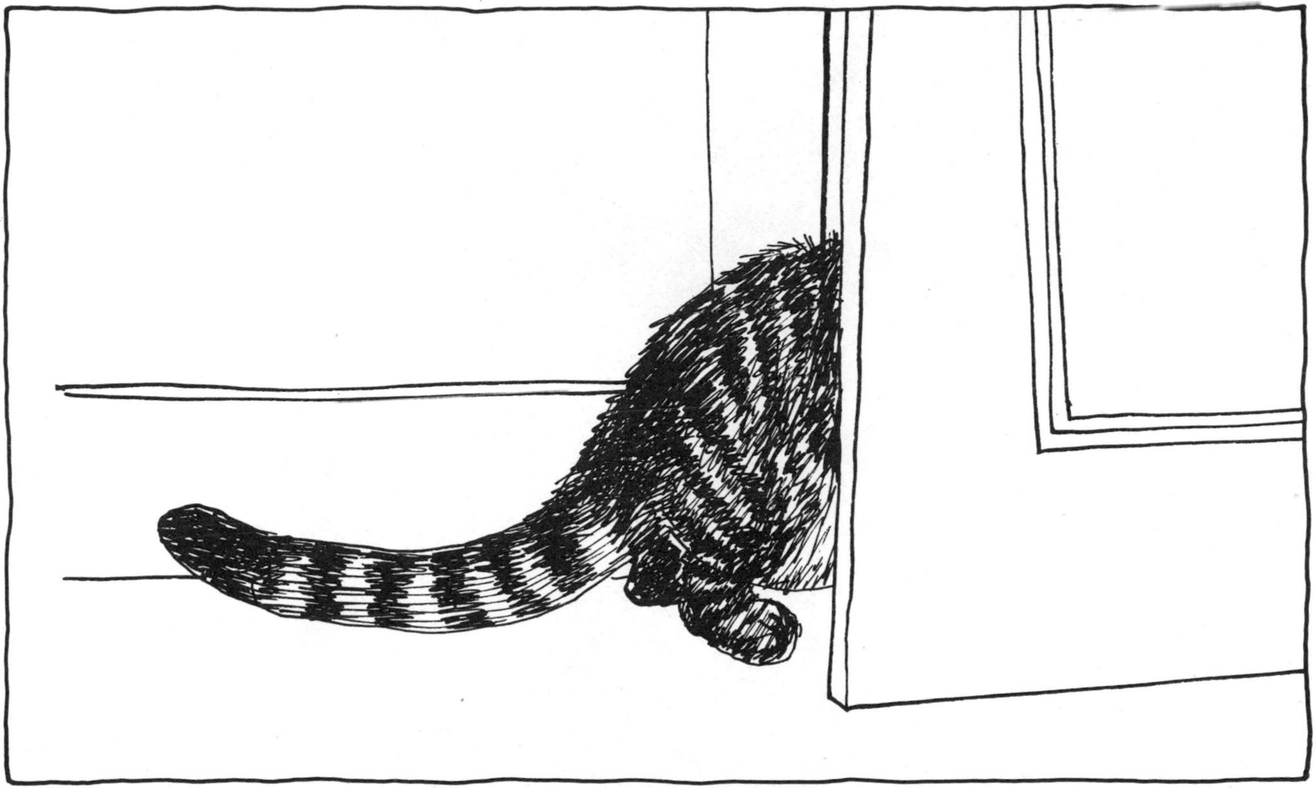

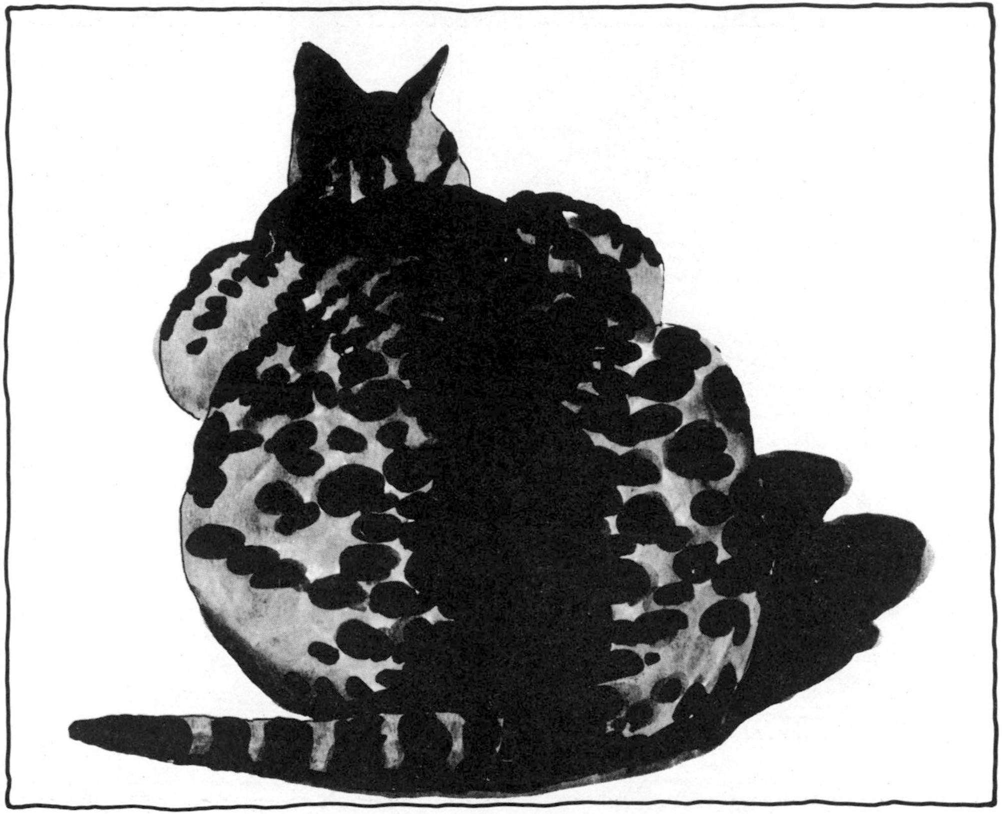

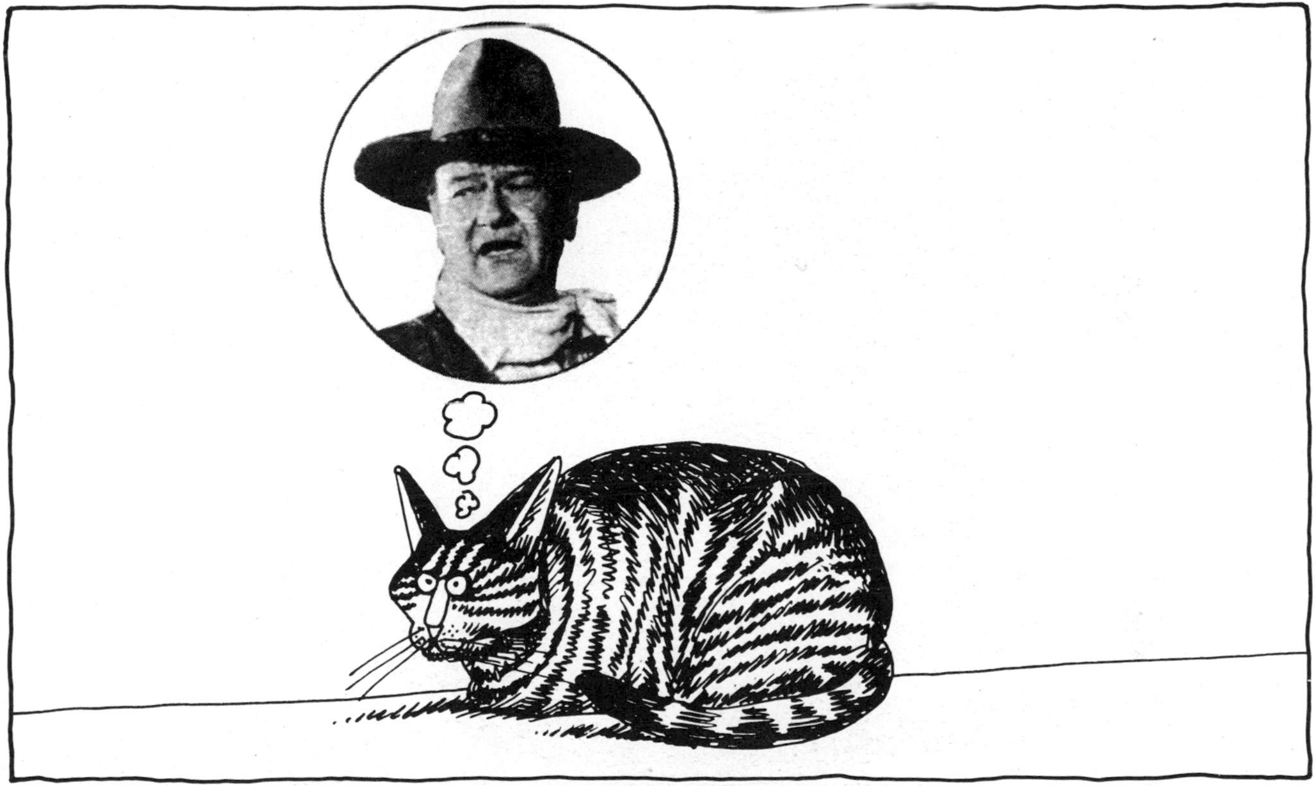

CATS CAN SEE THINGS WE CAN'T

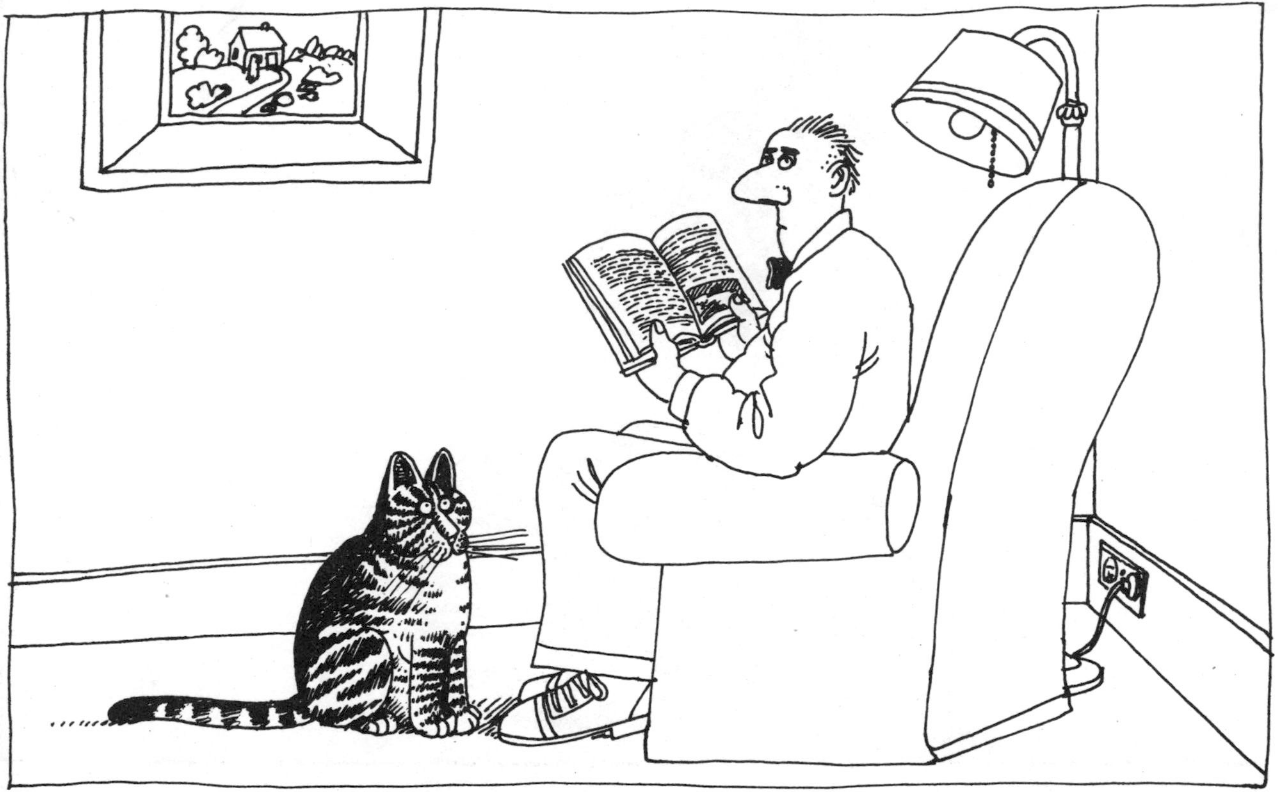

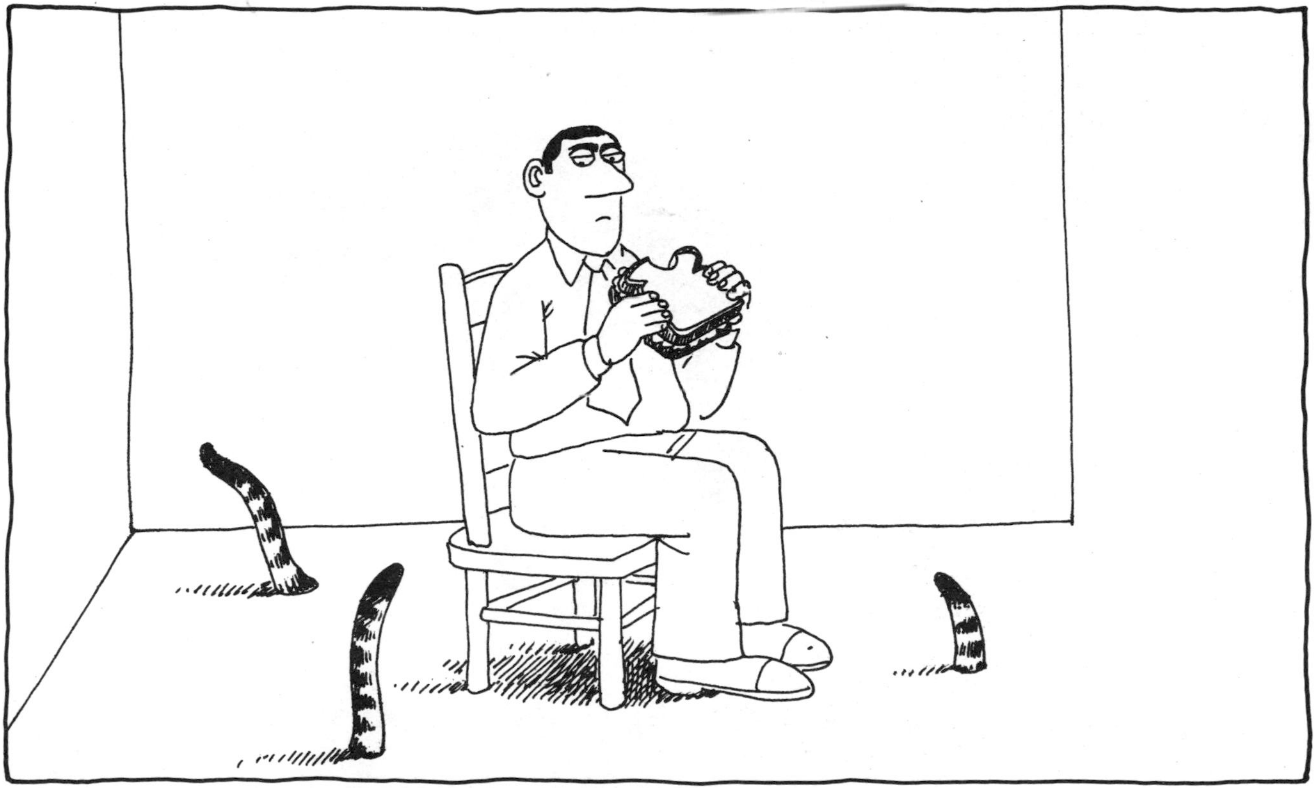

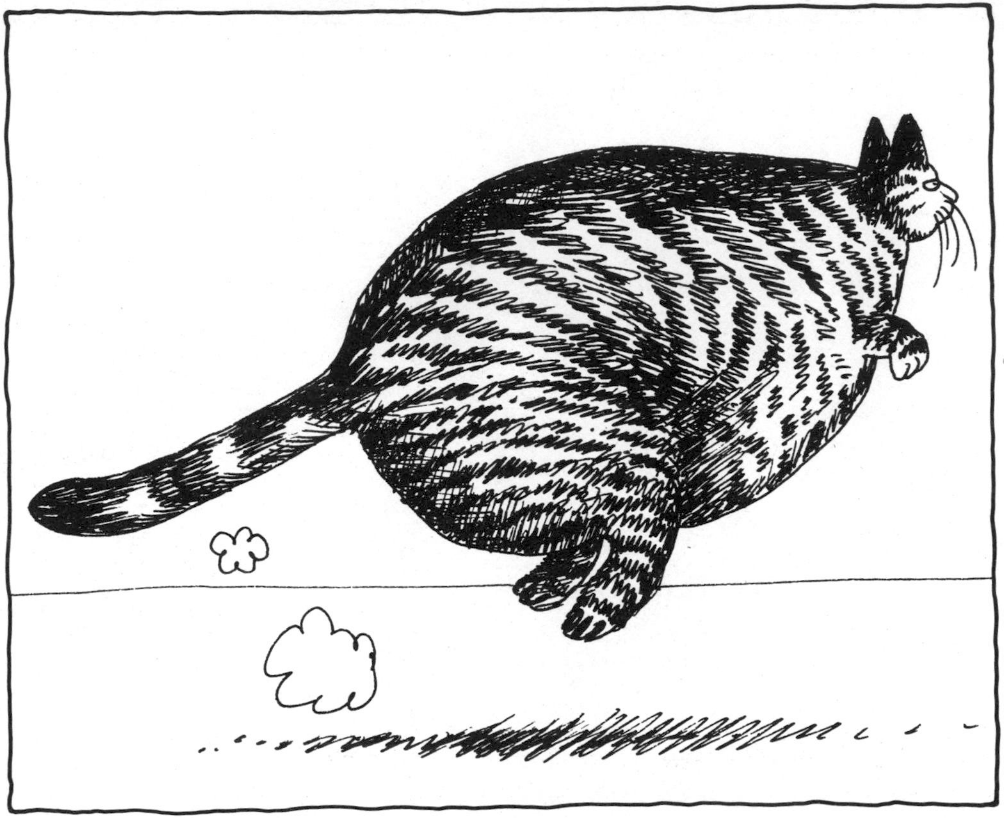

SIAMESE WICKER CAT FIGHTING SUIT

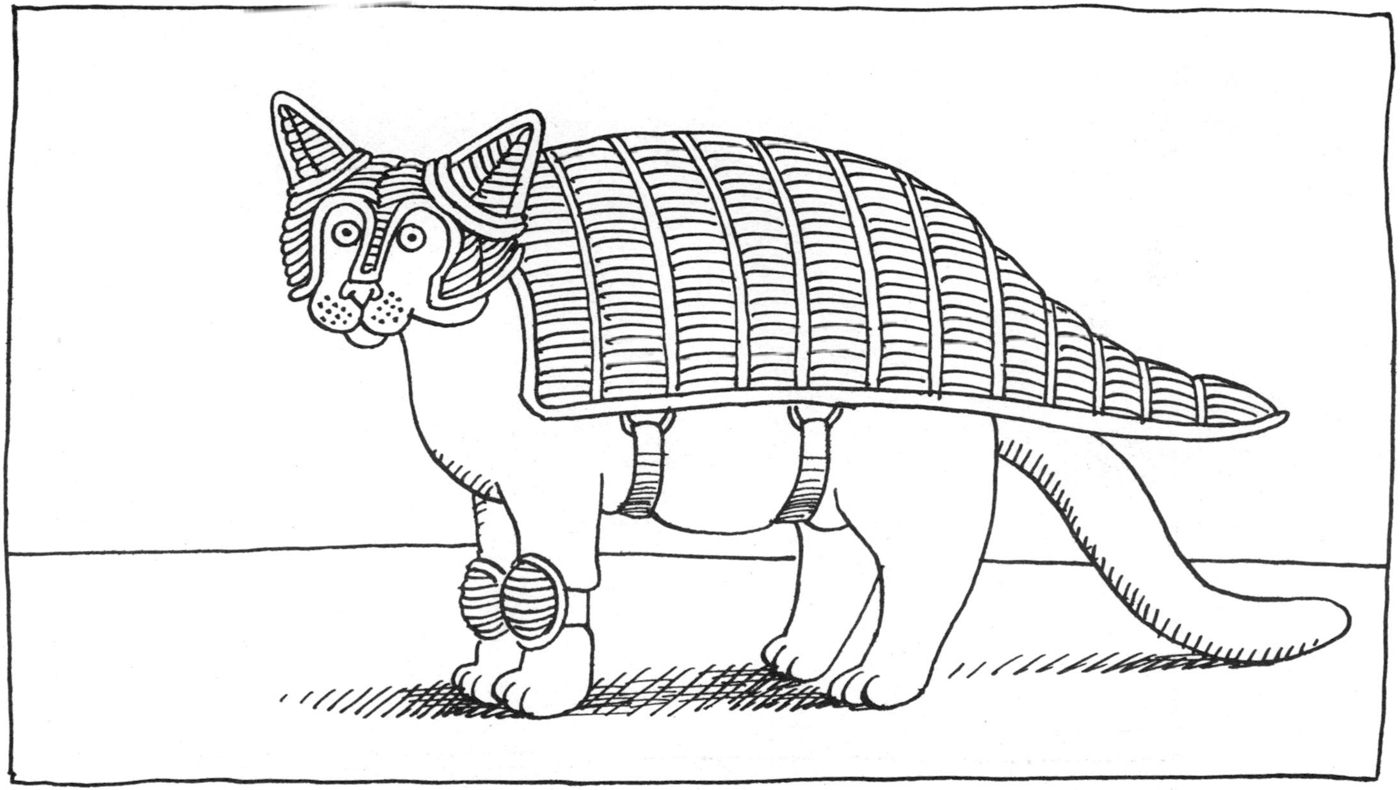

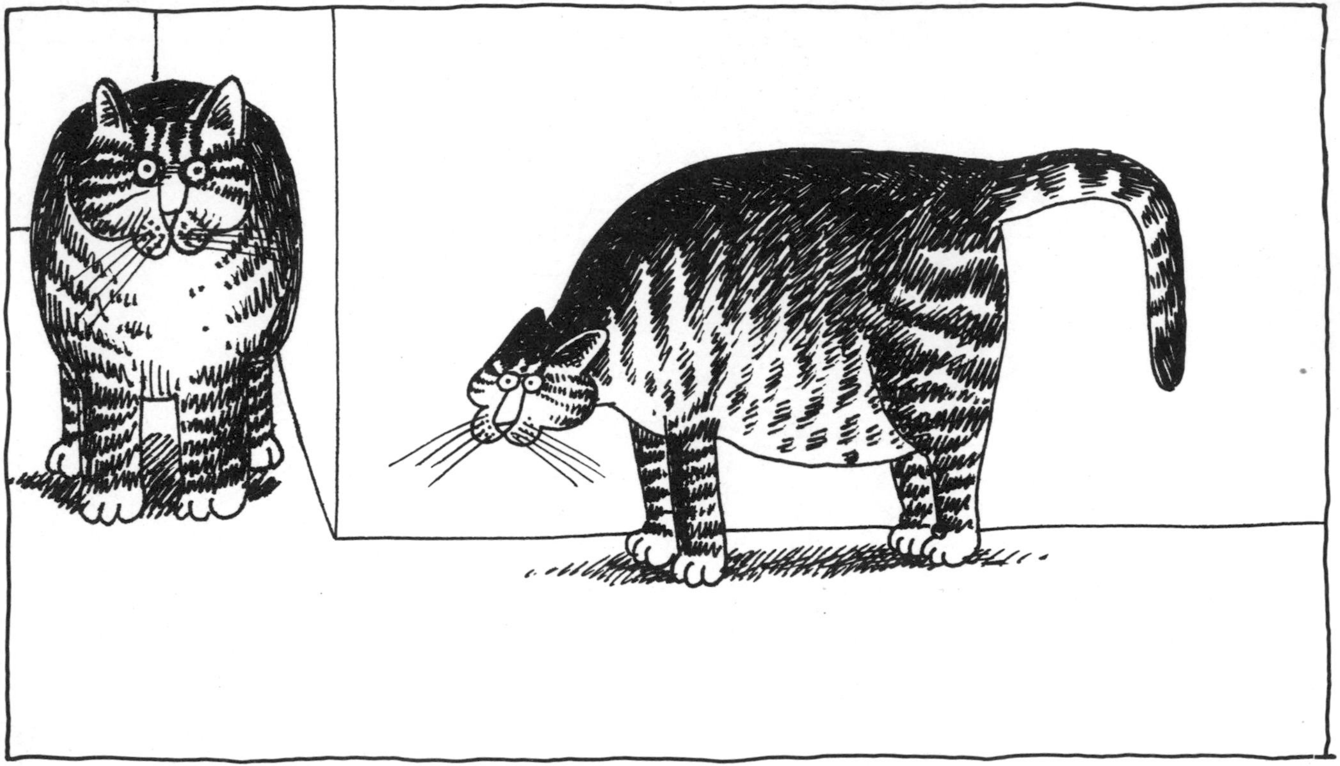

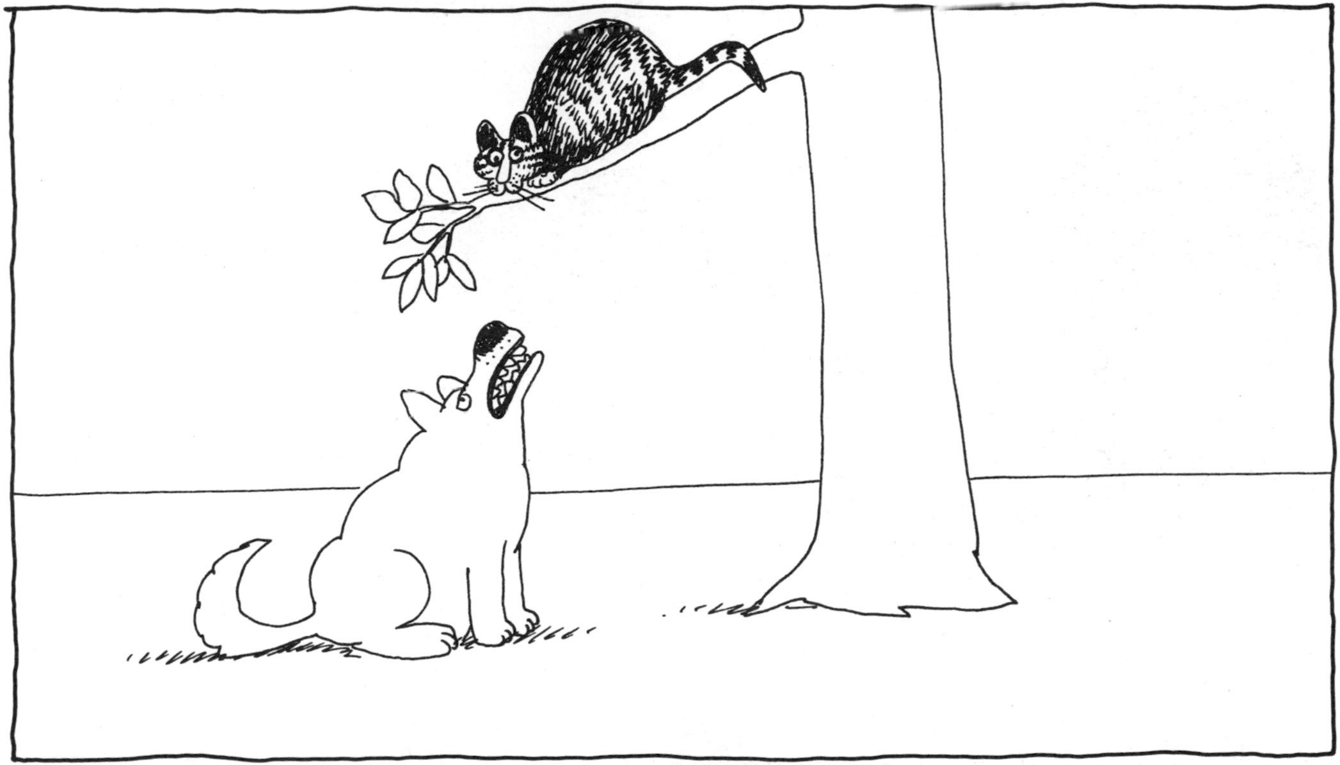

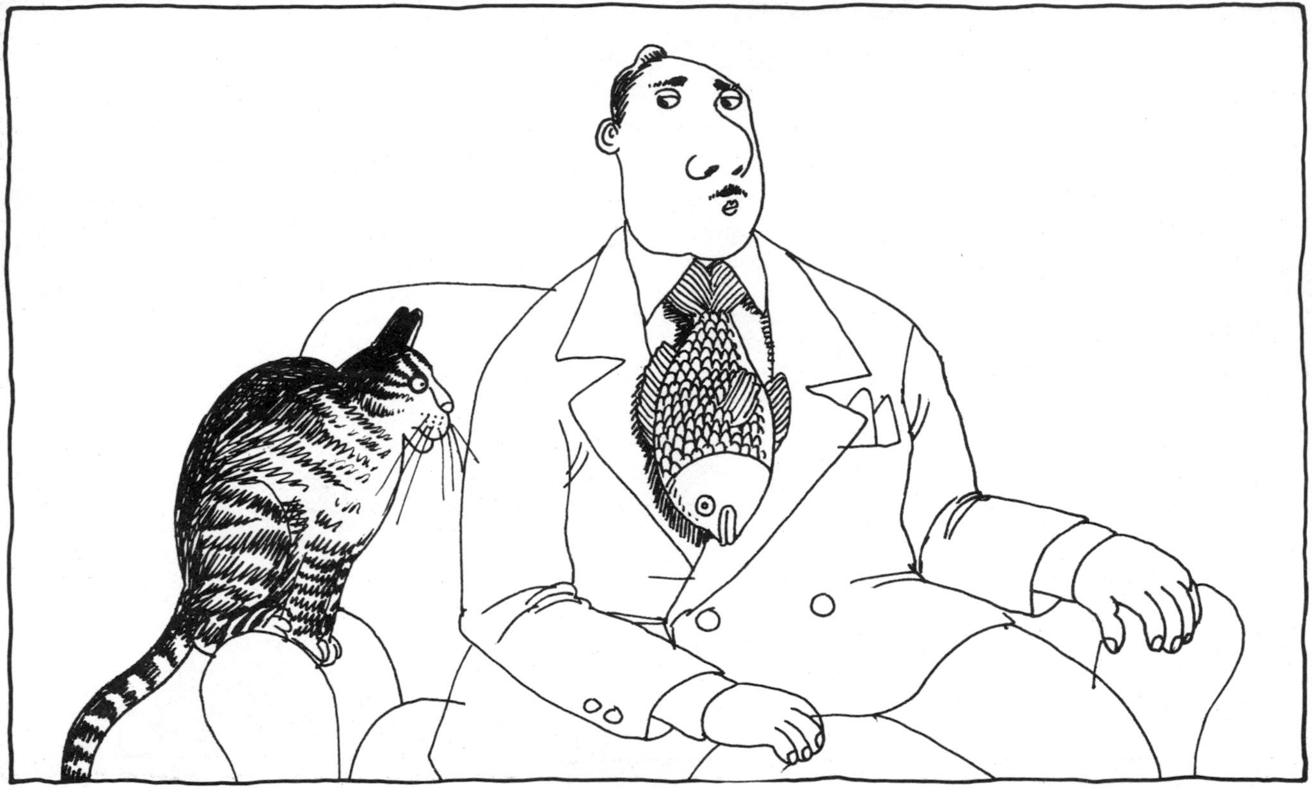

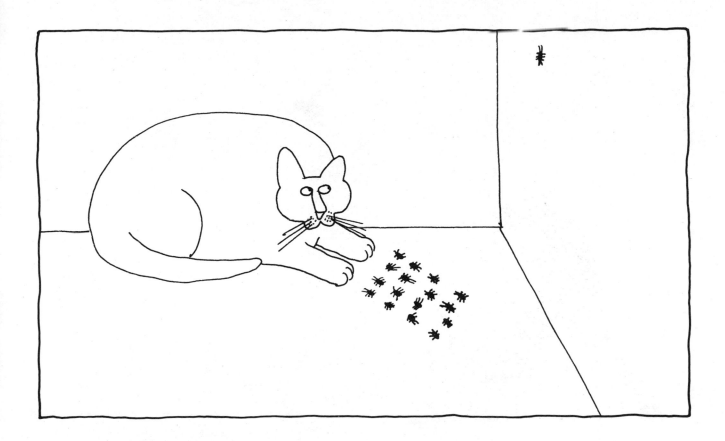

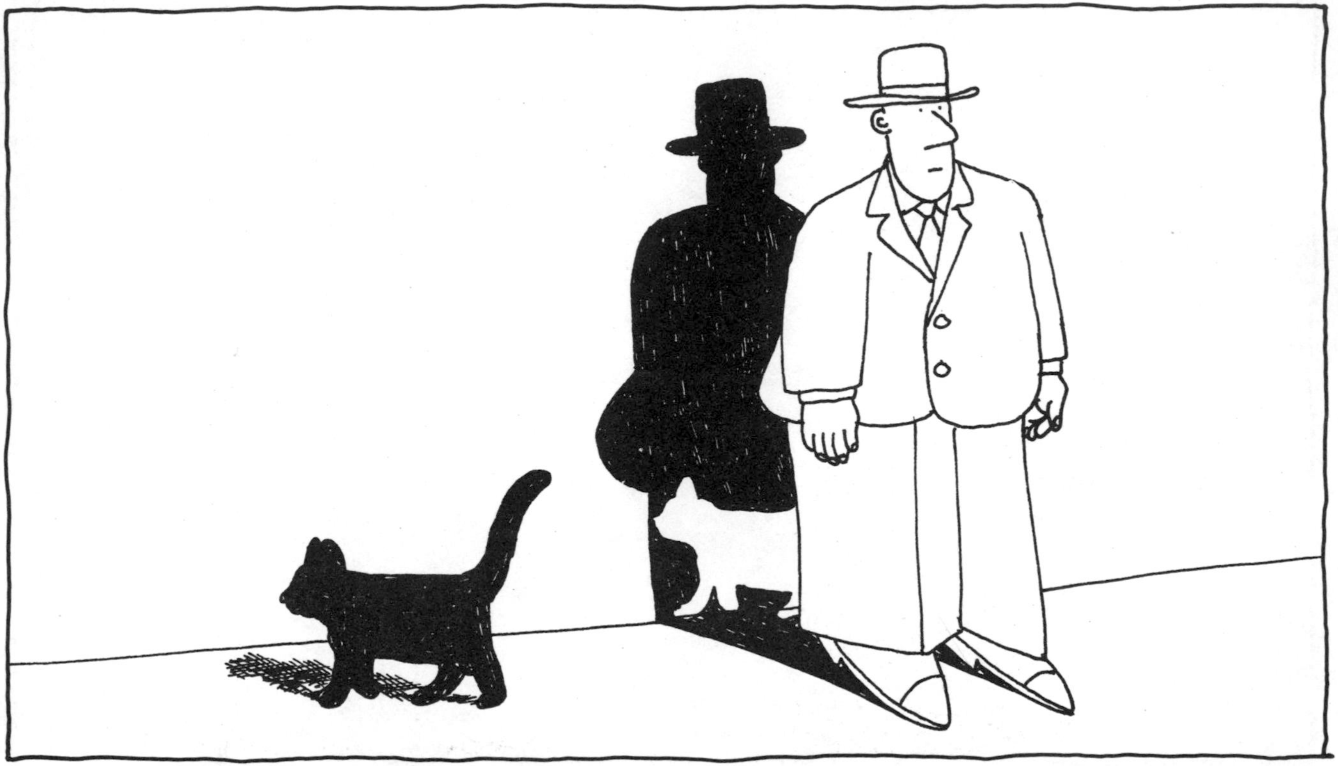

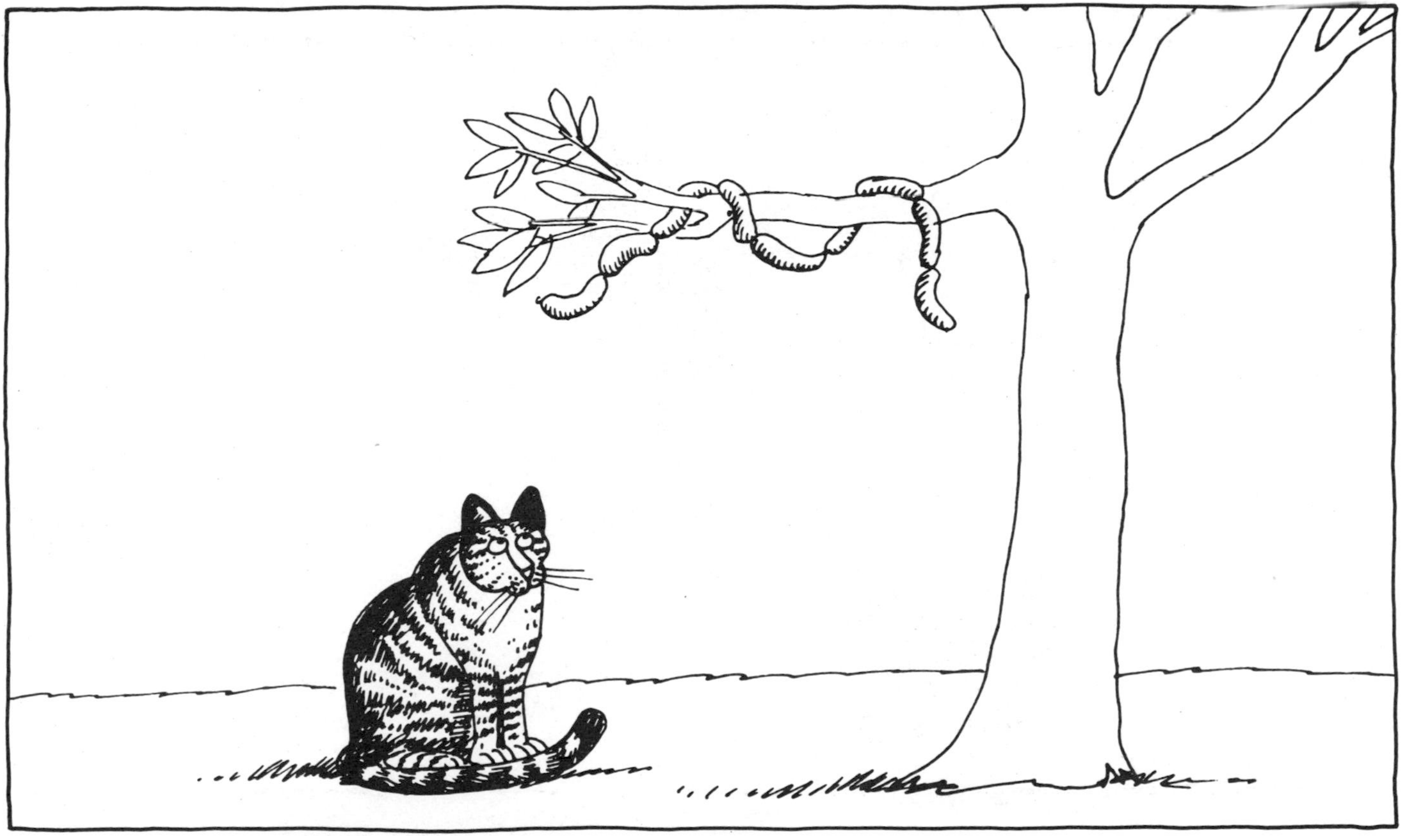

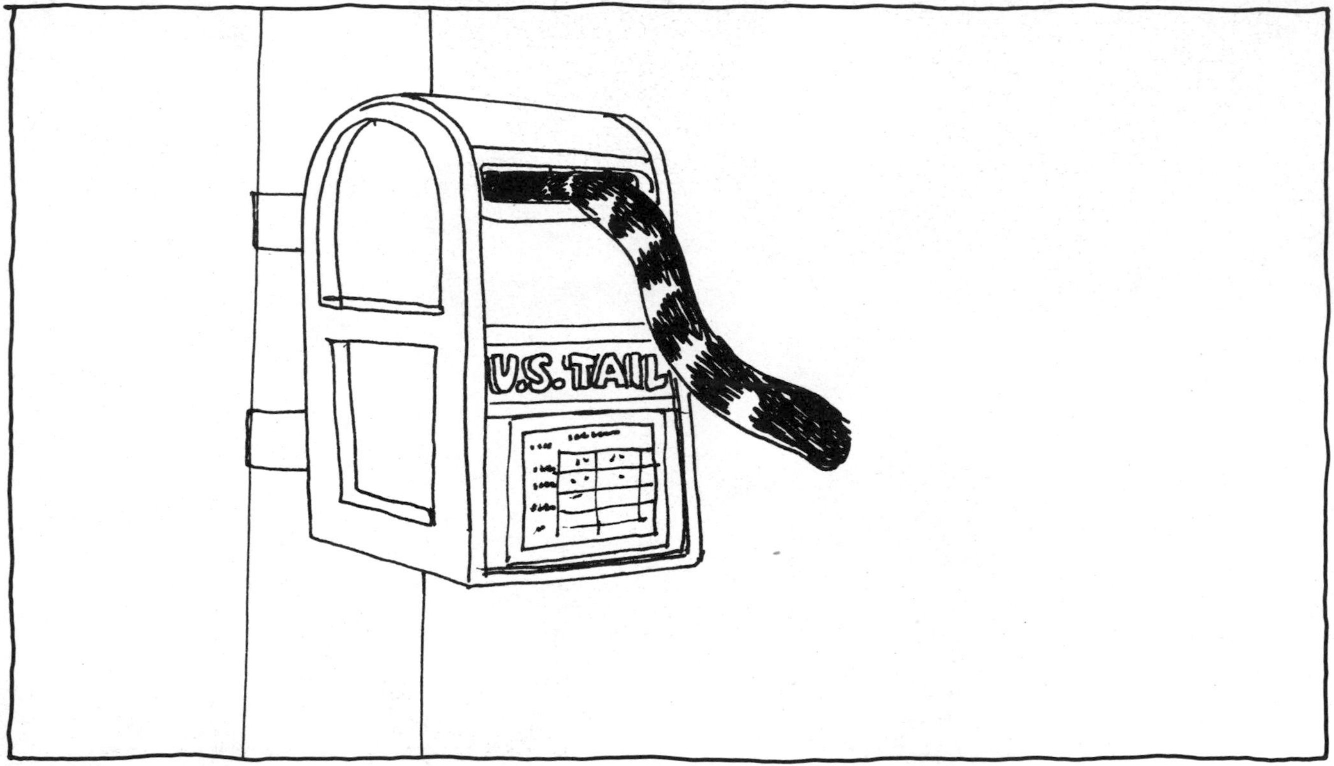
U.S. TAIL

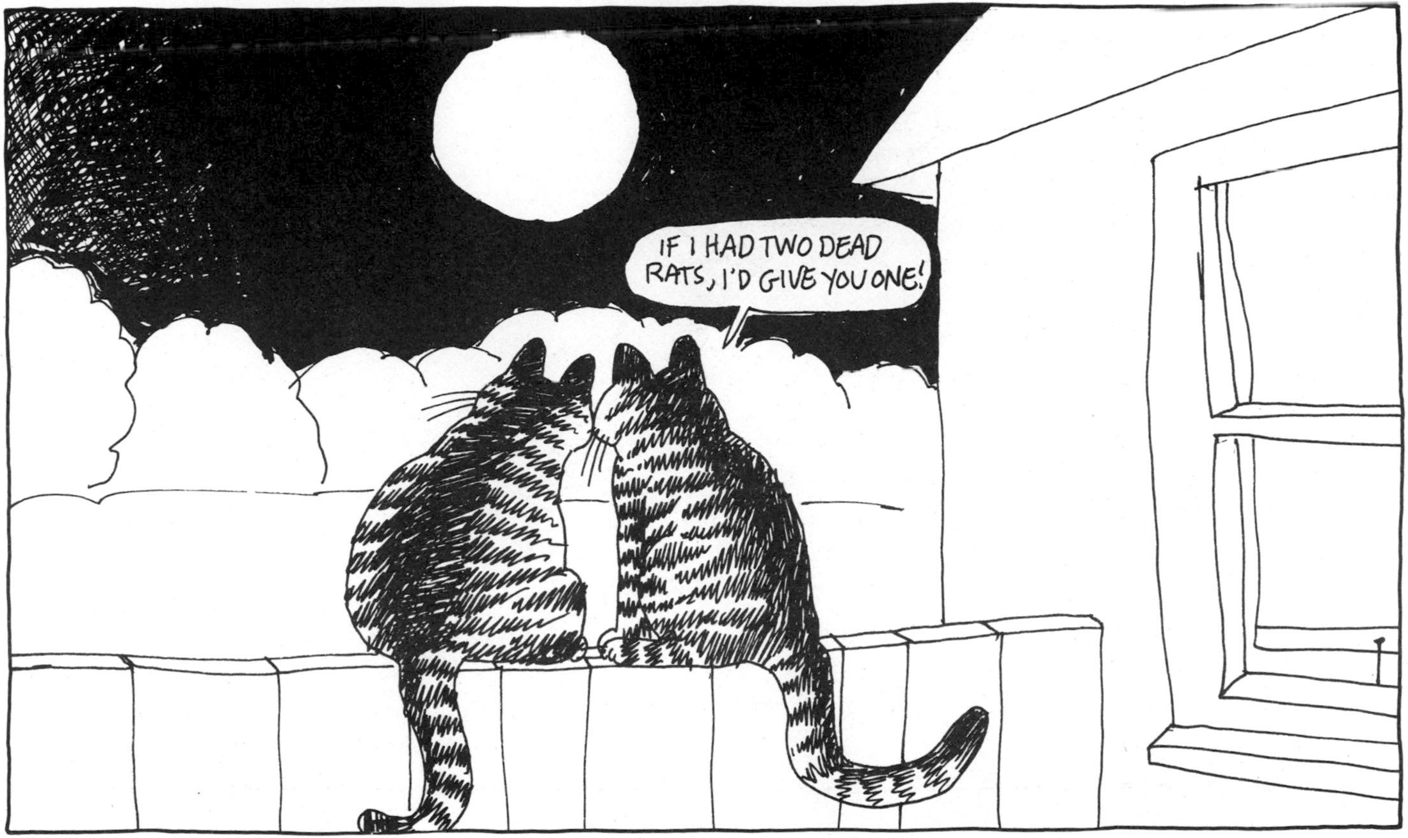
IF I HAD TWO DEAD RATS, I'D GIVE YOU ONE!

How to draw a Qat

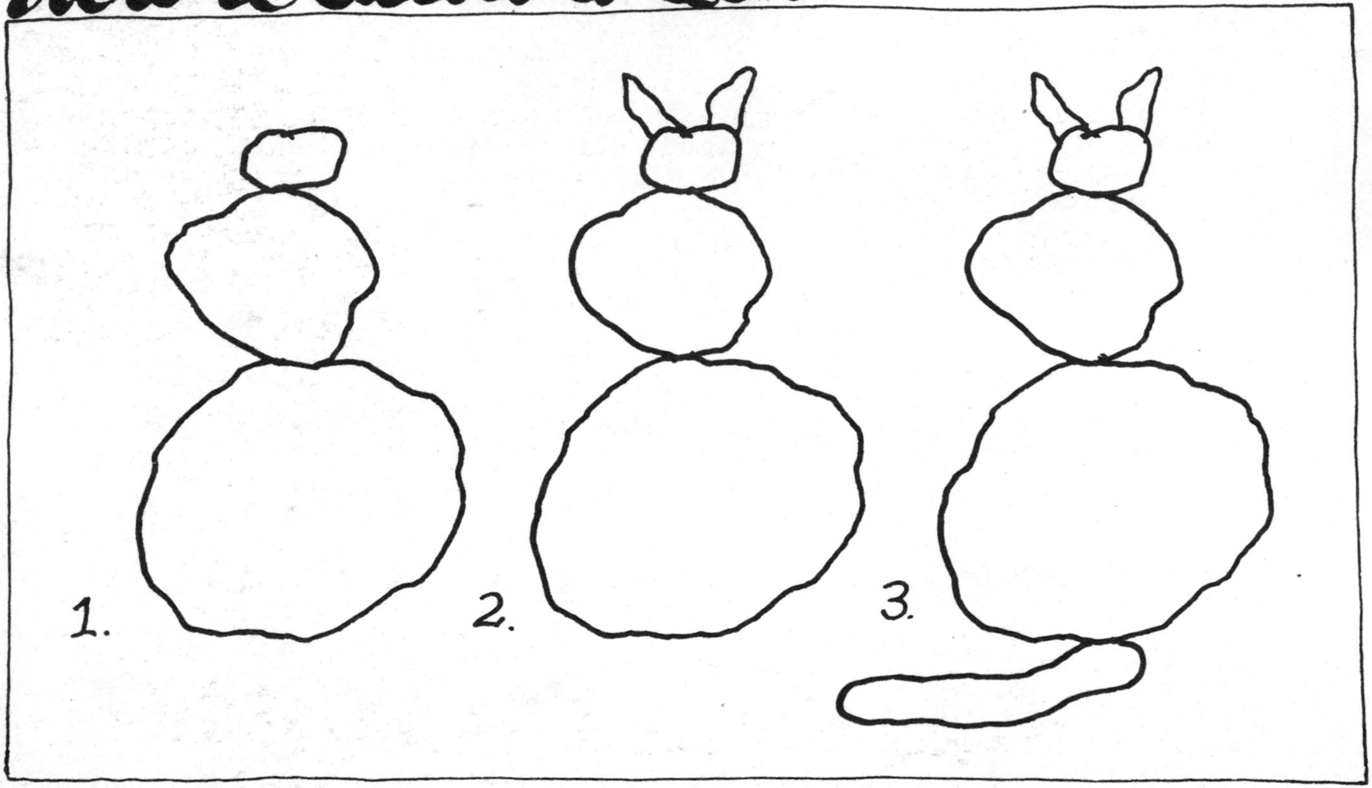
1.
2.
3.